Puerto Rico and the Origins of US Global Empire

Drawing on a postcolonial legal history of the United States' territorial expansionism, this book provides an analysis of the foundations of its global empire. Charles R. Venator-Santiago argues that the United States has developed three traditions of territorial expansionism with corresponding constitutional interpretations, namely colonialist, imperialist, and global expansionist. This book offers an alternative interpretation of the origins of US global expansion, suggesting it began with the tradition of territorial expansionism following the 1898 Spanish-American War to legitimate the annexation of Puerto Rico and other non-contiguous territories. The relating constitutional interpretation grew out of the 1901 *Insular Cases* in which the Supreme Court coined the notion of an unincorporated territory to describe the 1900 Foraker Act's normalization of the prevailing military territorial policies. Since then the United States has invoked the ensuing precedents to legitimate a wide array of global policies, including the 'war on terror'.

Puerto Rico and the Origins of US Global Empire: The disembodied shade combines a unique study of Puerto Rican legal history with a new interpretation of contemporary US policy. As such, it provides a valuable resource for students and scholars of the legal and historical disciplines, especially those with a specific interest in American and postcolonial studies.

Charles R. Venator-Santiago is Associate Professor with a joint appointment in El Instituto: Institute for Latino/a, Caribbean, and Latin American Studies at the University of Connecticut. He is also a board member of the Latino/a Critical Theory (LatCrit) organization and President of the Puerto Rican Studies Association (PRSA).

Law and the Postcolonial: Ethics, Politics, & Economy

Series edited by: Prof Denise Ferreira da Silva, Queen Mary University of London, Dr Mark A. Harris, La Trobe University, and Dr Brenna Bhandar, SOAS, UK

Law and the Postcolonial: Ethics, Politics, & Economy seeks to expand the critical scope of racial, postcolonial, and global theory and analysis, focusing on how the global juridico-economic apparatus has been, and continues to be, shaped by the Colonial and the Racial structurings of power. It includes works that seek to move beyond the previous privileging of culture in considerations of racial and postcolonial subjectivity to offer a more comprehensive engagement with the legal, economic and moral issues of the global present.

Titles in this series include:

State Violence and the Execution of Law
Biopolitcal caesurae of torture, black sites, drones
Joseph Pugliese

The Pirate Myth
Genealogies of an imperial concept
Amedeo Policante

Puerto Rico and the Origins of US Global Empire
The disembodied shade
Charles R. Venator-Santiago

Forthcoming:

Genocidal Democracy
Neoliberalism, mass incarceration and the politics of urban gun violence
John D. Marquez

Postcolonial Capitalism
Justice, global labour and racial violence
Denise Ferreira da Silva and Rashne Limke

Puerto Rico and the Origins of US Global Empire

The disembodied shade

Charles R. Venator-Santiago

Routledge
Taylor & Francis Group
a GlassHouse Book

First published 2015
by Routledge
2 Park Square, Milton Park, Abingdon, Oxon, OX14 4RN

Simultaneously published in the USA and Canada
by Routledge
711 Third Avenue, New York, NY 10017

A GlassHouse Book
Routledge is an imprint of the Taylor & Francis Group, an informa business

British Library Cataloguing in Publication Data
A catalogue record for this book is available from the British Library

Library of Congress Cataloging-in-Publication Data
A catalog record has been requested for this book

ISBN: 978-0-415-66230-7 (hbk)
ISBN: 978-0-203-38086-4 (ebk)

Typeset in Garamond by
by FiSH Books Ltd, Enfield

For Maggie

Contents

Acknowledgements

I am greatly indebted to the editors of Routledge's Law and the Postcolonial: Ethics, Politics, & Economy series, Denise Ferreira da Silva, Mark Harris, and Brenna Bhandar for their patience, support and commitment to creating an intellectual space where I can share my work. I am also thankful to my constant companions and critics in this endeavor, Tayyab Mahmud, Francisco Valdes, and the LatCrit community.

This project grew out of series of arguments and criticisms with friends in the Department of Legal Studies at the University of Massachusetts, the Politics Department at Ithaca College, and El Instituto: Institute for Latino/a, Caribbean, and Latin American Studies as well as the Department of Political Science at the University of Connecticut. To all my colleagues who endured my constant delays, questions, rants, and complaints I am thankful for your patience.

I would be remiss if I did not acknowledge the support and patience that I have received from friends, colleagues and mentors throughout, including Mary Romero, Roberto Marques, Asma Barlas, Beth Harris, Guillermo B. Irizarry, Mark Overmyer-Velazquez, Marysol Asencio, Mark Boyer, Jennifer Fontanella, David Yalof, Blanca Silverstrini, Richard Delgado, Steve Bender, Farid Samir Benavides, and Alexander Betancourt.

I also need thank Magdalene, Alejo, Titi Nancy, Katia, Isabel, Ryan, Lily, Benito, Bob, Patricia, Fabian, and all of those family members who continue to tolerate my long disappearances and absences.

Earlier versions of my argument were published in the following:

- Venator-Santiago, C.R. (2006) 'Agamben's State of Exception and U.S. Territorial Law and Policy', *Studies in Law, Politics, and Society* (39): 15–56.
- Venator-Santiago, C.R. (2012) 'Inverted Totalitarianism and the U.S. Territorial Doctrine', *Revista de Pensamiento Jurídico* 30(3): 295–310.
- Venator-Santiago, C.R. (2013) 'Extending Citizenship to Puerto Rico, The Three Traditions of Inclusive Exclusion', *CENTRO: Journal of Puerto Rican Studies* (Spring): 50–75.

Chapter 1

A conceptual overview

> It is locality that is determinative of the application of the Constitution, in such matters as judicial procedure, and not the status of the people who live in it.
>
> (Justice William H. Taft, *Balzac v. People of Porto Rico*, 1922)

> This century-old doctrine informs our analysis in the present matter.
>
> (Justice Anthony Kennedy, *Boumediene v. Bush*, 2008)

Following the attacks of 11 September 2001, the administration of President George W. Bush began to develop an array of extraterritorial policies enabling the United States to selectively conduct a global war on terror. Simultaneously, Congress began to normalize these policies through the enactment of legislation enabling the Bush administration to conduct its indeterminate global campaign. The Bush administration also developed corresponding constitutional interpretations situating the power of the Executive or Commander-in-Chief outside of the scope of international and domestic constitutional law. The Supreme Court, however, entered the fray with a series of opinions that sought to temper the Bush administration's power without hindering its ability to conduct a global war on terror. A majority of the Court ultimately invoked a 'century-old' postcolonial interpretation of the Constitution that legitimized the United States' continued global war on terror.

The President, Congress, and the Court in large measure wrangled over the modalities of administration of territories rooted in three traditions of United States' territorial expansionism. Historically, the United States has developed at least three traditions of territorial expansionism with corresponding constitutional interpretations and policies. Throughout the nineteenth century, the United States developed a colonialist tradition premised on the annexation of new territories that could be subsequently organized into new states of the Union. Colonial territories were treated as parts of the United States for constitutional purposes. Simultaneously, the United States developed an imperialist tradition premised on the occupation of territories. Unlike colonial territories, occupied territories were ruled as possessions situated outside of the United States for constitutional purposes, regardless of their geographic location. Between 1898 and 1901, however, the United States developed a new tradition of expansionism, global in scope, that enabled it to *annex* new territories without binding Congress to colonize them into states of the Union. All territories acquired under the aegis of this third tradition, a postcolonial tradition of territorial expansionism, have since been ascribed a borderland status for constitutional purposes. More importantly, the United States' adoption of a postcolonial modality of territorial expansionism and administration marked its entry into the exclusive club of global empires.

Central to the Bush administration's policies were the construction of extraterritorial torture and detention camps as well as the ascription of alien subjectivities on suspected 'enemies' of the United States. Invoking his constitutional power as Commander-in-Chief of the armed forces, President Bush ordered the construction of camps in places like Guantánamo Bay, Cuba, Afghanistan, Iraq, as well as in other so-called 'black sites' throughout the world. In addition, persons ascribed the status of a terrorist were treated as 'enemy combatants' or 'enemy aliens' who could be kidnapped, tortured, subjected to extraordinary rendition, placed under surveillance, and in some cases subjected to extrajudicial assassination or execution (The Constitution Project 2013). The Bush administration situated the camps and the detained subjects *outside* of the United States, regardless of the geo-political location of the camps [*Hamdi v. Rumsfeld,* 542 US 507 (2004)].

Working with the US Congress, the Bush administration further crafted laws, policies and corresponding constitutional interpretations of the status of extraterritorial spaces housing torture and detention camps as well as the status or subjectivity of the bodies of enemy aliens (Yoo 2006; Bruff 2009; Cheney and Cheney 2011). To paraphrase Alexis de Tocqueville, the Bush administration sought to legalize its war on terror policies in order to counterbalance the democratic impulses of US civil rights and international human rights law (Mayer 2000: 263–270). Territories like Guantánamo Bay, the Bush administration argued, were located in an extraterritorial space situated *outside* of the United States for both constitutional and international law purposes, yet within the purview of the Commander-in-Chief's sovereign power. It followed that because camps located in places like Guantánamo Bay, Cuba were outside of the United States for constitutional purposes, and because they were outside of the US, they were outside of the scope of international law, which only regulated the conduct of states within their sovereign borders. Thus, the Bush administration consistently argued, detainees held in US torture and detention camps could not invoke constitutional (civil rights) or human rights to challenge the military's power over the bodies of detainees. Similarly, the Bush administration ascribed a special alien status on detainees in order to bar them from invoking constitutional rights and privileges such as the *writ of habeas corpus* or human rights protecting detainees against torture and other forms of cruelty. Enemy aliens' and enemy combatants' bodies were in themselves outside of the reach of legal rights that could interfere with the military's power, or so the Bush administration argued. Stated differently, the Bush administration, with the aid of its congressional collaborators, sought to develop laws, policies and constitutional interpretations that situated both territories and enemy bodies outside of the law (constitutional and/or international) yet within the purview of its plenary authority or sovereign power of the Commander-in-Chief, the military title or rank of the US President.

Simultaneously, the United States Supreme Court, the final arbiter or interpreter of the US Constitution, consistently tempered some of the Bush administration and Congress' war on terror policies and legal interpretations. The Court chose the question of the legality of the torture and detention camps located in Guantánamo Bay, Cuba as a juridical arena to temper or place some limits on the Bush administration's war on terror policies. Although the Court issued a series of rulings on various dimensions of the legal status of Guantánamo Bay and the detainees held in the corresponding camps, it did not rule on the corresponding constitutional questions until 2008. More specifically, in *Boumediene v. Bush* [553 US 723 (2008)], the Court ruled on the constitutionality of the Bush administration's policies denying detainees access to a *writ of habeas corpus*, a privilege that enabled persons held in US camps to challenge their incarceration by forcing the US military to justify the basis for holding a detainee. A majority of justices invoked colonialist territorial jurisprudence as legal precedents to place limits on the power of the Commander-in-Chief over detainees arguing that '(e)ven when the United States acts outside its borders, its powers are not "absolute and unlimited" but are subject "to such restrictions as expressed in the Constitution"' (553 US 723, 765). Yet, even though the court was willing to place constitutional limits on the sovereign power of the President, the Court refused to treat camps held within the sovereignty of the United States as constitutional parts of the nation-state. Instead, a majority of the justices invoked the territorial precedents established by the so-called 'Insular Cases,' a 'century-old doctrine,' to describe the constitutional status of Guantánamo Bay and the detainees held in the corresponding camps. Unlike colonialist territorial precedents, which treated territories as parts of the United States for constitutional purposes, the precedents established by the Insular Cases enabled the United States to selectively rule acquired territories as foreign localities for constitutional purposes. Thus, while colonialist territorial jurisprudence essentially bound the US to extend the full bill of rights and other protections such as the *writ of habeas corpus* to territories held within the sovereign power of the US, the Insular Cases authorize the US government to extend only 'fundamental' rights and protections to territories held within its sovereignty.

The precedents established by the Insular Cases, and more specifically in *Downes v. Bidwell* [182 US 245 (1901)], enabled the US to acquire and/or annex territories and selectively rule them as unincorporated territories or foreign localities in a domestic or constitutional sense. My contention is that the ensuing body of law, also known as the doctrine of territorial incorporation, has since enabled the US to acquire (and/or annex) territories and subsequently rule them as postcolonial 'borderland' territories that can be selectively situated in liminal constitutional spaces. This borderland legal or constitutional status has since enabled the US government to select when and how to extend or withhold constitutional provisions, including civil rights and privileges, to unincorporated territories and their residents or inhabitants (including detainees). To re-appropriate Judge Juan R. Torruella's (1988) argument, since 1901 the doctrine of territorial incorporation has enabled the United States to selectively rule acquired territories as separate and unequal constitutional possessions.

In sum, since 11 September 2001, the United States has anchored its legal justification for a global war on terror on a postcolonial interpretation of the Constitution. The United States began to develop a postcolonial territorial tradition of expansionism in the aftermath of the 1898 Spanish–American War in order to rule Puerto Rico and the other annexed territories primarily inhabited by non-white populations. Simultaneously, the United States began to constitute itself as a global empire. Since then, the Supreme Court has at times invoked a postcolonial interpretation of the Constitution to temper the contours of the more extreme or imperialist impulses of Congress and the President. Unfortunately, critics of US global empire and its current war on terror more often than not neglect to take into account this legal history.

THE POSTCOLONIAL ORIGINS OF US GLOBAL EMPIRE

Legal actors and scholars generally read the legal history of US territorial law and policy in two ways. Legal actors within the Bush administration conceptualized US territorial jurisprudence as an undifferentiated collection of cases addressing the status of territories within the United States. Legal actors in the administration did not recognize jurisprudential differences between rulings about annexed and occupied territories or the ensuing interpretations used to legitimate different types of US expansionism. More specifically, this reading obscured differences among legal rationales used to legitimate colonialist, imperialist and global forms of US territorial expansionism. More importantly, this reading of US territorial legal history enabled the administration to draw upon all territorial precedents, regardless of the status of the territory within the United States, and cherry-pick interpretations that could be used in multiple contexts. This approach enabled the Bush administration to draw upon imperialist legal precedents to formulate an interpretation that legitimated treating unincorporated territories as spaces located outside of the law, that could be ruled in a state of exception.

Alternatively, in my opinion, the prevailing reading among Liberal legal scholars and legal actors emphasizes a linear reading of the development of US territorial law and policy. Central to this interpretation is Max Farrand's classic work *The Legislation of Congress for the Government of the Organized Territories of the United States, 1789–1895*, which documents the legal history of the acquisition of US territories and their subsequent admission into the Union as states on an equal footing with the original thirteen. Focusing primarily on congressional legislation, generally known as organic or territorial acts, Farrand divides this history in two periods. During the first period (1789–1836), Congress began to enact territorial legislation defining its powers to govern new territories that could be subsequently organized into new states of the Union. During the second period (1836–1895), Farrand further argues, legislation aimed at consolidating the plenary power of Congress, and the United States more generally, to govern territories. Farrand's periodization framed nineteenth-century US territorial law and policy as an expression of nation-state building.

In *Territories and Dependencies of the United States*, William F. Willoughby draws on Farrand's periodization to construct a larger US territorial narrative that incorporates the annexation of non-contiguous islands like Hawai'i and the Spanish territories annexed during the War of 1898. Willoughby's narrative includes three periods. Situated between 1784 and 1853, the first period encompassed the annexation of the contiguous territories that would result in the legal construction of the continental United States. This period was primarily shaped by the settlement and colonization of the territories that would eventually result in the construction of 35 additional states (1905: 5–6). The second period, roughly situated between 1853 and 1898, was marked by the annexation of Alaska and the Howland and Baker islands. However, unlike the first period, Willoughby further argued, most of the Federal 'energies' were devoted to the colonization of the continental territories already possessed and was fairly unimportant in the larger history of US expansionism (6). The annexation of Hawai'i, Samoa, Puerto Rico, Guam, and the Philippines in 1898, Willoughby concluded, marked the beginning of a third period. To be sure, whereas territories previously annexed were organized into states that were admitted into the Union on an equal footing with the original thirteen, Willoughby argued,

> the United States was for the first time confronted with the possibility, if not certainty, that for an indefinite time to come, the territory under its sovereignty would have to be divided into two classes having different political status; the one constituting the United States proper and enjoying full political rights and privileges, and the other dependent territory in subordination to the former and having its form of government and the rights of its inhabitants determined for it
>
> (1905: 7–8).

This latter period, Willoughby reasoned, could be defined as a sort of unconscious imperialism premised on the annexation of islands populated by inferior races (4). It is important to note that Willoughby's narrative also included a discussion of the occupation of 'Indian territories,' but ultimately concluded that these territories would be absorbed into future states (73–74). In a sense, Willoughby's narrative of US territorial law and policy creates a linear history that begins with the colonization of the United States and develops into an imperialist tradition.

Gerald L. Neuman's more recent iteration of the development of the US territorial doctrine both echoes and expands Willoughby's conceptual map. Neuman identifies four phases in the development of the US territorial doctrine or rather the relevant jurisprudence. The first three phases correspond to Willoughby's narrative. However, in the fourth phase, spanning from the 1950s to the present, Neuman writes:

> ...the courts have recognized that constitutional limitations may apply even outside the boundaries of the United States. At the same time, the postwar rejection of colonialism has caused a reevaluation of the purposes for which territories may legitimately be governed. Thus far, despite continuing criticism of the *Insular Cases* doctrine, its approach has been subtly transformed rather than overruled.
>
> (Duffy Burnett and Marshall 2001: 185)

Stated differently, Neuman contends, since the 1950s the Supreme Court has progressively shifted away from a 'colonialist' to a more liberal territorial jurisprudence. Although Neuman recognizes the continued disparities present in US territorial jurisprudence, his rendition of the fourth phase suggests that the Court can re-interpret the Insular Cases in a more democratic and egalitarian way, at least within the parameters of the US Constitution.

At least two legal scholars have offered critical readings of the history of United States' territorial expansionism linking the Insular Cases to the current US war on terror laws and policies. Both Natsu Taylor Saito (2007) and Kal Raustiala provide linear readings of US territorial law and politics that incorporate debates about both US colonialism and imperialism. They establish connections between colonialist and imperialist traditions of US territorial acquisition and governance. However, Taylor Saito's narrative does not examine the legal history of US territorial expansionism leading her to obscure conceptual (and constitutional) differences within US territorial law and policy (2007: 22–23). In contrast, while Raustiala provides a critical reading that incorporates multiple traditions of territorial expansionism, his narrative only recognizes two types of territorial subordination, namely intra and extra-territorial subordination. Notwithstanding, like Neuman (2009), both Taylor Saito and Raustiala recognize some of the continuities between US territorial jurisprudence and the ongoing war on terror policies.

I have a different conceptual reading of the development of US territorial law and policy. My contention is that throughout the nineteenth century, the United States simultaneously developed two distinct traditions or strands of territorial expansionism with corresponding laws and policies, namely a colonialist and an imperialist. Between 1898 and 1901, the US developed a third postcolonial tradition, global in scope, to rule the newly annexed territories, Puerto Rico, Guam and the Philippines. Yet, while I recognize continuities among the first two traditions and the third, I also argue that it is possible to recognize substantive differences among the three traditions of territorial expansionism. Moreover, I argue that the three traditions or strands continue to coexist within a broader narrative of US territorial law and policy.

The reader should note that I am primarily concerned with a reading of US territorial law that has been both constitutive of corresponding policies and at times disconnected from actual events on the ground. To be sure, while traditional Liberal interpretations of US constitutional law emphasize the unmediated relationship between the state and the body of the subject of law, in US territorial law the status of the legal subject within the state is mediated by the constitutional status of the territory. Of course, this interpretation does not account for the ways that US legal and political actors treat the inhabitants (residents and/or detainees) of territories, but it helps to contextualize the source of legal authority invoked to justify their actions.

In many ways, my argument is anchored on a series of political and academic debates over the constitutional status of the Spanish territories acquired by the United States following the 1898 War (Torruella 1988: 24–32; Sparrow 2006: 31–56). Between 1898 and 1901, US political actors and academics generally gravitated to either the anti-imperialist or the imperialist camps. For the most part anti-imperialists generally embraced a colonialist view of territorial expansionism (for example Adams 1898; Randolph 1898; Baldwin 1899; Sumner 1899; Shipman 1900; Bacon 1901; and Fuller 1901). In contrast, imperialists typically embraced the unfettered right of the United States to occupy territories without legal and political restrictions (for example Langdell 1899; Thayer 1899; Beach 1899; Bosley 1900; and Russell 1900). However, the decade of the 1890s saw the rise of an influential group of so-called 'large policy' advocates or proponents of US global expansionism (Torruella 2007: 172–173). Large policy or global expansionists ultimately fueled the debates over the creation of what Abbott Lawrence Lowell (1899) described as a 'third-view' on expansionism, which proposed the creation of a new territorial status that combined elements from both the colonialist and imperialist traditions (for example Becker 1900; Burgess 1899; Costigan 1899; Fisher 1899; and Morse 1900). Since then, Puerto Rican legal scholars such as Raúl Serrano Geyls and Gorrín Perralta (1979), José Trías Monge (1980), Juan Torruella (1988), Rubén Nazario Velasco (1999), José López Baralt (1999), Efrén Rivera Ramos (2007), and José Julián Álvarez González (2009) have written important legal and political histories that expand the century-old academic debates in new and critical ways. The pages that follow draw on these academic debates as a conceptual frame of reference. I argue that it is possible to discern clear differences between the expansionist traditions and the ensuing territorial statuses by paying attention to five broad questions, namely: What is the intent of the acquisition of the territory? What is the status ascribed to the territory? What is the constitutional source of power authorizing US legal and political actors to rule a territory? What is the membership or citizenship status ascribed to the inhabitants of the acquired territory? and What civil rights extend to the territory? The legal and political history of the answers to these questions both reveals the continuities and discontinuities among the three types of US territorial expansionism, and highlights the differences between each type of territory.

By 1898, the US had developed fairly coherent corresponding bodies of law. United States colonialism was premised on the annexation of new territories, including non-contiguous territories such as Alaska and Hawai'i, which could be settled by white Anglo-Americans and subsequently organized for admission into statehood. Colonial territories were treated as parts of the United States for constitutional purposes. The constitutional authority to rule a colonial territory was anchored in the Territories Clause (US Constitution, Art. IV, Sect. 3, cl. 2) and the Admissions Clause (US Constitution, Art. IV, Sect. 3, cl. 1). By 1898, birth in a colonial territory was tantamount to birth in the United States. This meant that persons born in a colonial territory acquired the same citizenship or membership status as persons born in a state of the Union or the United States. More importantly, constitutional civil rights extended to colonial territories to the same extent as they extended to any part of the United States. In sum, colonial territories were situated *inside* the United States for constitutional purposes.

In contrast, US imperialism was premised on the strategic occupation of territories primarily for economic and/or military purposes. Although territories subject to US imperialism were subsequently annexed and granted statehood (for example Hawai'i), the general intent was to occupy a territory for strategic purposes. Territories subject to imperialist occupation were generally treated as foreign locations for constitutional purposes and domestic for international interests. Congress and the Commander-in-Chief held the power to selectively treat occupied territories as part of the United States. Unlike the colonialist tradition, the constitutional authority to rule an occupied territory was anchored on various constitutional provisions other than the Territories Clause, including the Commander-in-Chief Clause (US Constitution, Art. II, Sect. 2, cl. 1). Birth in an occupied territory was tantamount to birth outside of the United States. Finally, Congress held the power to enact legislation that could extend or withhold civil rights to the inhabitants of an occupied territory. It is important to emphasize that occupied territories could be held in a state of exception for the duration of the occupation. In sum, territories subject to imperialist occupation were selectively ruled as localities situated *outside* of the United States for constitutional purposes.

As I noted above, following the 1898 War, the United States began to develop a third type of territorial expansionism with a corresponding law and policy. The new territorial law and policy, initially crafted by the War Department, normalized by Congress and subsequently institutionalized by the Court in the Insular Cases, selectively combined elements from prior traditions. More specifically, the new laws and policies enabled the US to craft specific or particular policies for annexed and later leased territories, without binding the Federal government to established constitutional precedents and limitations.[1] The corresponding constitutional interpretation further enabled US legal and political actors to legitimize a new type of territorial expansionism, global in scope.

The main objective of the global expansionist tradition was to annex territories throughout the world for strategic purposes without binding Congress to subsequently organize a territorial government that could be admitted into the Union as a state. More specifically, the initial territorial policy was developed to govern the Spanish territories annexed in the aftermath of the 1898 War and primarily populated by non-Anglo-Saxon or non-white populations. Although United States citizens settled these territories, Congress did not enact legislation that enabled the settlement and subsequent organization of a colonial or territorial system of government. In fact, the early organic or territorial acts were designed to enable the military and US corporations to exert a hegemonic presence in these territories. Even though the United States admitted five new contiguous (Oklahoma, New Mexico, and Arizona) as well as non-contiguous (Hawai'i and Alaska) states into the Union after 1898, Congress has refused to enact binding legislation admitting any territory acquired since into the Union. The intent of the annexation of new territories after 1898 has been postcolonial in scope.

As I suggested before, US global expansionists developed a new territorial status tantamount to a postcolonial borderland space between 1898 and 1901. Also known as the unincorporated territory, the new status enabled US law and policymakers to selectively rule annexed territories as foreign localities in a domestic or constitutional sense. In concrete terms, this meant that the US law and policymakers could enact legislation withholding or extending constitutional provisions to unincorporated territories. For example, two years after the United States annexed Puerto Rico, the initial legislation normalizing Puerto Rico's territorial status withheld the extension of the Uniformity Clause (US Constitution, Art. I, Sect. 8, cl. 1), which barred the imposition of discriminatory tariffs, duties, and other taxes within the United States, and imposed a 15 percent tariff on merchandise trafficked between the US and the island, effectively treating Puerto Rico as a foreign country for trade or commercial purposes.[2] Rather than treating Puerto Rico as a colonial part of the United States for constitutional purposes, Congress enacted tariff legislation that selectively treated an annexed territory as an occupied space. The Court's affirmation of this principle in the 1901 Insular Cases has since provided the precedent enabling the US law and policymakers to selectively treat annexed and leased territories as foreign locations for constitutional purposes.

In the Insular Cases, the Court also anchored the power of Congress to govern unincorporated territories on an expanded interpretation of the Territories Clause. Prior to 1898, Congress' power to enact territorial (colonial) legislation was limited by prevailing constitutional doctrines applicable to the United States. The new interpretation, however, enabled Congress to enact legislation that selectively withheld or extended constitutional provisions to unincorporated territories so long as it did not infringe on the 'fundamental' or natural rights of the local inhabitants. To this extent, while the new interpretation departed from colonialist territorial precedents, it was not as extreme as the imperialist territorial tradition, which empowered US legal and political actors to rule occupied territories under martial law or in a state of exception. In a sense, the new interpretation of the Territories Clause enabled the United States to rule unincorporated territories somewhere between a colonial and an occupied territory.

The United States also developed a corresponding subjectivity allowing for the affirmation of the inclusive exclusion (Ophir *et al.* 2009) of the inhabitants of unincorporated territories within the US global empire. For the most part, the United States' legal and political actors agreed that the non-Anglo-Saxon inhabitants of the newly annexed unincorporated territories should be selectively excluded from acquiring equal membership within the polity. Whereas by 1898 persons born in a colonial territory acquired a constitutional citizenship (US Constitution, 14th Amendment), with the support and collaboration of the Supreme Court, Congress enacted a series of racial laws that conferred an array of non-constitutional citizenships and nationalities to persons born in unincorporated territories. The general effect of these membership laws was to affirm the unequal inclusion of the inhabitants of the unincorporated territories, while simultaneously excluding or barring them from equal or constitutional citizenship. More substantively, while persons residing in colonial territories were entitled to the same civil rights and protections available to the inhabitants of the United States more generally, the inhabitants of unincorporated territories were only entitled to mere 'fundamental rights' and protections. In sum, the new subjectivity affirmed the separate and unequal constitutional status of persons born and residing in unincorporated territories.

For the most part, the prevailing critiques of the US war on terror laws and policies have been anchored on a liberal paradigm of subjectivity and have for the most part ignored the centrality of US territorial law and policy. At least two strands of the liberal paradigm have dominated the debates. One strand, perhaps best described as the pragmatic strand, has focused on the detainees' access to rights as a precondition for justice. Liberal legal advocates and other critics have argued that US war on terror policies deny detainees access to basic civil and/or human rights (Cole 2003; Olshansky 2007). The pragmatist critique describes the relationship between the US government and the detainee as an unmediated relationship between a state and a body. It also situates the legal and political history of the corresponding debates within a larger story of rights, obscuring the role of US territorial law and policy in the corresponding debates. The core legal problem with US war on terror policies is that they deny the detainee equal access to basic civil and/or human rights, while obscuring the relationship between the war on terror policies and US global expansionism.

A second strand of critique has mostly looked to Giorgio Agamben's revisiting of Carl Schmitt's (1931/2003; 1950/2002) notion of the 'state of exception'. Drawing on the work of Schmitt, Hannah Arendt, Michel Foucault and others, Agamben has suggested that the US war on terror has employed a state of exception to rule the bodies of detainees. According to this argument, following the attacks of 11 September 2001, the United States' government apparatus normalized a state of emergency response and began to create camps within its sovereignty where the law could be suspended. The inhabitants (detainees) of these camps are stripped of all legal and political garments and reduced to a sort of 'naked life' or pure 'biological life' subject to the unmediated power of the US state apparatus. Yet, while Agamben emphasizes the centrality of the territorial space in determining the status of the detained body, his analysis of the underlying legal history of US law and policy is grounded on a liberal story of the individual's access to rights and privileges. Agamben situates the constitutional origins of this logic within a story of the legal history of the suspension of the *writ of habeas corpus* during episodes of martial law in US history (2003: 19–20). In Agamben's story, camps and their corresponding states of exception are part of a liberal US legal history that focuses on the access of individuals to rights and privileges. Again, like liberal pragmatists, Agamben's analysis obscures the centrality of US territorial law and policy, or more precisely how US global empire has shaped the legal foundations of war on terror policies developed by the Bush administration, policies that sought to create camps ruled by a state of exception.

CHAPTER OUTLINES

One of the key objectives of this book is to offer a postcolonial interpretation of US constitutional law as a precondition for understanding the legal foundations of United States global expansionism. The pages that follow offer an alternative interpretation of US constitutional law and more specifically the legal history of US territorial law and policy. Although I anchor my arguments on traditional sources of US law, readers looking for a formalist or functionalist interpretation will be disappointed. I am reading traditional sources of law through political lenses informed by a decolonial concern. Aside from the conceptual critiques offered by a postcolonial approach, the starting point of this argument is historical. Readers seeking a social explanation will be sorely disappointed. I provide an interpretation of the law (here understood as a political institution) that will help establish a baseline for other forms of research. Between 1898 and 1901, US law and policymakers developed a new interpretation of the Territories Clause that enabled the US government to annex territories throughout the globe without binding the law and policymakers to treat the new acquisitions as constitutional parts of the United States or place them on a path to admission as a state of the Union.

The book is divided into three overlapping periods that explain the origins and development of the United States global empire. My first contention is that the United States has developed three traditions of territorial expansionism. Between the founding and 1898, I argue, the United States simultaneously developed a colonialist and an imperialist tradition of territorial expansionism with corresponding constitutional interpretations. In Chapter 2 I develop a typology consisting of five dimensions of US territorial expansionism to explain the legal and political differences between United States' colonialism and imperialism. As I noted earlier, this typology uses the following five questions as guides for understanding the development of different forms of territorial expansionism, namely: 1) What is the intent of acquiring the new territory? 2) What is the territorial/constitutional status ascribed to the acquired territory? 3) What is the constitutional source of power for the ensuing territorial laws and policies? 4) What is the membership status of the inhabitants of the acquired territory? and 5) What are the constitutional rights available to the subjects inhabiting the acquired territory? I demonstrate that a critical reading of the legal history of US territorial expansionism can clarify the differences between both traditions.

I also argue that between 1898 and 1901 the United States began to develop a third or postcolonial tradition of territorial expansionism that would enable it to strategically annex new territories throughout the world without binding Congress to past colonialist precedents. I situate the origins or foundation of US global expansionism in the constitutional debates that took place during this period. Central to my argument is the claim that the United States specifically used the case of Puerto Rico to test and develop a corresponding constitutional interpretation. Unlike the colonialist tradition, the United States sought to annex new territories without binding the US government to colonialist legal and political precedents, including treating the newly annexed territories as states-in-the-making. Chapters 3, 4, and 5 draw on the case of Puerto Rico to explain the nuances of the third tradition of US territorial expansionism, the US global empire. My discussion also draws on the five-point typology of US territorial expansionism to both compare and contrast the global expansionist tradition with nineteenth-century colonialism and imperialism and to explain how contemporary laws and policymakers use this tradition to affirm US global hegemony.

Chapter 3 provides the historical context for the annexation of Puerto Rico and the development of the territorial dimensions of the new constitutional interpretation, or the first three questions of my typology. The chapter explains the context shaping the military annexation of Puerto Rico and ensuing legal debates over the constitutional status of the island. The chapter is limited to a discussion of the first three questions of my typology. The main goal of the chapter is to describe the origins of the unincorporated territorial status and the constitutional debates shaping its definition. I argue that the new territorial status confers a borderland status on unincorporated territories.

Chapters 4 and 5 discuss the creation of a corresponding borderland subjectivity. More specifically Chapter 4 provides a historical overview of the extension of US citizenship to Puerto Rico. Chapter 5 describes the competing debates over the extension of personal or fundamental constitutional rights to Puerto Rico. The chapters explain how the US global empire uses inegalitarian and undemocratic laws and policies to affirm the separate and unequal status of Puerto Rico's inhabitants within the US global empire. In broader terms, the chapters use the creation of a Puerto Rican subjectivity to understand how the US began to use a 'functional approach' to administer the subjects inhabiting unincorporated territories.

The third part of this book examines how contemporary law and policymakers continue to use a 'century-old' territorial doctrine to shape the contours of US global empire. I argue that many of the contemporary US laws and policies used to legitimate US global empire are anchored on the Insular Cases. I use the case of the US war on terror as an example of the more extreme and insidious expression of US global empire and demonstrate how the corresponding laws and policies invoke the constitutional precedents established by the case of Puerto Rico. Chapter 6 examines how the Supreme Court used the doctrine of territorial incorporation to temper Congress and the Bush administration's imperialist policies for the torture and detention camps located in Guantánamo Bay, Cuba. The chapter focuses on the debates over the relationship between the territorial status of Guantánamo Bay and the US war on terror. Chapter 7 completes the story by discussing how the precedents established by the Insular Cases have shaped and informed a series of US government policies addressing the status of subjects and/or enemy aliens suspected of engaging in acts of terror against the United States. The main objective of these chapters is to demonstrate that the current US war on terror laws and policies are in large measure a continuation of a century-old tradition of US global expansionism informed by postcolonial legal precedents.

NOTES

1 For an alternative postcolonial interpretation see generally Lanny Thompson's *imperial archipelago* (2010). Thompson's argument is primarily anchored in cultural representations and at times misses the nuances that are present in legal documents.

2 It is important to note that the 1900 Foraker Act imposed a lower tariff on Puerto Rico than the tariff on foreign goods established by the 1897 Dingley Act. Nonetheless, the Foraker tariff treated Puerto Rico as a foreign country rather than as a part of the United States for commercial and constitutional purposes.

Chapter 2

Nineteenth-century territorial expansionism

> Thus, it was at the adoption of the Constitution, the United States, as a geographical unit and as a governmental conception both in the international and the domestic sense, consisted not only of states, but also of territories, all the native *white* inhabitants being endowed with citizenship, protected by pledges of a common union, and, except as to political advantages, all enjoying equal rights and freedom, and safeguarded by substantially similar guaranties, all being under the obligation to contribute their proportionate share for the liquidation of the debt and future expenses of the general government.
>
> (Justice White, *Downes v. Bidwell*, 182 US 244, 320, 1901)

Throughout the nineteenth century the United States simultaneously developed a colonialist and an imperialist tradition of territorial expansionism with corresponding constitutional interpretations. Although both traditions were premised on the acquisition of new territories for the purpose of nation-state building, each tradition can be differentiated in five ways. First, whereas United States' colonialism was premised on the *annexation* of new territories that could be settled and subsequently organized for the purposes of making new states for the Union (Randolph 1898; Baldwin 1899), the imperialist tradition was premised on the mere *occupation* of territories for strategic military and/or commercial purposes (Thayer 1899; Langdell 1899). Second, while colonial territories were treated as constitutional parts of the United States, occupied territories were selectively ruled as foreign countries. Third, whereas colonial expansionism was moored on interpretations of the Territories Clause of the Constitution (US Constitution, Art. IV, Sect. 3, cl. 2), imperialist expansionism was anchored to a host of other constitutional provisions. Fourth, while the Bill of Rights was ultimately extended to colonial territories, the extension of rights to occupied territories was subject to the will of the Federal government. Finally, whereas birth in a colonial territory was tantamount to birth in the United States for citizenship purposes, birth in an occupied territory was tantamount to birth in a foreign country. These distinctions are crucial to understanding the nature of nineteenth-century United States' expansionism and explain how power was organized to rule the citizens and subjects inhabiting the territories between the founding of the United States and 1898. More importantly, as US anti-imperialists and imperialists argued in 1898, these principles defined United States territorial law and policy prior to the annexation of Puerto Rico and the other Spanish territories.[1]

THEORIZING THE US COLONIAL–IMPERIAL DUALITY

Contemporary theorists tend to invoke at least three linear interpretations of nineteenth-century US territorial expansionism, obscuring the differences between colonialism and imperialism in US constitutional law and history. Marxist scholars argue that imperialism is a higher stage of capitalist development and tend to situate the origins of imperialism in the late-nineteenth century or more precisely between 1875 and 1914. They argue that imperialism grew out of a new phase of capitalist development grounded in the search for new markets and sources of raw materials resulting in a territorial division of the world among international (and later global) empires. For example, Eric Hobsbawm writes:

> The crux of the Leninist analysis (which frankly based itself on a variety of contemporary writers, both Marxian and non-Marxian) was that the new imperialism had economic roots in a specific new phase of capitalism, which, among other things, led to the 'territorial division of the world among the great capitalist powers' into a set of formal and informal colonies and spheres of influence.
>
> (1989: 3, 60–61)

Echoing Hobsbawm's argument, Alex Callinicos situates the origins of US imperialism during the same period or between the years following the Civil War and World War I (2009: 144). While both scholars recognize earlier forms of US expansionism they bind imperialism to an international form of capitalist development contingent on the acquisition of new territorial markets without intending to annex new colonies.

Alternatively, some theorists invoke Hannah Arendt's periodization to analyze the development of nineteenth-century expansionism. In *The Origins of Totalitarianism,* Arendt drew on the British expansionist experience to argue that imperialism emerged in response to the 'incongruity of the nation-state system with the economic and industrial developments in the last third of the nineteenth century' (2004: 159). Like the Marxists, Arendt further claimed that imperialism 'grew out of colonialism,' which she described as a form of expansionism premised on 'national conquests' and 'true empire-building Roman style' (Ibid.). Whereas colonialism was premised on the annexation of new territories that could be settled in order to expand the national borders of the empire, imperialism 'started its politics of expansion for expansion's sake' (Ibid.).

In contrast, while Michael Hardt and Antonio Negri also embrace a linear analysis of the development of US expansionism, they anchor their interpretation on Bruce Ackerman's liberal narratives of US constitutional exceptionalism (2000: 167–168). In *Empire,* Hardt and Negri construct a narrative of the historical development of a US 'imperial notion of sovereignty' that parallels Ackerman's story of the development of three constitutional regimes. In *We the People,* Ackerman examines the 'jusgenerative' effects of three constitutional regimes in fostering democratic interpretations of the US constitution. Ackerman explains how on three constitutional periods, namely the Founding, Reconstruction, and the New Deal, prevailing regimes managed to reinstate constitutional interpretations that affirmed the democratic rights of 'We the People' or the people of the United States. In Hardt and Negri's narrative, between the founding and the Civil War the United States developed a first phase of territorial expansionism premised on the conquest of the western frontier. A second, perhaps an intermediary phase, resulted from the tensions created by the conquest of the West during the 1890s and marked the beginning of the development of US imperialism. Finally, between World War I and the New Deal, the United States developed a new form of imperialism of global dimensions.

Notwithstanding the ideological differences informing these narratives, all agree on a linear history of the development of US territorial expansionism, which situates colonialism at the beginning of a historical narrative of expansionism and places imperialism at the tail end. While Hardt and Negri offer a more nuanced (and at times convoluted) interpretation of this history, all agree that in response to changing economic landscapes the United States developed an imperialist or international form of expansionism between the period following the Civil War and World War I. Yet, none of these theorists examine or engage the nineteenth-century literature on the constitutional justifications for US expansionism. None contemplates the possibility that the United States simultaneously developed a colonialist and an imperialist tradition of territorial expansionism. If anything, these linear conceptions of US expansionism obscure a more complex political history.

In addition, it is possible to discern at least two sources of US territorial expansionism, namely a popular sovereignty and state-sponsored forms of expansionism. Popular sovereignty expansionism consisted of individuals or groups of settlers seeking to acquire and settle a territory for the purposes of constructing future states for the Union (Boydston 2005; Sizemore 2013). Examples of this tradition abound and are readily discerned from the histories of the colonization of Native American territories, Texas (Reichstein 1989), the Jefferson Territory (Trinklein 2010), the Mormon State of Deseret (1872: Misc. Doc 165), Hawai'i (Dudley and Agard 1993), Isle of Pines, Cuba [*Pearcy v. Stranahan,* 205 US 257 (1907); Rodríguez Torres

2011]. In these and other cases, groups of US citizens migrated to territories and began to organize territorial government on their own initiative and with their own funding. Their goal was to subsequently organize a territorial government that could enable it to become a state of the Union. In the cases of Liberia (1827: H. Rept. 101) and Samaná Bay, Dominican Republic, US citizens sought to construct colonial outposts to resettle black Americans. In some instances, as the experience of Native Americans and the Guano Islands (Skaggs 1994) attest to, individuals and corporations (corporate persons) sought to conquer territories for mere profiteering. In the case of William Walker's occupation of Nicaragua his goal was to conquer a nation and profit from the occupation. In some instances what began as popular sovereignty initiatives, transformed into state-sponsored forms of colonialism (for exampleTexas and Hawai'i) and imperialism (for example the Native American territories).

In contrast, state-sponsored territorial expansionism is premised on the government's formal annexation or occupation of territories. Presumably, the colonialist tradition resulted in the organization of territories that could become states of the Union, while imperialist tradition sought to merely occupy territories for strategic purposes. Although annexed territories were populated by settlers the structural dimensions of the colonization process were placed under the purview of Congress. Notwithstanding the importance of popular sovereignty expansionism, my focus in this book is limited to state-sponsored forms of territorial expansionism. More specifically, the pages that follow examine the development of laws and policies used to formally acquire and govern territories annexed and/or occupied, both inside and outside the current continental borders by US legal and political actors (Raustiala 2009: 16).

Finally, as I will expand below, it is important to note that the history of US territorial expansionism also contains anomalies that escape easy classification. For example, US Native American law and policy throughout the nineteenth century developed in piecemeal fashion and contains significant contradictions. More importantly, Native Americans in the United States have experienced an array of colonialist and imperialist policies. Notwithstanding, my contention is that overall the US government has ruled Native Americans as occupied domestic dependent nations or tribes bound to quasi or semi-sovereign localities. Likewise, it is important to further note that US territorial law and policy also grew out of both efforts to legitimate expansionism over time as well as an array of political goals. Suffice it to say that I do not intend to provide a homogenizing narrative of US colonialism and imperialism, but I do intend to argue that it is possible to discern distinct constitutional policies that substantively differentiate each tradition from the other.

THE ACQUISITION OF US TERRITORIES

Despite the Constitution's silence on the question of territorial acquisition, the United States embraced expansionist laws and policies since its inception (Grupo 1984; Sheridan for Congressional Research Service 1985; López Baralt 1999). Whether one looks to the 1754 'Plan of the Union' (Grupo 1984, 1: 3), Article XI of the 'Articles of Confederation', or the 1789 Northwest Ordinance (Onuf 1987), little doubt should remain that since its founding the United States envisioned itself as an empire with boundaries extending beyond those of the original thirteen states. While it is true that the Constitution did not contain language defining the power of the United States to acquire new territories beyond the original compact of thirteen states, the Territories Clause enumerated the powers of Congress to govern annexed territories and possessions until these were admitted as states of the Union.[2] To be sure, between its inception and 1853 the United States annexed all the territories presently comprising the continental landmass of the Union and carved 35 new states. Alaska and Hawai'i, the two non-contiguous states of the Union, were annexed in 1867 and 1898 respectively.

Throughout this period, the United States used four methods of expansionism to acquire new territories. Since its inception the United States began to annex territories adjacent to the thirteen original states in order to buffer the presence of European empires and dispossessed Native Americans (Farrand 1905). The United States purchased parts of the Northwest Territories (1783) (Native Americans); Louisiana (1803) (France); East and West Florida (1819) (Spain); parts of the Southwest (1852) (Mexico); and Alaska (1867) (Russia). In other instances, the United States acquired territories through treaties following expansionist wars (for example, Mexican-occupied Southwest). Wars of annexation included the future President Andrew Jackson's campaigns against the Spanish empire and Seminoles in order to acquire the Florida territories (1814–1819) and the US–Mexico War (1846–1848). The Monroe Doctrine of 1823 also stands as the core policy enabling the United States to strategically annex and/or occupy new territories to forestall European forays into the Western Hemisphere (Alvarez 1924). Military incursions were also linked to economic interests. For example the 1803 Louisiana purchase entailed control of the Mississippi River, a key financial artery of North America (Brown 1918/2000; Levinson and Sparrow 2005). The later acquisition of the Mexican province of California was in large measure driven by a desire for gold (Harlow 1982). In at least two instances, namely in the cases of the Republics of Texas (1845) and Hawai'i (1898), the United States signed joint resolutions authorizing the annexation of both territories. However, in the latter case, the United States enabled a rebellion that undermined the Hawaiian sovereignty and subsequently installed a puppet government that signed the joint resolution authorizing the annexation of the former Republic to the United States. In most cases, however, the annexation of territories was driven by either the threat of war or actual aggression. In contrast, the Unite States primarily occupied territories for military, commercial (Guano Islands) (Skaggs 1994)[3], or both purposes (Native American territories).

Overall, it is also important to note that racist ideologies asserting white supremacy as well as complementary narratives of Anglo-American exceptionalism fueled nineteenth-century United States' territorial expansionism. In *Race and Manifest Destiny* Reginald Horsman documents how throughout the nineteenth century US law and policymakers consistently invoked racist ideologies, fueled by narratives of 'Manifest Destiny' and Anglo-Saxon or Anglo-American exceptionalism, to legitimate the right of Anglo-Saxon Americans to annex the territories presently comprising the United States. Horsman argues that by the 1850s, the decade during which the US finished annexing all contiguous territories comprising the 48 continental states of the Union, US expansion was viewed as an affirmation of white Anglo-Saxon supremacy. In *Beneath the United States*, Lars Schoultz further documents how nineteenth-century US foreign policymakers invoked Manifest Destiny and other racist narratives of Anglo-American exceptionalism to legitimate the US forays into Latin America. Moreover, the legal histories of territories annexed and/or occupied throughout the nineteenth century are littered with racist provisions and references affirming the supremacy of white settlers and occupiers more generally. In sum, my point is that scholars across disciplines have demonstrated that racist narratives of Manifest Destiny and Anglo-American exceptionalism both fueled and affirmed nineteenth-century US expansionism.

THE QUESTION OF INTENT

United States' colonialism has been premised on the annexation of territories for the purpose of enabling white settlers to create new states for the Union. Throughout the nineteenth century, law and policy makers repeatedly affirmed this principle. For example, in *Dred Scott v. Sandford* (1856), Chief Justice Roger B. Taney summarized this argument through a description of Louisiana territory's history:

> At the time when the territory in question was obtain by cession from France, it contained no population fit to be associated together an admitted as a state; and it therefore was absolutely necessary to hold possession of it, as a Territory belonging to the United States, until it was settled and inhabited by a civilized community capable of self-government, and in a condition to be admitted on equal terms with the other States as a member of the Union.
>
> (60 US 393, 448)

Once acquired, territories were typically ascribed a tutelary status, tantamount to that of a ward or a child in a state of pupilage. During this period the President, acting on behalf of Congress, organized a local territorial government that could grow to petition admission into the Union.

United States colonial legislation was also premised on the ability to regulate the settlement of white subjects in order to manage the creation of new states. The 1789 Northwest Ordinance, the first law enacted by the nascent US Congress, provided the basic ideological blueprint for the development of a colonialist territorial policy (Farrand 1896; Taylor, Jr. 1987). Originally designed to regulate the settlement of the Northwestern territories (presently comprising the states of Indiana, Ohio, Michigan, Illinois, Wisconsin and parts of Minnesota), the Northwest Ordinance authorized the President to organize and manage a colonial government until Congress determined that the territory was ready for admission into the Union (Onuf 1987). The 1789 Ordinance enabled property-owning 'free male inhabitants' to colonize territories and progressively acquire local powers of self-government contingent on population growth. Upon reaching a population of 60,000 inhabitants, the territory could petition admission into the Union as a state (Taylor Jr. 1987: 43). While it is important to note that the Northwest Ordinance included provisions protecting the land rights of Native Americans (Art. 3), the law enabled the colonial annexation of lands inhabited by Native Americans. Moreover, while the ordinance included a provision barring slavery in the Northwestern territories, the same provision affirmed the prevailing fugitive slave laws (Art. 6) enabling bounty hunters to routinely kidnap black inhabitants. To the extent that the Northwest Ordinance served as an ideological framework for subsequent territorial legislation, this law affirmed the notion that white settlers should colonize annexed territories.

However, by 1804, following the annexation of the Orleans (presently Louisiana) territories, Congress began to use organic or territorial acts to essentially organize new territories and prepare them for statehood. Again, although the history of the statehood processes of the 37 states admitted into the Union since the original thirteen is not uniform or for that matter coherent, by 1898 it is possible to discern some patterns in the development of organic acts. For example, most organic acts provided for the original organization of a local or territorial government under the supervision of the President. Once the Federal government deemed these territories to be worthy of admission, it would enable the territorial government to draft a state constitution and begin the admissions process. Again, while recognizing that not all statehood processes followed the same rules, by 1898 organic or territorial acts generally spelled out a colonial process leading to the future admission of new states. All territories annexed prior to 1898 and ruled under the colonialist tradition were subsequently admitted as new states of the Union.

Simultaneously, the United States recognized at least three types of imperialist territorial occupations with corresponding constitutional interpretations. Historically, the most common type of US imperialism has been the occupation of territories for military purposes. Whether the United States was occupied by a foreign power [*United States v. Rice,* 4 Wheat. 246 (1819)] or was itself engaged in the occupation of a territory [*Fleming v. Page,* 50 US 603 (1850)], the Supreme Court typically recognized that a military occupation was temporary and contingent on the duration of a conflict. The intent of military occupations also varied widely, ranging from the occupation of territories for strategic purposes, to commercial interests, or in some cases for mere ideological desires (for example, 'Manifest Destiny'). The point is that throughout the nineteenth century the United States' imperialism at times invoked military imperatives in order to legitimate the occupation of territories.

United States legal actors also recognized the temporary occupation of territories for mere commercial purposes. The disputes arising from the Union's occupation of Southern businesses in the decade following the Civil War provide a clear example of a domestic form of imperialist occupation. In some instances, the Union occupied Southern businesses and/or territories well after the cessation of hostilities in order to generate revenues that could be used to offset the costs of the Civil War [*New Orleans v. Steamship Company,* 87 US 387 (1874)]. The disputes arising from the temporary occupation of the so-called Guano Islands located within the purview of Peru and Haiti (for example Navassa) provide the clearest examples of international imperialist occupations for commercial purposes (Skaggs 1994). To be sure, as early as 1856, Congress had enacted legislation authorizing individuals and businesses to occupy any 'discovered' island while exploiting guano or bird manure deposits used in the production of agricultural fertilizers. As the Supreme Court later suggested in *Jones v. United States* [137 US 202 (1890)], companies could retain plenary control over the Guano Islands while they harvested the local guano deposits. While it is likely that in most cases military occupations entailed securing the economic interests of the United States, US legal actors also developed constitutional interpretations legitimating the occupation of territories for exclusive commercial or economic purposes.

United States' imperialists developed distinct policies to legitimate the occupation and acquisition of Native American tribal nations and territories for an array of strategic purposes, including the creation of new states for white settlers. However, and notwithstanding fleeting debates over the possible creation of a Cherokee state (Oklahoma) (Sheridan 1985: 40–42) or the assimilation of individuals under the terms of the 1887 Dawes Act, the Federal government did not contemplate the colonization or creation of Native American states. Instead, as I will discuss in more detail below, the Federal government ruled Native American territories as domestic dependent nations subject to a 'ward'-like or tutelary status within the Anglo-American polity [*Cherokee Nation v. Georgia*, 30 US 1, 17 (1831)]. For the most part, throughout the nineteenth century the Federal government ruled Native American nations and territories as occupied semi-sovereign or domestic dependent nations.

This of course is not to say that the history of US territorial occupation has been uniform or consistent. For example the case of the annexation of Mexico provides multiple examples of different forms of US expansionism. Following the Mexican secession from Spain, Mexico inherited the rights and responsibilities of the 1819 Treaty of Adams-de Onís including 'imperial sovereignty' over the Southwestern territories west of the Mississippi (Thorpe 1909, 6: 3475–3476). Soon after, US settlers began to colonize the Texas territory and subsequently managed to wage a successful rebellion leading to the creation of the Republic of Texas in 1835. In 1838 the United States signed a convention with the nascent Republic and formally annexed Texas in 1845. The following year the United States formally attacked Mexico and subsequently occupied the Port of Tampico as well as various ports in California, Mexico. Throughout the remainder of the war, the United States ruled the Port of Tampico as an occupied or foreign country [(*Fleming v. Page* (1850)]. However west of Texas and north of the Rio Grande, the US annexed large parts of the present day Southwest (including New Mexico, California), and in 1853 signed the Gadsden Purchase acquiring the remaining Southwestern territories. These territories were subsequently organized into states of the Union. The point is that the United States both occupied and annexed parts of Mexico. The latter resulted in the colonization and subsequent creation of the states of California, Colorado, Nevada, New Mexico, and Arizona.

In the case of Hawai'i, the United States had long recognized the Republic of Hawai'i and its sovereign representatives. However, by 1893, with the assistance of the United States Navy, a group of US fruit companies organized the overthrow of the Republic and imposed a series of puppet rulers. Between 1893 and 1898 the United States military occupied Hawai'i with the intent of establishing a commercial foothold in the Pacific region. During this period, the United States ruled Hawai'i as an occupied country. However, in 1898 the US formally annexed the Republic of Hawai'i and in 1900, Congress enacted a territorial act incorporating Hawai'i as a colonial territory destined to become a state of the Union. While it is not readily evident that the original intent of the US occupation was to colonize Hawai'i, by 1900 Congress had authorized the colonization of the archipelago and placed it on a path to statehood. Although not all territories were initially acquired with the purposes of creating new states, once annexed they were ruled as colonial territories and placed on a path to eventual statehood.

In sum, nineteenth-century US law and policy recognized a distinction between the annexation and occupation of territories. Territories subject to colonialism were annexed with the intention of creating new states. In contrast, territories subject to imperial occupation, including Native American territories, were generally held for strategic (military and commercial) purposes without being treated as potential states in the making. Even in the case of Hawai'i, Congress first enacted legislation authorizing the annexation of the Republic before placing the islands on a path to statehood. By 1898, US legal actors recognized distinctions between the goals informing the annexation and occupation of new territories.

STATUS

The status of territories ruled by each tradition can be differentiated in two ways. First, legal actors sought to situate an acquired territory within the definition of the United States for constitutional purposes. Territories were either a part of the United States or not. Second, and related, lawmakers also took measure of the location of a territory. While annexed territories were clearly situated inside of the US sovereignty, occupied territories were situated either outside of the United States or in its interstices, namely in anomalous places under the control of the US government. What is important to keep in mind, however, is the fact that US legal actors recognized a clear difference in the statuses ascribed to annexed and occupied territories.

The colonialist interpretation treated annexed territories as constitutional parts of the United States. One of the earliest and most cited articulations of this interpretation was established in *Loughborough v. Blake* (1820), a Supreme Court ruling affirming the constitutionality of a tax imposed on the District of Columbia. In *Loughborough* Chief Justice Marshall wrote:

> Does this term designate the whole, or any particular portion of the American empire? Certainly this question can admit but one answer. It is the name given to our great republic, which is composed of States and territories. The district of Columbia, or the territory west of Missouri, is not less within the United States, than Maryland or Pennsylvania; and it is not less necessary, on the principles of our constitution, that uniformity in the imposition of imposts, duties, and excises, should be observed in the one, than in the other.
>
> (18 US 317, 319)

Not only did Chief Justice Marshall equate the status of the District of Columbia to that of a territory, but he also established that annexed territories were part of the definition of the United States for constitutional purposes. These interpretations helped moor US colonial policy on constitutional soil.

In contrast, the imperialist tradition ascribed at least four distinct statuses to occupied territories. Imperialist constitutional precedents enabled the

United States to selectively treat territories subject to military occupation as foreign countries for constitutional purposes. For example, following the 1812 War the Supreme Court established in *US v. Rice* that while under British occupation, the port of Castine, Maine became a foreign port for the purposes of US revenue laws (17 US 246, 254). Similarly, following the Civil War the Supreme Court established that territories occupied by the Confederacy could be treated as foreign territories, even after the same Court had established that indissoluble nature of statehood. Although in *Texas v. White* [74 US 700 (1868)] the Supreme Court established that Southern states that joined the confederacy had not ceased being states of the Union during the Civil War, in *New Orleans v. Steamship Company* (1874) Justice Noah H. Swayne reasoned:

> Although the city of New Orleans was conquered and taken possession of in a civil war waged on the part of the United States to put down an insurrection and restore the supremacy of the National government in the Confederate States, that government had the same power and rights held by conquest as *if the territory had belonged to a foreign country and had been subjugated in a foreign war.*
>
> (87 US 387, 394) (emphasis mine)

According to this logic domestic territories such as Maine (then a district of Massachusetts) and the state of Louisiana (then part of the Southern Confederacy) occupied by either a foreign or domestic enemy could be treated as foreign countries for constitutional purposes throughout the duration of the occupation and a subsequent transitory period. Territories subject to military occupation could be treated as foreign countries situated outside of the United States for constitutional purposes.

In contrast, a second and the core constitutional precedent used by United States' legal actors to legitimate the military occupation of sovereign or foreign territory was established to regulate profiteering during the 1846–1848 US–Mexico War. In *Fleming v. Page* (1850) the Supreme Court addressed the power of the collector of the port of Philadelphia, PA to collect duties or tariffs on goods and merchandise imported from the port of Tampico, Mexico in 1847 by the US trading firm of Fleming and Marshall. At the time, the port of Tampico was under US occupation and governed by military authorities 'acting under the orders of the President' (50 US 603, 614). Writing for the court, Chief Justice Taney argued that while:

> It is true, that, when Tampico had been captured, and the State of Tamaulipas subjugated, other nations were bound to regard the country, while our possession continued, as the territory of the United States, and to respect it as such...But yet it was not a part of this Union. For every nation which acquires territory by treaty or conquest holds it

> according to its own institutions and laws. An the relation in which the port of Tampico stood to the United States while it was occupied by their arms did not depend upon the laws of nations, but upon our own Constitution and acts of Congress.
>
> (50 US 603, 615)

At the time, the Chief Justice further reasoned, Congress had not enacted legislation extending the 'boundaries of the United States' (50 US 603, 616). Subsequent interpretations of this precedent have established that the United States can selectively govern an occupied territory as a domestic possession for international interests, while simultaneously treating it as a foreign territory for domestic purposes.

In a sense, the precedent established by *Fleming* granted the US government a power to define occupied territories as a temporary borderland space. In the absence of congressional legislation, the President or Commander-in-Chief was authorized to selectively treat an occupied territory as either part of the United States or a foreign country for constitutional purposes. Likewise, Congress could enact legislation achieving the same objective. What is important to note, however, is that territories subject to imperialist occupation remained foreign countries until the United States annexed them. To this extent, the borderland status ascribed to occupied territories was temporary or contingent on the occupation.

Territories occupied for commercial purposes were ascribed a temporary status as a Federal possession and situated in the interstice of the states and the Federal government. For example, in *Jones v. US* (1890), the Court concluded that Island of Navassa, a Guano island, was a territorial possession appurtenant or belonging to the Federal government, but situated outside of the states or districts (137 US 202, 216). To this extent the Guano Islands' status was contingent on its commercial utility. In terms of their constitutional locations, the islands were situated in an anomalous space outside of the jurisdictions of the states or districts, but within the purview of the Federal government, at least while occupied by corporations. This status can be read as an extraterritorial variant of the Native American domestic dependent nation, a status discussed below.

Since the founding, the United States ascribed at least two contradictory territorial statuses to Native American tribes or nations. Francis Paul Prucha notes that between 1778 and 1868 the United States ratified upwards of 367 treaties with various Native American nations (1994: 1). The treaty system recognized some Native American tribes as independent or sovereign nations. In *Dred Scott,* Chief Justice Taney summarized this interpretation in the following language:

> (t)hese Indian Governments were regarded and treated as foreign Governments, as much so as if an ocean had separated the red man from

> the white; and their freedom has constantly been acknowledged, from the time of the first emigration to the English colonies to the present day, by the different Governments which succeeded each other. Treaties have been negotiated with them and their alliance sought in war.
>
> (640 US 393, 404)

Notwithstanding, Congress effectively terminated the treaty system under the terms of the 1871 Indian Appropriations Act establishing that:

> No Indian (sic) nation or tribe within the territory of the United States shall be acknowledged or recognized as an independent nation, tribe, or power with whom the United States may contract by treaty; but no obligation of any treaty lawfully made and ratified with any such Indian nation or tribe prior to March third, eighteen hundred and seventy-one, shall be hereby invalidated or impaired.
>
> (Revised Statutes §2079 1874: 363)

As such the coercive acquisition of Native American territories by the United States was tantamount to the imperialist occupation of sovereign nation-states.

In contrast, during the 1830s, in a series of Supreme Court rulings generally known as the *Cherokee Cases,* Chief Justice Marshall invented an alternative territorial status situating Native American nations in an anomalous zone located within the geographical limits of the United States, but outside of the states (*Cherokee Nation v. Georgia,* 30 US 1 (1831); *Worcester v. Georgia,* 31 US 515 (1832); Shattuck and Norgren 1991; Norgren 1996). More precisely, Chief Justice Marshall described this new status in *Cherokee Nation v. Georgia* in the following terms:

> Though the Indians are acknowledged to have an unquestionable, and, heretofore, unquestioned right to the lands they occupy, until that right shall be extinguished by a voluntary cession to our government; yet it may well be doubted whether those tribes which reside within the acknowledged boundaries of the United States can, with strict accuracy, be denominated foreign nations. They may, more correctly, perhaps, be denominated domestic dependent nations. They occupy a territory to which we assert a title independent of their will, which must take effect in point of possession when their right of possession ceases. Meanwhile they are in a state of pupilage. Their relation to the United States resembles that of a ward to his guardian.
>
> (31 US 1, 17)

The new interpretation established that domestic dependent nations although located within the geographical boundaries of the United States, were not a part of the nation-state for constitutional purposes. Yet, while these legal constructions acquired a semi-sovereign status, the Court refused to equate the domestic dependent nation to a sovereign nation in an international sense. The domestic dependent nation was relegated to the penumbras of a space located somewhere between a state and the Federal government.

My point, however, is that both territorial statuses ascribe degrees of sovereignty and nationality that are fundamentally different from those of territories subject to colonial annexation. In the former instance, the notion that Native American territories possess a sovereign status in an international sense suggests that US territorial policy merely affirms a Federal form of imperial occupation. In the latter case, even when accounting for the tutelary or 'ward like' nature of the domestic dependent nation, the prevailing narrative ascribed a semi-sovereign or national status on Native American territories. To this extent, using the prevailing nineteenth-century grammar, it is possible to describe the US presence in Native American territories as a form of indefinite imperialist occupation.

SOURCES OF POWER

Chief Justice John Marshall established the basic interpretation of the constitutional source of US colonialism in *American Insurance Co. v. Canter* [26 US 511 (1828)]. According to the Chief Justice, the power to govern annexed territories was anchored on either the treaty of territorial annexation or the so-called Territories Clause (US Constitution, Art. 4, Sect.3, cl. 2). While annexation treaties generally contained basic guidelines for the initial governance of a territory, the Territories Clause empowered Congress to 'make all needful rules and regulations, respecting the territory, or other property belonging to the United States' (Id.). Typically, Congress enacted organic or territorial legislation to organize and govern a colonial territory while the President implemented and administered the relevant legislation during the period between annexation and statehood. In the absence of congressional legislation, the Supreme Court affirmed in *Cross v. Harrison* (1853) the power of the President to administer annexed territories until Congress enacted relevant legislation (57 US 164, 194). What is important to emphasize, however, is that the Territories Clause was invoked to govern colonial territories, public lands, and other territories that were treated as parts of the United States for constitutional purposes.

In contrast, the power to govern territories subject to imperialist occupation was grounded in an array of constitutional provisions other than the Territories Clause. The United States did not invoke the Territories Clause to rule any occupied territory throughout the nineteenth century or for that matter ever. The constitutional power to rule territories subject to military occupations was typically anchored on two clauses delineating the President's executive powers rather than on the Territories Clause. The Commander-in-Chief Clause (US Constitution, Art. II, Sect. 2, cl. 1) granted the President the power to manage the armed forces occupying a territory. As Commander-in-Chief, the President held a plenary power to oversee the implementation of US policies during a belligerent occupation. However, almost a decade before the Civil War, in *Cross v. Harrison* the Supreme Court affirmed the power of the President to govern a domestic occupied territory (California) after the cessation of hostilities and until Congress enacted legislation to govern the annexed territory (57 US 164; Lawson and Seidman 2004: 179–182). In addition, the Treaties Clause (US Constitution, Art. II, Sect. 2, cl. 2) also empowered the President to manage an occupied territory during a transitional period leading to the implementation of a treaty. This latter power, however, was incidental to the implementation of treaties. My point is to emphasize that United States' imperialism relied on the despotic powers of the President to rule occupied territories, domestic or international (Rossiter 2004).

Congress could also invoke a wide array of enumerated powers to authorize the President, corporations, and even individuals to rule territories occupied for commercial purposes. For example, in 1856 Congress enacted legislation authorizing citizens and corporations to rule over discovered territories that contained guano deposits, so long as these territories did not belong to the United States or another sovereign nation-state (11 Stat. 119). This power, anchored in the Commerce Clause (US Constitution, Art. 1, Sect. 8, cl. 3), enabled individuals and corporations to exercise a plenary power over their employees in certain commercial territories.

Before the 1880s, David E. Wilkins argues, 'relations between tribes and the United States were largely determined either by treaties or the so-called Indian trade and intercourse acts' (1997: 67). As previously noted, under prevailing interpretations the Treaties Clause granted the President the power to implement and administer a treaty. In contrast, the 'Indian trade and intercourse acts' were typically anchored on the Commerce Clause, which granted Congress the power 'to regulate Commerce with foreign Nations, and among several States, and with Indian Tribes.' According to Wilkins, prior to the Supreme Court's ruling in *The Cherokee Tobacco* [78 US 616 (1870)], Native American territories 'were not regarded as included in congressional enactments unless the tribe had given its explicit consent and unless they were expressly included in the law' (55). However, as Wilkins further notes, *The Cherokee Tobacco* ruling established that general congressional acts would now apply to Native American territories unless Congress explicitly excluded them. The key implication, of course, is that Native American nations were now selectively governed as parts of the United States unless

Congress chose to exclude them from a law. Again, notwithstanding the inherent contradictions of the latter interpretation, what is important to note is that throughout the nineteenth century US imperialism primarily anchored its constitutional power to govern Native American territories on the Treaties and Commerce Clauses while eschewing the Territories Clause.

In *Tribes, Treaties, and Constitutional Tribulations*, Vine Deloria Jr. and David E. Wilkins note that the Property or Territories Clause did not play a prominent role in Congressional deliberations or Federal court rulings addressing Native American matters (1999: 80). Even as the United States absorbed Native American nations into its boundaries, US legal actors avoided using the Territories Clause. In fact, in *US v. Kagama* (1886) the Court even tried to disembowel prevailing interpretations of the Territories Clause in order to affirm the Federal government's imperialist regulation of tribal sovereignty. To be sure, writing for the Court, Justice Miller argued that the power of Congress:

> to organize territorial governments, and make laws for their inhabitants, (arose), not so much from the clause in the constitution in regard to disposing of and making rules and regulations concerning the territory and other property of the United States, as from the ownership of the country in which the territories are.
>
> (118 US 375, 380)

In sum, the constitutional sources of power for both the colonialist and imperialist traditions were anchored on different constitutional provisions throughout the nineteenth century. Colonial territories have always been governed under the purview of the Territories Clause. Although the *Canter* precedent suggests that the United States could invoke a treaty of territorial annexation as a source of law to rule a colonial territory, this interpretation was limited to a transitional period between the formal annexation of a territory and subsequent action by Congress. In contrast, US law and policy-makers have anchored the power to govern occupied territories in a range of constitutional provisions other than the Territories Clause. Unless territories subject to imperial occupation were treated as future states in the making, United States law and policymakers did not invoke the Territories Clause to govern occupied territories.

RIGHTS AND LIMITS OF POWER

Prevailing colonialist interpretations granted Congress a plenary 'political power' to govern annexed territories. Congress exercised its plenary authority in at least three ways. First, Congress acquired the power to create extra-constitutional institutions to rule a colonial territory. For example, as Chief Justice Marshall established in *American Ins. v. Canter*, Congress could create special territorial legislatures as well as non-Article 3 or rather extra-constitutional courts to rule a territory (26 US 511, 546). Stated differently, the colonialist interpretation recognized Congress' plenary power to create courts with different powers from those established by the judiciary article of the US constitution. Second, as noted above, Congress authorized the President to administer and manage the colonization process of a territory. Historically, all organic acts gave the President a plenary power to organize a local government, appoint the Governor and other members of the executive branch, and the local judiciary. Citizens settling a territory were for the most part excluded from meaningful participation in the governance of a territory. Finally, citizens and subjects who migrated to a colonial territory lost their right to participate in the national political process until the territory became a state of the Union. Granted, the latter disenfranchisement of citizens was primarily a product of the undemocratic nature of the US constitution (Dahl 2003; Levinson 2006), a constitution that limits political power to the representatives of the states while excluding the residents of territories and citizens more generally from substantive participation in the republic.[4] The political disenfranchisement of the residents of colonial territories was ultimately justified as a temporary measure contingent on the statehood process, an arbitrary political process controlled by Congress (McCarthy, Poole, and Rosenthal 1998).

Yet, while US colonialist law and policy curtailed the political rights of the residents of territories, it recognized the entitlement of citizens residing in a territory to the same constitutional civil rights available to those residing in a state of the Union. Again, in *American Ins. v. Canter* Chief Justice Marshall established the basic principle defining the extension of civil rights to the territories:

> This treaty is the law of the land, and admits the inhabitants of Florida to the enjoyment of the privileges, rights, and immunities, of the citizens of the United States. It is unnecessary to inquire, whether this is not their condition, independent of stipulation. They do not, however, participate in political power; they do not share in the government, till Florida shall become a state. In the mean time, Florida continues to be a territory of the United States; governed by virtue of that clause in the Constitution, which empowers Congress 'to make all needful rules and regulations, respecting the territory, or other property belonging to the, United States.'
>
> (26 US 511, 542)

To this extent, residence in a territory was tantamount to residence in the United States. Again, to the extent that any constitutional rights were applicable to a national space, territories were treated as a part of the United States.

Subsequently Chief Justice Taney invoked this principle in *Dred Scott v. Sandford* to affirm the rights of citizens to own other humans (as property) and challenge the 1820 Missouri Compromise, a law that essentially barred the extension of slavery to the Northern US territories. Chief Justice Taney reasoned that:

> The powers of the Government and the rights and privileges of the citizen are regulated and plainly defined by the Constitution itself. An when the Territory becomes a part of the United States, the Federal Government enters into possession in the character impressed upon it by those who created it. It enters upon it with the powers of the citizen strictly defined, and limited by the Constitution, from which it derives its own existence, and by virtue of which alone it continues to exist and act as a Government and sovereignty. It has no power of any kind beyond it; and it cannot, when it enters a Territory of the United States, put off its character, and assume discretionary or despotic powers which the Constitution has denied it.
>
> (60 US 393, 449)

In fact, Chief Justice Taney rejected the idea that Congress could enact legislation that subordinated citizens residing in a territory to a subject status:

> There is certainly no power given by the Constitution to the Federal Government to establish or maintain colonies bordering on the United States or at a distance, to be ruled and governed at its own pleasure; nor to enlarge its territorial limits in any way, except by the admission of new States.
>
> (Id. at 446)

In the latter case, I read Chief Justice Taney's use of the term 'colonies' to describe territories subject to imperialist occupation. To this extent the principle, initially introduced by Chief Justice Marshal in *Canter* and reaffirmed throughout the nineteenth century by the Supreme Court, barred the United States from enacting legislation that would infringe the constitutional rights and liberties of the residents of territories destined to become states of the Union.

Notwithstanding Supreme Court jurisprudence, legal actors and scholars alike debated *how* the bill of rights extended to territories that did not possess the same status as a state of the Union. Four competing interpretations prevailed throughout the nineteenth century. One interpretation suggested that upon annexation the constitution was operative in a colonial territory *ex propio vigore* or on its own force in every place subject to the US government's authority [*Loughborough v. Blake*, 18 US 317]. To this extent colonial citizens could invoke the bill of rights to limit the powers of Congress in a territory. A second interpretation suggested that Congress only extended *fundamental* rather than the *full* panoply of civil rights to the territories through organic acts (Willoughby 1905: 21). Certainly, most organic acts passed throughout the nineteenth century contained provisions enumerating the rights available to the residents of the territories. More importantly, in some instances (for example Iowa and Alaska), territorial governments did not grant the right to a trial by jury to some accused criminals. Yet, following the enactment of the Fourteenth Amendment in 1868, Congress passed legislation recognizing the extension of the Constitution in the colonial territories. More precisely, §1891 of the Revised Statutes (RS) provided that:

> The Constitution and all laws of the United States which are not locally inapplicable shall have the same force and effect within all the organized Territories, and in every Territory hereafter organized as elsewhere within the United States.
>
> (US Congress 1874: 333)

Stated differently, the bill of rights was as operative in the colonial territories as it was in a state of the Union or any other part of the United States. Finally, in 1890 the Supreme Court in *Mormon Church v. United States* established that the bill of rights existed in the territories 'rather by inference and the general spirit of the constitution from which congress derives all its powers, than by any express and direct application of its provisions' (136 US 1, 44). What is important to emphasize, however, is that by 1898 law and policy makers agreed that the bill of rights was operative in a colonial territory in the same ways that it was operative in any other part of the United States.

In contrast, imperialists asserted the plenary or absolute power to govern occupied territories (Gardiner 1899). According to Westel W. Willoughby:

> (T)he power of the President, as Commander-in-Chief of the army and navy, is practically absolute over conquered territory. And also, that this power persists after the formal annexation of the territory in question to the United States and until Congress legislates for its government. It would appear, however, that during this latter period, the President's power is not as absolute as in the period prior to annexation. Absolute power, according to American constitutional doctrine, is only justified by military necessity, and, therefore, with the cessation of hostilities and the annexation of the territory by which it is brought within the general province of the American doctrine, there spring up certain limitations upon the President's governing power.
>
> (1929: 463)

For many, under prevailing nineteenth-century interpretations, the President could govern a territory subject to military occupation with plenary, absolute, or unconstrained force.

As Commander-in-Chief, the President held a plenary and absolute power to determine which civil rights to withhold or extend to *any* territory subject to military occupation. For the most part, the military administered the implementation of a system of justice (for example military commissions) and extended some fundamental due process rights to accused 'enemies' or other subjects of a US occupation. However, as the Supreme Court affirmed in *Ex Parte Milligan* [71 US 2 (1866)], the military also held a plenary power to withhold the extension of basic due process guarantees like the *writ of habeas corpus*, creating what Clinton Rossiter described as a 'constitutional dictatorship' (2004: 230) or Giorgio Agamben a 'state of emergency' (2003: 20–21). Suffice it to say during the nineteenth century, aliens and citizens alike inhabiting a territory subject to a US military occupation could find themselves with little or no access to basic due process and civil rights.

Islands subject to commercial occupation were ruled in like manner to territories subject to military occupations. Although the 1856 Guano Islands Act gave corporations an almost absolute power to rule, Section 1 of the Act also relegated these islands to the President's power to manage the foreign affairs of the United States (*Jones v. US*, 137 US 202, 217). To this extent, the President exercised a plenary power over the islands. On the matter of rights, while the Congress and the Court recognized the personal property rights of businessmen to temporarily own Guano islands, the Court did not rule on the question of the civil rights of the citizens and or subjects inhabiting these corporate enclaves. To this extent, it is possible to argue that the extension of civil rights to commercial islands was contingent on congressional legislation.

In the case of Native Americans, throughout the nineteenth century the Federal government developed competing and contradictory doctrines of plenary power to legitimate the subordination of tribal nations. For example, as previously noted, the Federal government conducted treaties with Native American nations affirming tribal sovereignty, while simultaneously occupying tribal territories. Likewise, the *Cherokee Cases* affirmed the 'semi-sovereign' status of Native American nations for state purposes which located them outside of the US jurisdiction, but simultaneously established the Federal government's plenary power to govern tribal nations as 'wards' in a state of pupilage. Notwithstanding the contradictory Federal Native American law and policy, by 1898 the United States had all but abandoned the treaty system and affirmed the Federal government's plenary or prerogative power authorizing Congress to enact governing legislation for Native American territories and the President to administer these localities (Taylor Saito 2007).

Deloria Jr. and Wilkins demonstrate that prior to 1898 the United States did not extend the bill of rights to Native American tribes or nations (1999: 96–138). Tribal members residing in a domestic dependent nation were generally ruled by tribal governments and entitled to the corresponding rights. Throughout the nineteenth century Native American territories were selectively situated outside of the United States for the purposes of extending constitutional civil rights to its non-white residents. For example, both the 1866 Civil Rights Act and the Fourteenth Amendment contained language limiting the extension of rights to persons 'subject to the jurisdiction' of the United States. To the extent that the US withheld the extension of the bill of rights to tribal nations, the residents of these territories were excluded from the protections afforded by the bill of rights. As a result Congress held a plenary power to enact legislation extending civil rights to the residents of Native American territories.

Although both the colonialist and imperialist traditions were premised on the subordination of the citizen and/or subject inhabiting the respective territory, fundamental differences existed between the two traditions. To be sure, although the Federal government retained a plenary political power to govern annexed territories, this power was limited by the extension of civil rights to the racially eligible citizens. In contrast, the government retained a plenary power to rule occupied territories. Unless the US government extended rights to the inhabitants of occupied territories, by legislation, treaties, or simple administrative orders, it is possible to argue that these territories could be ruled in what Giorgio Agamben (2003) has described as a 'state of exception.' Unlike annexed territories, which were a part of the United States for constitutional purposes, the United States retained the power to suspend the rule of law in an occupied territory and govern the inhabitants of those localities as mere bodies subject to the power of the state. Suffice it to say that the imperialist tradition has always granted the United States a plenary power to rule the inhabitants of occupied territories as subjects without providing them access to civil rights.

CITIZENSHIP

By 1898, inhabitants of colonial territories could acquire a US citizenship in at least five ways. Racially eligible residents of a colonial territory typically acquired a US citizenship through the initial annexation treaty. Until 1952, United States' immigration and naturalization laws limited the ability to acquire US citizenship for persons deemed white and/or of African descent (Haney-Lopez 1996). Prior to 1898, all annexation treaties either provided for the collective naturalization of the racially eligible inhabitants of an annexed territory or promised to do so at some future time (Thorpe 1909). In the case of the 1848 Treaty of Guadalupe Hidalgo, however, Articles 8 and 10 enabled Mexicans who wished to retain their citizenship to also retain equal property rights in the newly annexed territories. Article 9 also granted Mexicans equal access to civil rights while residing in an annexed territory until they chose to procure a US citizenship (USGAO 2004: 27–28). Notwithstanding the nuances in the language of the nineteenth-century treaties of territorial annexation, all treaties guaranteed the extension of citizenship to the racially eligible inhabitants of annexed territories.

Congress could also enact special legislation conferring citizenship on the inhabitants of the territories. The most common form of legislation was the organic or territorial act, which at times included provisions conferring citizenship on the inhabitants of the territories. Lawmakers could also enact special legislation providing for the collective naturalization of the residents of an annexed territory. These laws, however, generally complemented the territorial annexation treaties.

By 1898, birth in an annexed territory was tantamount to birth in the United States for citizenship purposes. Although the original Constitution did not include a citizenship provision, in 1866 Congress enacted the Civil Rights Act conferring birthright citizenship on most persons born in the United States, which included states and territories. Native Americans and the children of ambassadors or diplomats were, however, excluded from this law. In 1868, Congress enacted the Fourteenth Amendment reproducing the citizenship provision of the Civil Rights Act. Like the 1866 Civil Rights Act, the scope of the Birthright Citizenship Clause of the Fourteenth Amendment also included the territories (Flack 1908: 63). Following the Civil War Congress extended the citizenship provision of the Fourteenth Amendment to annexed territories through both Revised Statutes §1992 and §1995, in the latter specifically stating that birth in the Oregon territory was tantamount to birth in the United States. Alexander M. Bickel (1973) has since argued that the Supreme Court extended the Birthright Citizenship Clause of the Fourteenth Amendment to the territories in the *Slaughterhouse Cases* [83 US 36 (1873)]. Finally, in 1898 the Supreme Court ruled in *United States v. Wong Kim Ark* (169 US 649) that all persons born in the United States, including persons born in a territory, were entitled to a birthright citizenship. Suffice it to say that by 1898 any person, excluding Native Americans and the children of diplomats, born in a colonial or annexed territory acquired a US citizenship at birth. Stated differently, birth in a colonial territory was tantamount to birth in the United States.

Finally, in *Boyd v. State of Nebraska* (1892) the Supreme Court established that the statehood admission process was tantamount to a collective naturalization process (143 US 135, 170). The Supreme Court essentially reasoned that the admission of a state into the Union represented a sort of marriage between the states and the territories, including the inhabitants of a territory. If Congress was ready to admit a new state, it was also ready to admit its inhabitants. To this extent, persons eligible to acquire a US citizenship and residing in a territory that was converted into a state automatically became US citizens as a result of the extension of statehood to the territory.

In contrast, for the most part the United States treated occupied territories as foreign countries for citizenship purposes. In *Inglis v. Sailor's Snug Harbor* [3 Peters 99 (1830)], Luella Gettys argued, the Supreme Court established that 'a child born in New York of British parents, after the British took possession of it during the Revolutionary War, was born a British subject under the protection of the British government and not under the State of New York' (1934: 21). This interpretation suggested that persons born to an occupier (parent) in occupied territories acquired a derivative form of *jus sanguinis* (blood right) citizenship. To this extent, the racially eligible children of US citizens born in an externally occupied territory could claim a parental or derivative citizenship. This principle also applied to external territories such as the Guano Islands occupied for commercial purposes. However, it is not readily evident that domestic territories under Federal occupation became foreign countries for citizenship purposes. To be sure, while the *New Orleans v. Steamship Company* ruling established that the United States could selectively treat a domestic territory subject to military occupation as a foreign country, it is not clear that this principle applied to the question of citizenship following the enactment of the 1866 Civil Rights Act or the Fourteenth Amendment. Suffice it to say, that with the exception created by a domestic insurrection or civil war, US imperialism treated territories subject to military and commercial occupation as foreign countries for citizenship purposes.

Prior to the enactment of the 1924 Indian Citizenship Act, Native Americans were selectively barred from acquiring US citizenship in two ways. Generally speaking, throughout the nineteenth century, Native Americans were ruled as an inferior race incapable of being US citizens. An 1856 opinion by Attorney General Caleb Cushing summarized the Federal government's ideology:

> In fine, no person of the race of Indians is a citizen of the Unite States by right of local birth. It is an incapacity of his race.
>
> (7 Opinion of Attny. Gen. 746, 750 [Andrews 1856])

Unless Congress enacted a specific statute providing for the naturalization of a particular individual or nation (Getches, Wilkinson, and Williams 1998: 164), US law barred Native Americans on racial grounds from acquiring United States citizenship.

Following the enactment of the 1866 Civil Rights Act and later the Fourteenth Amendment, however, the Court adjusted the latter logic to bar Native Americans born in the United States from acquiring a US citizenship.

More specifically, Congress and the Court argued that Native American tribes held a semi-sovereign status selectively located outside of the jurisdiction of the United States and therefore Native Americans could be excluded from acquiring citizenship at birth within the United States. In *Elk v. Wilkins* the Supreme Court provided constitutional cover to this interpretation establishing that:

> Indians born within the territorial limits of the United States, members of, and owing immediate allegiance to, one of the Indian tribes, (an alien though dependent power,) although in a geographical sense born in the United States, are no more 'born in the United States and subject to the jurisdiction thereof,' within the meaning of the first section of the fourteenth amendment, than the children of subjects of any foreign government born within the domain of that government, or the children born within the United States, of ambassadors or other public ministers of foreign nations.
>
> (112 US 94, 102)

For purposes of US citizenship laws, the Court's interpretation effectively treated Native Americans as 'stateless aliens' (McGovney 1911: 328). After all, let us remember that while the Federal government recognized the domestic dependent nation status of Native American territories, it also subordinated these territories to an anomalous or borderland status located in the penumbras of the law. What is important to note is that in 1898, for citizenship purposes, birth in a Native American territory was tantamount to birth outside of the United States.

CONCLUSION

To sum up, what is important to note is that by 1898 the United States had developed two traditions of territorial expansionism that effectively affirmed what Karl Raustiala has described as a form of Westphalian territoriality (2009: 11). Annexed territories subject to colonialism were governed as constitutional parts of the United States. In contrast, occupied territories were ruled as foreign localities situated outside of the United States. Even in instances where the United States selectively ruled occupied territories as domestic for constitutional purposes, the ensuing status was temporary and contingent on the duration of the occupation. Of course, as the experience of Native Americans attests, temporary occupations can be indefinite.

This latter ontological distinction is important because it provides clear precedents for the creation of a new postcolonial expansionist tradition in the United States. For the most part (perhaps excepting the cases of Mexico and Hawai'i), the imperialist tradition was premised on the mere occupation of a territory. There was no intention of colonizing a territory in order to organize it as a future state of the Union. Even in the case of the occupation of Native American territories, which are still occupied by the United States at the time of this writing, there was no intention of creating new states primarily inhabited by members of a tribe or nation. Notwithstanding, the imperialist tradition also affirmed the creation of borderland territories that could be selectively ruled as domestic for constitutional purposes. However, these anomalous statuses were contingent on the duration of the occupation, or in the case of Native American territories, until they disappeared. In the following chapter, I will argue that the United States drew on the imperialist tradition to develop a postcolonial form of expansionism that enabled the Federal government to selectively rule permanently annexed territories as foreign localities in a domestic or constitutional sense. Thus, while the basic principles informing a postcolonial tradition of territorial expansionism were present throughout the nineteenth century, it is not until 1898 that the United States begins to develop a new tradition of territorial annexationism that eschews the acquisition of territories for the purpose of creating new states.

NOTES

1 Prevailing interpretations of what I describe as the colonial/imperialist debates focus on a series of academic debates published in the Harvard, Yale, and Columbia University law schools flag ship law reviews (Torruella 1988: 24–32; Sparrow 2006: 41–46). However, as I will discuss in more detail in Chapter 3, it is not clear whether these debates were organic to the legal academy or whether they were reminiscent of academics providing intellectual heft to the prevailing political debates of the period. Suffice it to say that notwithstanding the source of the debates, the historical interpretations of the corresponding constitutional precedents are fairly accurate.

2 Max Farrand documents that Gouverneur Morris introduced the Territories Clause to authorize Congress to rule the Northwest Territories or territories possessed at the founding and was opposed to the admission of new states (1913: 143–145). However, as noted above, whether one looks to the Articles of Confederation or simply looks to the Federalists' view of the strategic (both military and economic) importance of the Louisiana Purchase, it should be clear that Gouverneur Morris' position was held by a minority of the founders of the United States.

3 The acquisition of the Guano Islands provides an early example of US imperialism centered on the temporary acquisition of non-contiguous or non-continental territories for mere profit. However, while the foundations for this type of imperialism were outlined during the nineteenth century, the relevant constitutional interpretations began to take form after the 1898 Spanish–American War (Duffy Burnett 2006).

4 It is true that most organic acts, including the 1789 Northwest Ordinance, have contained provisions authorizing the election of either a delegate or resident commissioner to the Federal House of Representatives (none in the Senate), but these territorial representatives have been barred from voting on congressional legislation. At most, territorial delegates and/or resident commissioners have been allowed to vote in committee, but these representatives have been barred from substantive participation in political decisions that impact US citizens residing in the territories (e.g. decision to fight in wars, the development of economic policies, etc.).

Chapter 3

Large Policy expansionism, the Third View, and the unincorporated territory

> What I am contending for just now is the power of the Government, without any qualification whatever, to annex, either by treaty or by war, any territory, anywhere on the face of the globe that any other independent sovereignty could annex by war or by treaty.
>
> Senator Joseph B. Foraker (R-OH) (1899)[1]

During the 1890s, the United States began to develop a 'Large Policy' or global form of expansionism premised on the annexation of territories strategically situated throughout the world (Torruella 2007: 172). Large Policy advocates sought to annex islands for the purpose of building coaling and naval bases to create a strategic buffer zone against possible attacks by existing global empires. They also sought to assert sufficient hegemony throughout the world in order to join the elite club of global empires. Although the United States began to annex non-contiguous territories as early as 1867 (Alaska) and by 1893 it had acquired the sovereign Republic of Hawai'i, the annexation of Puerto Rico, Guam and the Philippines in the aftermath of the Spanish–American War of 1898 marked the United States' first shift in domestic law and policy from a colonialist or imperialist power to a global power.

However, prevailing constitutional doctrines used by the United States to legitimate its nineteenth-century territorial expansionism proved inadequate for the political challenges posed by the annexation of non-contiguous territories inhabited by non-white populations. As previously noted the colonialist tradition treated annexed territories as constitutional parts of the United States. In contrast, the imperialist occupation of territories was premised on the temporary occupation of a territory and was not cost effective or conducive to the development of long-term or stable administrative policies. Following the 1898 Spanish–American War, proponents of the global form of territorial expansionism introduced a new constitutional interpretation that combined features from both the colonialist and imperialist traditions. Sometimes described as the 'Third View,' the ensuing constitutional interpretation enabled the United States to annex new territories and selectively govern them as foreign countries in a constitutional or domestic sense (Lowell 1899: 176). From a domestic perspective, this meant that annexed territories such as Puerto Rico could be governed as separate and unequal territorial possessions of the United States.

Although the ideological foundations of the Large Policy or Third View form of US territorial expansionism are traceable to the late 1880s and early 1890s, the constitutional interpretations of this form of territorial expansionism emerge from a series of legal and political debates that took place between 1898 and 1901. More specifically, the legal and political debates over the US insular or territorial law and policy used to govern Puerto Rico and the other islands acquired during the 1898 Spanish–American War established the constitutional framework for the new theory of US expansionism. The initial constitutional interpretation of the status of Puerto Rico was first introduced by the War Department during a two-year transitional military dictatorship following the occupation of Puerto Rico on 25 July 1898 (Friedrich 1950; Lawson and Seidman 2004). The President and Congress began to normalize a tempered interpretation of the military's new territorial law and policy with the 1898 Treaty of Paris and the 1900 Foraker Act. In 1901 the Supreme Court further tempered and began to provide constitutional cover to the new territorial law and policy in a series of rulings generally known as the 'Insular Cases.' The ensuing interpretation or doctrine, also known as the doctrine of territorial incorporation, garbed the development of a global form of United States territorial expansionism or empire in constitutional terms. While the court has since modified the constitutional interpretations underlying the logic of US global empire, the basic legal framework was established between 1898 and 1901.

THE ROAD TO US GLOBAL EMPIRE

Critics of US global empire are prone to either ignore the substantive literature about the global dimensions of 1890s United States' territorial expansionism as well as the corresponding constitutional debates over the so-called 'Third View' expansionism (Lowell 1899) and/or subsume them into nineteenth-century narratives about the emergence of US imperialism. In the former case, scholars writing about United States' expansionism during the 1890s and the annexation of Puerto Rico have readily provided substantive evidence documenting the global ambitions of US law and policymakers (Weston 1972; LaFeber 1986; Torruella 2007). In the latter case, scholars tend to make two arguments. First, there is a tendency to obscure the difference between traditional forms of imperialist territorial occupation and Third View territorial annexationism by either equating the two or using the term imperialism to describe both forms of expansionism without recognizing the corresponding narratives of power.

In addition, critics often situate the origins of US global empire in the vicinity of the Second World War ignoring the legal precedents established amidst the 1898 Spanish–American War. Prevailing interpretations posit that the United States began to acquire the necessary superpower to assert control of global networks of military bases and markets following the Second World War (Wolin 2008: 20). Even Hobsbawm, who recognized the shift in United States' territorial policy following the 1898 War, also concludes that the US did not become a global Empire until the Second World War (2008: 75–76). In fact, Hobsbawm treats the US annexation of Puerto Rico and the other Spanish territories as an expression of a 'regional' form of expansionism dismissing the conceptual shift that occurred in US law and policy debates of the period (Ibid.). This instrumental approach 'clouds' our ability to understand the conceptual foundations of a new type of power, a power grounded on a new logic of global territorial expansionism.

In the epilogue of *Global Intrigues* Judge Juan R. Torruella coined the notion of 'Large Policy exponents' to describe the global ambitions of a cabal of US law and policy makers driving a new form of territorial expansionism during the 1890s (2007: 172). This cabal of global expansionists, Torruella notes, included political figures such as Theodore Roosevelt, Brooke Adams, Senator Henry Cabot Lodge, Admiral Alfred T. Mahan and other expansionists who embraced the period's 'hawkish,' and Anglo-American narratives of 'Manifest Destiny' exceptionalism (Ibid.). Like prior narratives of expansionism, Large Policy or global expansionism was premised on both the strategic acquisition of territories for military and economic purposes as well as the affirmation of white supremacist narratives. However, the ensuing form of global expansionism was also premised on the legal construction of a new territorial status that expanded the powers of the government while curtailing the ability of local inhabitants from invoking constitutional limits on the empire's rule.

Mark Rusell Shulman (1995) situates the origins of the United States' pursuit of a global military policy between 1882 and 1993 with the emergence of 'Navalism' or the pursuit of sea power. During this period, the US Navy began to develop seaborne strategies premised on establishing buffer zones to protect the nation from the potential threats of global powers. Retired Admiral Alfred T. Mahan (1898), perhaps the most influential military strategist of the period, further proposed the annexation of islands throughout the world with the intention of constructing strategic Naval coaling stations and other military installations. The ultimate objective was to secure a global network of bases that could affirm the seaborne supremacy of the US Navy. These bases would also enable the US to create a strategic buffer zone to forestall attacks by other global empires. By 1893, the Navy had secured the occupation of the sovereign Republic of Hawai'i and began to explore the occupation of islands throughout the Americas and the Pacific Ocean (Weston 1972; Schoultz 1998; Rodríguez Beruff 2007).

However, notwithstanding its early military forays, the United States would not begin to develop a new expansionist law and policy until it annexed the Spanish territories following the 1898 War (LaFeber 1986).

The Large Policy or Navalist approach also represented what Carl Schmitt describes in the *Nomos of the Earth* as both a closure of past forms of closed territorial colonialism and an entry into an open new world. As Schmitt and others (Skorownek [1982]/1990), argue by the 1890s the United States had conquered its western frontiers achieving a sort of continental closure of the nation-state. Entry into the global club of empires, or as Schmitt describes, the 'new world,' propelled the US into an open world of new geographical lines or boundaries and corresponding ideas. The 1898 War became the founding catalyst of this shift (Schmitt [1950]/2002: 316–317). The special annexation of non-contiguous territories for strategic purposes both enabled the United States to see itself as a global empire and to join the exclusive club of global expansionists.

It is important to note that the move from a colonial or imperial to a global tradition of expansionism is marked by at least two important ideological shifts in the United States. First, during the late-1880s and mid-1890s, legal and political actors began to envision the United States as a power that could permanently annex territories throughout the world without being bound to colonialist precedents, including binding the Federal government with constitutional limitations afforded to the local inhabitants or by ascribing a colonial territorial status on annexed territories. Second, and most importantly, the new interpretation sought to enable US legal and political actors to craft special laws and policies that could be adapted to the local exigencies of any annexed territory. To this extent territories could be ruled differently based on the local context or strategic needs of the US in any newly acquired territory (Thompson 2010).

United States' global expansionist law and policy was also fueled by domestic economic transformations and the search for global markets during the 1890s. Following the Civil War, the United States began to shift from an agricultural to an industrial or capitalist-based economy (Bensel 1990). David W. Brady's analysis of the 1890s' partisan realignment, or more specifically the elections propelling the Republican Party to power in the United States, created the conditions that cemented the key economic policies associated with the new form of US expansionism (1988: 52–53). Central to the Republican Party's economic policies were three policies, namely the affirmation of the gold standard, the passage of the 1897 Dingley Tariff Act, and the use of the Navy to affirm US expansionism encompassing the annexation of Hawai'i, the purchase (sic) of the Spanish islands, and the operation of the Nicaraguan canal. Brady argues that Republicans believed that continued reliance on the gold standard would facilitate free enterprise and US growth as a world economic power (54). In addition, the Dingley Tariff enabled the US to place a 25 percent tax or duty on imported or international goods protecting domestic markets and wages from external destabilization. Finally, Brady's argument suggests, Republicans believed that the United States should annex new territories and use the Navy to protect the economic investments and interests of US corporations doing business in these localities. The annexation of non-contiguous territories was seen as both an opportunity to develop new markets for US corporations as well as to form bridges to international markets. Suffice it to say that global expansionists were driven by the desire to develop the United States' growth as a world economic power.

At least two racist narratives of Anglo-American exceptionalism fueled US global expansionism (Weston 1972). One narrative, which I will discuss in further detail in the following chapter, invoked the 'White Man's Burden' to civilize the non-Anglo-Saxon inhabitants of territories subject to US annexation. For the most part, this ideology was premised on representing 'conquered' populations as infantile 'savages' in need of paternal and civilizing supervision (Mendez Saavedra 1992). Racist narratives of Anglo-American exceptionalism also embraced a Manifest Destiny ideology to differentiate between colonial and other types of annexed territories. Whereas colonial territories, traditionally considered constitutional parts of the United States, imbued their rightful inhabitants with the Anglo-American morals and values necessary for membership in the US polity, other territories fostered alienation and difference. For global expansionists, Spanish territories like Puerto Rico and the Philippines imbued their inhabitants with alien mores, values, and cultural traditions, differences that barred these inhabitants from assimilating US Anglo-American traditions and institutions. Again, as I will discuss in further detail below, the ensuing policies of US global expansionism were anchored on the affirmation of Anglo-American racial supremacy and the governance of inferior or less civilized races. More importantly, to the extent that contemporary US law and policymakers continue to invoke the interpretations that framed the Large Policy and Third View expansionism they are invoking racist laws and policies that were designed to 'civilize' 'barbarians.'[2]

WAR AND THE MILITARY IDEOLOGY

The cabal of 'Large Policy' advocates used the administration of President William H. McKinley and more specifically the 1898 Spanish-American War as a staging point to craft a new form of global expansionism. The war itself was triggered by the mysterious explosion of the *USS Maine* in the port of Havana, Cuba on 15 February 1898. In April of the same year, President McKinley requested congressional authorization to wage war against Spain in both the Caribbean (Cuba and Puerto Rico) and Pacific (the Philippines and Guam) theaters. On 25 July 1898, following a series of disastrous battles in Cuba, General Nelson A. Miles occupied Puerto Rico without resistance.

In theory, the hostilities between Spain and the United States ceased by 12 August 1898 when both nation-states began to develop the protocols for the negotiations of the 1898 Treaty of Paris (TOP). However, it is important to note that while hostilities between Spain and the United States theoretically ceased, Filipinos continued to wage war against the US occupation (Trask 1981; Wooster 1993). Spain and the United States reached a final agreement to end the War on 10 December 1898 and the US Senate ratified the Treaty of Paris on 11 April 1899 effectively ending the Spanish–American War. In sum, Puerto Rico remained an occupied Spanish territory between 25 July 1898 and 11 April 1899, when it was formally annexed to the United States. Since 11 April 1899, however, Puerto Rico has remained a separate and unequal unincorporated territory.

On 18 July 1898, President McKinley issued General Orders 101 authorizing the occupation of Cuba and the other Spanish ultramarine territories (Trías Monge 1991: 68–69). President McKinley commanded the military to occupy the islands in order to sever the 'political relations of the inhabitants' with Spain and to create the conditions that would enable the 'establishment of a new political power' (US Congress, H. Doc. 1484: 2177). The General Orders granted the military an 'absolute and supreme power' over the 'political condition of the inhabitants, the municipal laws of the conquered territory, such as affect private rights of persons and property and provide for the punishment crimes' (Ibid.). The military was tasked not only with occupying the Spanish territories, but also with the development the key legal and political institutions that both enabled the US to rule the islands and laid the groundwork for future congressional action. In his capacity as Commander-in-Chief, the President asked the Department of War to appoint military governors to rule the occupied Spanish territories until Congress enacted appropriate organic or territorial legislation.

Simultaneously, the US government began to negotiate the terms of a peace agreement with Spain. Also known as the 1898 Treaty of Paris, the ensuing peace treaty also began to normalize the initial military government's policies, first outlined in the General Orders 101 and the scope of power authorized by subsequent military orders issued to rule Puerto Rico and the other annexed Spanish territories. This was the first treaty of territorial annexation that neglected to treat ceded or annexed territories and their inhabitants as formal parts of the United States. Instead, the treaty sought to establish the plenary and absolute power of the US government to develop local territorial policies that selectively combined colonialist and imperialist institutions in order to rule occupied and annexed territories.

The Senate ratification debates were polarized along political parties and ideological visions of US expansionism. For the most part, senators from the Democratic Party embraced anti-imperialist arguments and opposed the annexation of Puerto Rico and the other Spanish territories. Like other anti-imperialists, they anchored their arguments on an array of colonialist interpretations of past territorial precedents. For example, Senator Donald Caffery (D-LA) invoked a narrative of Anglo-Saxon exceptionalism to reject the annexation of Puerto Rico. Central to his argument was the belief that the annexation of a territory bound Congress to treat it as a state-in-the-making. To be sure, the anti-imperialist senator summarized the colonialist interpretation in the following manner:

> The argument, in brief, is that inhabitants of a Territory belonging to the United States, no matter how acquired, are citizens of the United States; that as such they can not be held outside of the Constitution; that the Constitution contemplates no other than a federated government of States; that consequently new Territories must as soon as practicable be admitted as States.
>
> (32 Cong. Rec. 436)

Colonialist territorial precedents not only bound the United States to treat the non-white inhabitants of Puerto Rico as equal citizens, but also bound Congress to subsequently admit the island as a state of the Union.

In contrast, Republican senators favored the ratification of the Treaty of Paris on both imperialist and global expansionist grounds. For the most part, Republican senators favored the annexation of Puerto Rico on strategic military and economic grounds. Evidence of this interpretation is readily available throughout the Senate ratification debates. For example, Senator John C. Spooner (R-WI) argued:

> Porto Rico has become, with the development of our country, of great importance to us. It stands as an important outpost. Its relation to the Caribbean Sea and to the great waterway connecting the two oceans, which this nation is determined to have, is such that we ought to possess it and defend it and take care of it, giving to the people there as much of self-government as is possible.
>
> (32 Cong. Rec. 1384)

The annexation of Puerto Rico, Senator Spooner further argued, affirmed the United States' power as a world empire. In 1899, Senator Spooner summarized the global expansionist view in the following manner:

> I am a commercial expansionist. I believe in building up the trade of the United States. I am in favor of an interoceanic canal, not only for the purposes of national defense, but for its benefit to the trade of the future. I am in favor of acquiring naval stations all over the world where the interests of this government would be subserved thereby-resting places for our commerce. I am in favor of lines of cable

> connection in every conceivable direction where they would promote the interests of the United States.
>
> (32 Cong. Rec. 1385–86)

Both imperialist and global expansionists agreed that territorial annexation could help cement the United States' power as a global empire.

The United States essentially acquired four islands from Spain, namely Cuba, the Philippines, Guam, and Puerto Rico, and developed four distinct territorial laws and policies to govern these. In the case of Cuba, the United States modified its imperialist tradition making occupation contingent on the economic exploitation of the island. To be sure, while the debates over the annexation of Cuba predated the Spanish–American War, on 20 April 1898 Congress enacted the Teller Amendment barring the United States from annexing Cuba. Article One of the Treaty of Paris forced Spain to relinquish 'all claim of sovereignty over and title to Cuba' while granting the United States the power to 'occupy' the island 'for the protection of life and property' (US Congress 1910: S. Doc. 357, 1691). Soon after, Congress enacted the 1901 Platt Amendment, amending the Teller Amendment and granting the President the authority to both establish permanent naval coaling stations and occupy Cuba whenever it's economic interests were threatened by either international or domestic forces. The original occupation ended in 1903 with the cession of the Guantánamo Bay lands to the US military (Rodríguez Beruff 2007: 13). Read as a whole, the ensuing Cuban territorial law and policy recognized the conditional independence of the island contingent on the ability of a United States amoeba (and its corporate tentacles) to exploit the Cuban people. This form of imperialism established legal precedents affirming the US global empire's use of the military to occupy a territory in order to protect its economic interests and exploit it for mere economic gain.

In contrast, the Treaty of Paris provided for the annexation of three territories, namely the Philippines, Guam, and Puerto Rico. Soon after the annexation, Congress enacted legislation transferring control of the three islands to the War Department's Bureau of Insular Affairs. Unlike the cases of Puerto Rico and Guam, Filipino nationalists continued to wage military resistance against the United States following the 1898 occupation. Although the United States would continue to exercise hegemony over the Philippines for several decades, by 1946 the US government had formally recognized the archipelago's independence. Alternatively, Congress governed Guam as a Naval Coaling Station and military base between 1898 and 1950, when it enacted a special organic or territorial government to replace the military regime ruling the island. In the case of Puerto Rico, following the imposition of a two-year military dictatorship, Congress began to rule the island with a civilian government since 1900.

To varying degrees, the three islands were governed under the tenets of the Third View interpretation and the laws and policies adopted to rule these territories shaped the development of the nascent global expansionist tradition. However, the core constitutional precedents defining the global expansionist view were established by rulings and legislation addressing the status of Puerto Rico. In reality, US law and policy makers treated the Philippines as a hostile occupied territory and Guam as a military base. On the other hand, Puerto Rico was ruled as an annexed, albeit, unincorporated territory of the United States.

The second clause of Article Nine granted Congress a plenary and absolute power to rule Puerto Rico and its inhabitants. This clause established that '(t)he civil rights and political status of the native inhabitants of the territories hereby ceded to the United States shall be determined by Congress' (1910: S. Doc. 357, 1693). Congress was empowered to enact territorial legislation without being bound by the colonialist and/or imperialist precedents. In fact, subsequent interpretations of this clause further suggested that Congress was no longer bound or limited by the Constitution when legislating for the newly annexed territories. Stated differently, Congress, a constitutional creation, could now enact extra-constitutional legislation to govern Puerto Rico and the other territories without the restrictions established by colonialist territorial precedents.

Although the 1898 General Orders 101 and subsequent military orders laid the legal groundwork for the new territorial law and policy, the War Department began to develop the core institutions and corresponding constitutional interpretations in the fall of 1899. During the summer of 1899, President McKinley replaced Secretary of War Russell A. Alger with the well-known New York attorney Elihu Root and tasked him to develop a constitutional interpretation for the new territorial law and policy. Secretary Alger was simply unprepared to manage the War Department (Wooster 1993: 231) and much less able to participate in the development of a new expansionist territorial law and policy. Root later recalled President McKinley's invitation to replace Secretary Alger:

> … in the month of July, having just finished the labors of the year and gone to my country home, I was called to the telephone and told by one speaking for President McKinley, "the President directs me to say to you that he wishes you to take the position of Secretary of War." I answered "Thank the President for me, but say that it is quite absurd, I know nothing about war. I know nothing about the army." I was told to hold the wire, and in a moment there came back the reply, "president McKinley directs me to say that he is not looking for any one who knows anything about war or for anyone who knows anything about the army; he has got to have a lawyer to direct the government of the Spanish islands, and you are the lawyer he wants."
>
> (Bacon and Brown Scott 1970: xiv)

With the help of Charles E. Magoon, a legal aid in the War Department, the new Secretary of War subsequently developed a new constitutional interpretation that both weaved together the goals of the McKinley administration with the work of the military governors on the ground and provided the blueprints for the development of a global expansionist territorial law and policy (Kavass and Sprudzs 1903). The ensuing policy embodied the origins of a new expansionist policy global in scope.

The United States used a two-year military dictatorship to rule Puerto Rico between 25 July 1898, when General Miles occupied the island, and 1 May 1900. As noted above, during this period President McKinley charged the War Department with both developing local governing institutions for Puerto Rico (and the other territories) and crafting a broader territorial policy. Following 12 August 1898 agreement on the protocols of peace and the cessation of Spanish hostilities more generally, a series of military governors were appointed to both colonize Puerto Rico by dismantling local institutions (for example parliament) and enacting institutions that would affirm the United States hegemony over the island (for example military commissions and provisional courts). Legal scholars agree that Brigadier General George W. Davis (9 May 1899 – 1 May 1900), the last of the military governors appointed to rule Puerto Rico, developed the most influential institutions to govern the island (Delgado Cintrón 1988: 147–182; Trías Monge 1991: 68–81). In a report to Congress submitted in 1900, General Davis summarized his responsibilities as military governor as follows:

> Under the title 'Military government' has been presented a statement of conditions that determined the policy of the department commander with respect to the enforcement, change, or abrogation of local laws, and substitution for the local courts of other tribunals established by military order… The scope of these orders was very wide. Almost every branch of administration – political, civil, financial, and judicial – was affected by their provisions. It may be that the military governors exceeded their authority when they changed codes, the provisions which were not in conflict with the political character, institutions, and Constitution of the United States; but in the absence of instructions to the contrary, it was conceived to be the privilege and duty of the military commanders to make use of such means with a view to adapting the system of local laws and administration to the one which, judging from precedents, Congress be expected to enact for the island, thus preparing the latter for a territorial regime when Congress should be ready to authorize it.
>
> (US Congress H. Doc. 2: 45)

General Davis was tasked with developing local institutions that worked in the Puerto Rican context and were consistent with the War Department's emerging territorial law and policy. Secretary Root and General Davis' government reports provide the clearest examples of the nascent military territorial law and policy.

The main intention of the War Department was to develop a new territorial law and policy to govern strategically acquired islands permanently housing naval and military stations and potentially inhabited by non-white or Anglo-Saxon populations. For example, in a 1899 *Report on the Civil Government of Puerto Rico*, General Davis distinguished Puerto Rico from both US colonies and occupied territories:

> The conditions here are quite unlike any that existed in the sparsely settled western territories, which were acquired by purchase from France, by cession from Mexico, and under convention with Great Britain. They are unique in our history. We have no American precedent to which we can refer as an aid to decide the form of civil government should be set up.
>
> (US War Department, Davis 1899: 74–75)

Moreover, General Davis reasoned:

> Puerto Rico, unlike Dominica, Haiti, Venezuela, and many other republics, never was, is not, and probably never will be, independent. It is now a possession of the United States and must so continue until Congress decides otherwise. What ever government may be given to the island, it will be subject to the general control of Congress, and having no local army or navy, it would be without means and power to carry its local issues to the ultimate of armed repression and subjection of opponents.
>
> (1899: 74)

The military sought to create a new territorial status that would not bind US law and policymakers to prevailing colonialist precedents.

The War Department instead adopted the British colonial 'dependency' model to govern Puerto Rico and the other territories. As a 'dependency,' the United States could govern Puerto Rico indefinitely without binding Congress to grant the island statehood or independence, a territorial condition that would enable the military to permanently house strategic military installations in the island. Both Secretary of War Root (Bacon and Brown Scott 1970: 166–167) and Brigadier-General (1899: 76–82) argued that rather than Congress, the President would directly control Puerto Rico and the other dependencies. The President, in turn, was empowered to create a civil government to administer the island until Congress enacted alternative legislation. The President was further empowered to appoint a governor, an executive council and a local judiciary. The latter would include a Puerto Rican supreme court, a Federal court, and five district courts. In addition, the proposed government would enable Puerto Ricans to elect a legislative assembly with minor administrative powers. The dependency status granted the President a plenary authority to rule Puerto Rico indefinitely.

Moreover, dependencies could be governed as foreign countries for commercial purposes or more specifically for the collection of tariffs and duties. Following the US occupation of Puerto Rico the military began to collect tariffs and duties on goods trafficked between the island and the mainland. The military used the collected taxes to assist in financing the occupation of Puerto Rico. The dependency status would enable the President to continue to collect tariffs and duties on goods traded between Puerto Rico and the United States without the constraints of the Uniformity Clause (US Constitution, Art. I, Sect. 8, cl. 1). Under prevailing interpretations of the Uniformity Clause the Federal government was required to sustain a uniform system of tariffs and duties within the United States and could not enact discriminatory taxes, tariffs, or duties on merchandize trafficked between parts of the United States. According to Secretary Root, governing Puerto Rico as a dependency enabled the United States to selectively treat the island as a foreign country for purposes of the Uniformity Clause and use the tariff system to collect revenues from goods trafficked between the island and the mainland (1970: 162). These revenues would in turn be used to subsidize the US colonial occupation. From a constitutional perspective, this meant that Puerto Rico could be ruled as a separate and unequal territory within the Anglo-American sovereignty.

CONGRESS AND THE NORMALIZATION OF EMPIRE

The 1900 Foraker Act replaced the military dictatorship in Puerto Rico with a civil government based on the military's territorial institutions and policies. In his last report to the War Department, General Davis wrote:

> It has been pointed out that the course adopted is understood to have been, tacitly at least, approved by Congress, for with two slight exceptions, specified in the act of April 12, 1900, every order promulgated by the military governors has been confirmed by Congressional enactment, has become part of the supreme law of the land, and will so remain until abrogated or changed by Congress or by the legislative assembly of the islands.
>
> (US Congress 1902: H. Doc 2, 45–46)

Notwithstanding the enactment of the Foraker Act, the War Department's Bureau of Insular Affairs continued to administer the island's affairs. The Foraker Act became the first law to normalize the War Department's territorial policy. To this extent, the Foraker Act became the first legal expression of US global empire.

It is, however, worth noting that congressional lawmakers initially debated two different types of bills (Gould 1969; Cabranes 1979; Trías Monge 1980). In the House of Representatives, Congressman Sereno Payne (R-NY) initially introduced a bill extending the Dingley Tariff to Puerto Rico enabling the US government to collect tariffs and other taxes on merchandize trafficked between Puerto Rico and the mainland as well as between the island and the rest of the world. These temporary tariffs and taxes were meant to defray the costs of annexing Puerto Rico. In contrast, the Senate legislation introduced by Senator Joseph B. Foraker (R-OH) provided for the creation of a civil government for the island. Although the final version of the reconciled bill incorporated Representative Payne's revenue collection provision, Senator Foraker's version was broader in scope. Ultimately, a tempered version of Senator Foraker's bill prevailed.

Congressional debates over the Foraker Act echoed the debates over the ratification of the Treaty of Paris and were also polarized along partisan and ideological lines. Embracing an array of anti-imperialist positions, Democrats opposed the Foraker Act. For example, conservative Representative James D. Richardson (D-TN) opposed the annexation of Puerto Rico, but once annexed, he argued the island became a constitutional part of the United States and the Foraker Act 'unequal taxation of the island' disregarded and violated the Constitution (33 Cong. Rec. 1947). Alternatively, Representative Francis G. Newlands (D-NV), the author of the 1898 Newlands resolution providing for the annexation of the Republic of Hawai'i, argued that Congress was bound to treat Puerto Rico as an infant state in the making (33 Cong. Rec. 1998). Newlands' position advocated a form of colonial expansionism that challenged anti-imperialism. Suffice it to say that anti-imperialists opposed the enactment of territorial legislation that violated past colonialist constitutional precedents, constitutional precedents that bound Congress to treat Puerto Rico as a part of the United States and a state-in-the making.

In contrast, the Republican Party was divided between advocates of US imperialism and global expansionists. Representative Payne's initial bill (*HR 8245*) advocated for an imperialist policy by treating Puerto Rico as a foreign country for tariff purposes. He invoked at least three constitutional interpretations affirming the prevailing scholarly defense of the imperialist position (US Congress 1900 H. Rept. 249: 1–32). First, Representative Payne agreed that the definition of the United States was limited to the states and did not include territories (Ibid.: 6). Territories were temporary constructions located outside of the United States for constitutional purposes. Second, he argued that constitutional limitations only applied to states and not the territories. After all, the Constitution was a compact drafted by the original thirteen states to govern the relations between states of the Union, or so Representative Payne argued (Ibid.). Moreover, he claimed, the term United States held different meanings throughout the Constitution and in some contexts the term applied some constitutional limitations to the power of the Federal government over territories, and in other contexts it did not (Ibid.: 6–7). Representative George B. McClellan (D-NY) best summarized the position of the imperialist majority: 'Puerto Rico belongs to the United States, but is not a part of the United States and the Constitution only extends propio vigore over the States that compose the Union, and only extends over the territories by Congressional action' (33 Cong. Rec. 2063–64). Legislators advocating for US imperialism believed that the US could simply acquire new territories and rule them as mere possessions situated outside of the constitutional limits of the United States. Although the imperialist view did not prevail, it managed to temper the global expansionists' compromises with the anti-imperialist camp.

The Senate version of the bill sponsored by Senator Joseph B. Foraker (R-OH) (*S 2264*) both tempered Representative Payne's original proposal and reflected the global expansionist view. The final iteration of Senator Foraker's bill included tempered revenue raising provisions of the Payne bill. For example, the Foraker version reduced the 25 percent Dingley tariff to 15 percent and made it temporary rather than permanent. Rather than simply providing for the generation of income or revenue, the Foraker bill was an organic or territorial act modeled after General Davis' proposal. As I will discuss in more detail below, the proposed bill also departed from prior colonialist legislation and included institutions designed to rule Puerto Rico as an unincorporated territory. During the ensuing Senate debates Senator Joseph C. Spooner (R-WI) unequivocally argued that '(t)erritory belonging to the United States, as I think Puerto Rico and the Philippine Archipelago do, become a part of the United States in the *international sense*, while not being at all a part of the United States in the *constitutional sense*' (33 Cong. Rec. 3629). To the extent that Puerto Rico was treated as an international territory it could be treated as a separate and unequal territory for constitutional purposes.

Generally known as the Foraker Act, the final version of the bill essentially reproduced the key tenets of the military's interpretation. First, unlike all colonial organic or territorial acts, including the 1900 Government for the Territory of Hawai'i Act, the Foraker Act did not treat Puerto Rico as a state-in-the-making nor as a colonial territory. Quite the contrary, the Foraker Act enabled the United States to selectively govern Puerto Rico as a foreign country for an indeterminate amount of time. To be sure, Section Three of the Foraker Act extended a 15 percent Dingley Tariff on goods traded between the island and the mainland until 1902. The revenues generated from these taxes were reallocated to the President's budget for the island in order to lessen the financial burden of building US institutions in Puerto Rico and administering or colonizing the island more generally. Again, as noted above, selectively treating Puerto Rico (an annexed territory) as a foreign country for tax or commercial purposes represented a departure from prevailing interpretations of the Uniformity Clause, which were premised on treating all annexed territories as parts of the United States for constitutional purposes.

CONSTITUTIONALIZING GLOBAL EMPIRE

Within months the Supreme Court began to provide constitutional cover to the global expansionist view and institutionalized the corresponding laws and policies in a series of rulings generally known as the 'Insular Cases'. Efrén Rivera Ramos describes the Insular Cases as a series of rulings rendered between 1901 and 1922 and divided into three periods (2007: 74–75).[3] The first period is comprised of nine different opinions rendered in 1901, which introduced the basic constitutional interpretation legitimating the global expansionist view.[4] The new expansionist interpretation, since known as the doctrine of territorial incorporation, framed subsequent debates over the status of Puerto Rico and its inhabitants. A second period, Rivera Ramos further argues, encompassed a series of thirteen rulings rendered between 1903 and 1914 in which a majority of the Court embraced the doctrine of territorial incorporation.[5] Finally, by 1922 the Court expanded the scope of this doctrine to include territories inhabited by US citizens.[6] The United States has used this doctrine to rule all inhabited territories annexed since 1898.

Scholars agree that the basic premises of the new territorial doctrine were established in *Downes v. Bidwell* (1901) (Torruella 1988; López Baralt 1999; Duffy Burnett and Marshall 2001; Sparrow 2006; Rivera Ramos 2007). The case addressed the constitutionality of the military tariffs imposed on goods (in this case oranges) shipped from Puerto Rico and imported into the United States after the enactment of the Foraker Act. More specifically the key constitutional question was whether the Foraker Act's Section Three tariffs violated the Uniformity Clause by imposing the Dingley Act on goods traded between Puerto Rico and the mainland. A majority of five judges concurred in holding that while the treaty of cession made Puerto Rico a part of the sovereignty of the United States for international interests, the Treaty of Paris did not make the island a part of the 'United States' for domestic or constitutional purposes (182 US 244, 263). More importantly, Article Three did not incorporate Puerto Rico within the United States. Although a majority of five justices agreed with the holding, no single rationale managed to garner a majority of votes. In fact five different rationales encompassing the three expansionist views were filed.

Justice Henry B. Brown, the author of the now infamous *Plessy v. Ferguson* [163 US 537 (1896)], wrote the majority opinion in *Downes*. Drawing on imperialist precedents, Justice Brown reasoned that territories were not a part of the constitutional definition of the 'United States' and therefore the Uniformity Clause did not apply to Puerto Rico. Justice Brown argued that the Constitution was a compact among states of the Union and did not include territories (182 US 244, 251). It followed that the United States could govern Puerto Rico, and for that matter all acquired territories, as a possession 'appurtenant' and belonging to the United States without treating it as a part of the Union for constitutional purposes, at least not until Congress decided to invite the island to join the 'sisterhood of states' (Id. at 283). All territories, regardless of their status, Justice Brown reasoned, were located outside of the constitutional definition of the United States.

Moreover, Justice Brown, echoing the arguments of Secretary of War Root, anchored the power to govern territories on treaty law rather than the Territorial Clause. Citing Chief Justice Marshall, Justice Brown argued that 'the power to acquire territory by treaty implies, not only the power to govern such territory, but to prescribe upon what terms the United States will receive its inhabitants, and what their status shall be in what Chief Justice Marshall termed the "American Empire"' (182 US 244, 279). Thus, the annexation treaty would remain the source of law authorizing the governance of a territory until Congress determined whether it would grant the territory statehood or independence. By situating the power to rule Puerto Rico in the treaty, Justice Brown avoided the prevailing colonialist precedents and expanded the powers of the United States to rule a territory. Prevailing interpretations of the Territories Clause (colonialist) simply hindered the power of the US government to rule Puerto Rico by extending constitutional limits on US law and policy. It followed that Puerto Rico could be ruled as a separate and unequal territory belonging to the United States.

Justice Brown essentially extended the *Fleming* logic to *all* US territories acquired after the founding, regardless of the status of the territory. Annexed territories became mere possessions equal in status to occupied territories and Congress wielded the power to selectively treat these as part of the United States for domestic or constitutional purposes. Annexed territories also became US possessions for international purposes (182 US 244, 263). This logic enabled Justice Brown to conclude or find that Section 3 of the Foraker Act was constitutional because Puerto Rico was a mere possession of the United States (Id. at 287).

Four justices concurred with Justice Brown's holding, but rejected his reasoning. Although the four concurring justices filed two separate concurrent opinions, these reflected the global expansionist or Third View interpretation. Notwithstanding, Justice Edward D. White wrote the core concurring opinion that outlined the core principles of the doctrine of territorial incorporation, the doctrine that has since become the law of the land. Justice White unequivocally recognized the colonialist legal precedents, but limited the application of these precedents to territories settled by white citizens and subjects. In Justice White's words:

> Thus it was at the adoption of the Constitution, the United States as a geographical unit and as a governmental conception both in the international and domestic sense, consisted not only of states, but also of territories, all the native white inhabitants being endowed with citizenship, protected by pledges of a common union, and, except as to political advantages, all enjoying equal rights and freedom, all being under the obligation to contribute their proportionate share for the liquidation of the debt and future expenses of the general government.
> (182 US 244, 320)

In contrast, the new 'alien' territories represented a threat to the American empire (314–315). Puerto Rico and the newly annexed islands, 'inhabited with people utterly unfit for American citizenship' was perhaps better suited to house 'a naval station or a coaling station,' or 'an interoceanic canal' rather than a colonial territory (311).

The concurring justices, Westel W. Willoughby further noted, agreed on three core interpretations that became the basis for the ensuing doctrine of territorial incorporation (1929: 479–480). Justice White's opinion further articulated the core rationales of the concurring opinion and the doctrine of territorial incorporation more generally. Justice White established a clear difference between so-called annexed 'incorporated' territories, or territories that could be settled by white citizens and subsequently admitted as states into the Union (182 US 244, 311), and 'unincorporated' territories 'inhabited with people utterly unfit for American citizenship and totally incapable of bearing their proportionate burden of the national expense' and only fit to sustain 'naval' or 'coaling' stations (182 US 244, 311). To this extent, the differentiation between incorporated and unincorporated territories enabled the US to establish new borders within the nation-state by designating some territories as part of the United States and selectively treating other annexed spaces as foreign localities.

Justice White's argument also applied the *Fleming* logic to the case of Puerto Rico, but instead of simply treating all annexed territories as occupied possessions, he used the standard of 'incorporation' to differentiate between territories. He summarized the basic status of the unincorporated territory in the following language:

> The result of what has been said is that while in an international sense Porto Rico [sic] was not a foreign country, since it was subject to the sovereignty of and was owned by the United States, it was foreign to the United States in a domestic sense, because the island had not been incorporated into the United States, but was merely appurtenant thereto as a consequence.
> (182 US 244, 341)

The *Fleming* precedent was developed to rule either occupied sovereign countries or parts of their territories. In the case of Puerto Rico, the United States severed the island's relationship to Spain and annexed it. Puerto Rico ceased being a part of Spain and unlike Cuba did not become a sovereign country. Moreover, while the Foraker Act recognized Cuba's right to 'independence,' it did not do so in the case of Puerto Rico. Rather than rejecting a century of colonialist jurisprudence or extending the principle of *Fleming* to all annexed territories, Justice White simply invented a new territorial category, the unincorporated territory, to differentiate between *annexed* territories that were governed as constitutional parts of the United States and those that could be selectively governed as foreign localities in a domestic or constitutional sense. This legal construction enabled him to avoid repudiating more than a century of colonialist and imperialist jurisprudence.

It is important to note, however, that Justice White's use of the word 'incorporation' departed from prior usage. Before 1898, organic or territorial legislation used the word 'incorporation' to describe the collective naturalization process of the inhabitants of annexed territories and not the status of the territory itself. Justice White, however, used the notion of incorporation to describe the 'territorial' status of Puerto Rico and the other non-contiguous territories annexed as a result of the Spanish–American War, territories inhabited by non-white populations. Justice White invoked a narrative of Anglo-Saxon exceptionalism in order to ascribe an anomalous status on Puerto Rico tantamount to that of an alien territory. The notion of incorporation, previously applied to alien bodies, was now applicable to alien territories, or territories not amenable to white settlement.

More importantly, the distinction between 'incorporated' and 'unincorporated' territories has never existed in the Constitution. Advocates of the global expansionist view developed this legal construction in order to justify the separate and unequal treatment of *annexed* territories. Justice White's interpretation merely dressed the difference created by the military and the ensuing tempering legislation in a constitutional garb. It followed that annexed territories could now be selectively governed as occupied territories liminally situated somewhere in between an incorporated territory and a foreign country for domestic or constitutional purposes. Annexed unincorporated territories, although situated within the United States for international purposes, could now be situated in a constitutional borderland mostly contingent on the will of US legal actors.

The concurring justices, Willoughby further noted, reached consensus on two interrelated interpretations about the power of congress. First, although treaties gave the US government the power to annex new territories, only Congress held the power to incorporate a territory by either express or implied legislation. To this extent, the Foraker Act did not contain language expressly or implicitly incorporating Puerto Rico or its inhabitants. In the former, the very nature of Article Three affirmed the explicit exclusion of Puerto Rico, whereas the latter was affirmed by the absence of a collective naturalization provision, an example of an implicit or tacit form of incorporation (182 US 244, 332). Second, in legislating for unincorporated territories, Congress was not bound to the colonialist precedents. Both interpretations rejected Justice Brown's imperialist reading of the powers of the United States by anchoring the power to govern unincorporated territories in a more expansive interpretation of the Territories rather than the Treaty Clause. In sum, the ensuing territorial doctrine enabled Congress to invoke different interpretations of the Territories Clause to govern incorporated and unincorporated territories. In the latter case, the global expansionist could now selectively draw on both colonialist and imperialist precedents to craft interpretations of the status of unincorporated territories.

Notwithstanding these disagreements, it is also important to note that although the majority of judges agreed on granting Congress more expansive powers under the Territories Clause, these powers were not absolute. While the majority of the Court was unwilling to extend the bill of rights to Puerto Rico, the Court affirmed the principle that Congress possessed the power to withhold or extend 'fundamental' rights to the inhabitants of Puerto Rico. To be sure, as Justice Brown argued:

> Whatever may be finally decided by the American people as to the status of these islands and their inhabitants, – whether they shall be introduced into the sisterhood of states or be permitted to form independent governments, – it does not follow that in the meantime, a waiting that decision, the people are in the matter of personal rights unprotected by the provisions of our Constitution and subject to the merely arbitrary control of Congress. Even if regarded as aliens, they are entitled under the principles of the Constitution to be protected in life, liberty, and property.... We do not desire, however, to anticipate difficulties which would naturally arise in this connection, but merely to disclaim any intention to hold that the inhabitants of these territories are subject to an unrestrained power on the part of Congress to deal with them upon the theory that they have no rights which it is bound to respect.
>
> (182 US 244, 283)

Four justices, including Chief Justice Melville Fuller, dissented and filed two separate opinions. Both opinions embraced a colonialist interpretation of the status of annexed territories and the Territories Clause. The dissent rejected the differentiation between 'incorporated' and 'unincorporated' territories and argued for the use of colonialist precedents to judge the constitutionality of the Foraker Act. Nonetheless, even if we were to accept this 'occult' legal construction, the Chief Justice's dissent suggested, the

Foraker Act organized a civil territorial government for Puerto Rico and included a District Court for Puerto Rico that possessed the same jurisdiction as Federal District and Circuit Courts (182 US 244, 391). These provisions were colonial in nature and reproduced US institutions in Puerto Rico. To this extent, Chief Justice Fuller read the Foraker Act as a partial affirmation of United States' colonialist territorial policy tantamount to the incorporation of the island (King 1950: 266).

Chief Justice Fuller argued that the ensuing differentiation between territorial statuses empowered Congress to govern Puerto Rico and other unincorporated territories 'like a disembodied shade, in an intermediate state of ambiguous existence for an indefinite period; and more than that, that after it has been called from that limbo, commerce with it is absolutely subject to the will of Congress, irrespective of the constitutional provisions' (182 US 244, 372). The notion of the disembodied shade described a separate and unequal borderland territorial status, a place situated in what contemporary legal scholars would describe as the penumbras of the law.

Likewise, the dissent rejected Justice Brown's interpretation of the Treaty Clause and sought to anchor the power to govern Puerto Rico in the Territories Clause. However, the dissent also unequivocally rejected the global expansionist view. Again, Chief Justice Fuller's argument illustrates the colonialist critique of the Third View:

> The logical result is that Congress may prohibit commerce altogether between states and territories, and may prescribe one rule of taxation in one territory, and a different rule in another. That theory assumes that the Constitution created a government empowered to acquire countries throughout the world, to be governed by different rules than those obtaining in the original states and territories, and substitutes for the present system of republican government a system of domination over distant provinces in the exercise of unrestricted power.
>
> (182 US 244, 373)

The dissent rejected the imperialist and global expansionist view and would have treated Puerto Rico as a colonial territory declaring the Foraker Act's tariffs altogether unconstitutional.[7]

In sum, the majority of the Court's opinion in *Downes* gave constitutional legitimacy to the global expansionist view. Through the affirmation of the Foraker Act a majority of the Court affirmed the military's territorial policies. The notion of an unincorporated territory became tantamount to that of a disembodied shade, a territory that could be ruled as a separate and unequal borderland. More importantly, as Chief Justice Fuller recognized, underpinning Justice White's theory was an effort to enable the US government to exercise power over territories throughout the world. Read as part of a larger global expansionist policy, *Downes* and the Insular Cases more generally established the constitutional origins of the US global empire.

The doctrine of territorial incorporation gave constitutional legitimacy a form of US global expansionism tantamount to what Carl Schmitt described two decades later in *The Crisis of Parliamentary Democracy* as a 'modern' form of 'imperialism.' Schmitt summarized the new logic of territorial expansionism in the following terms:

> Modern imperialism has created countless new governmental forms, conforming to economic and technical developments, which extend themselves to the same degree that democracy develops within the motherland. Colonies, protectorates, mandates, intervention treaties, and similar forms of dependence make it possible to day for a democracy to govern a heterogeneous population without making them citizens, making them dependent upon a democratic state, and at the same time held apart from this state. That is the political and constitutional meaning of the nice formula 'the colonies are foreign in public law, but democratic in international law.'
>
> ([1923]/1988: 10)

The new logic of global expansionism enabled the United States to develop locally distinct laws and policies to rule Puerto Rico and its other unincorporated territories according to the strategic needs of the US global empire. The shift to a new form of global expansionism also marked the moment that the US joined the club of global empires.

CONTINUITIES AND DISCONTINUITIES

To sum up, I want to note three important conclusions. First, my contention is that the unincorporated territorial status is a legal construction that grew out of the tempering of a military territorial law and policy. The War Department drew on the British dependency model to rule annexed territories without constitutional limits and without binding the US more generally to past expansionist precedents. Both the 1898 Treaty of Paris and the 1900 Foraker Act began to normalize and codify a tempered interpretation of the military's proposed territorial law and policy, an interpretation that could be reconciled with a constitutional interpretation. To this extent, while the Supreme Court's affirmation of the Foraker Act gave this interpretation a tempered constitutional garb, I argue, the justices were merely affirming a new territorial law and policy developed to enable the US to become an empire global in reach and scope.

Second, the new interpretation gave the United States pragmatic flexibility to administer annexed territories without binding the government to an outcome. As previously noted, US colonialism was premised on the annexation of territories for the purpose of creating new states of the Union. In contrast, the imperialist interpretation empowered the United States to occupy new territories without binding Congress to annexing it. Of course, as the experience of Hawai'i demonstrates, the occupation did not foreclose future annexation. To this extent, the global expansionist interpretation echoed the imperialist tradition. While Congress was no longer bound to treat *annexed* unincorporated territories as states in the making, this status did not foreclose the possibility that one day Congress could incorporate a territory and/or granted statehood. Likewise, as the case of the Philippines also demonstrates, the United States could also de-annex unincorporated territories and grant them independence. Although the primary intent or goal in annexing islands throughout the world was to build strategically situated coaling stations and naval bases, more generally, the global expansionist interpretation gave Congress and US legal actors a pragmatic flexibility to annex territories for indefinite periods of time without being bound to make them states of the Union.

Notwithstanding the latter argument and without providing much evidence, Natsu Taylor Saito argues that US lawmakers 'turned to their colonial experience with American Indians for legal as well as military precedent' to determine the status of Puerto Rico and the other Spanish territories annexed in the aftermath of the War of 1898 (2007: 23). Citing the work of Rivera Ramos, she suggests that the Supreme Court drew on the doctrine of plenary powers developed in the Cherokee Cases to craft the unincorporated territorial status for Puerto Rico. Taylor Saito does not describe the actual status of Puerto Rico or explain the continuities and discontinuities between unincorporated territories and other types of territories. Later citing the work of José A. Cabranes, Taylor Saito concludes that the unincorporated status enabled the US government to exert a plenary authority to colonize Puerto Ricans (Ibid.: 24–25).

This of course is not to say that the precedent established by the occupation of Native American domestic dependent nations does not help explain the unincorporated territorial status. As Kal Raustiala has previously noted (and I think Taylor Saito would agree), prior to 1898, the United States selectively situated domestic dependent nations inside and outside of the United States (2009: 46) and located these legal constructions in an anomalous or borderland place between a state and the Federal government. Like unincorporated territories, in 1898 domestic dependent nations were also ruled as separate and unequal spaces within the Anglo-American polity. Both types of localities were also racialized and postcolonial. To this extent, and conceptually speaking, it is clear that the US government invoked similar narratives of exceptionalism to construct the domestic dependent nation and the unincorporated territories.

The question is whether the unincorporated territorial status is constitutionally different from the domestic dependent nation. I agree with T.

Alexander Aleinikoff that there are clear distinctions between the two statuses. In *Semblances of Sovereignty* Aleinikoff writes:

> Nor are tribes analogous to governments in US territories. Indian sovereignty is to some degree more expansive: it is deemed inherent, while territorial governmental power is a product of congressional designation. Furthermore, the Constitution does not directly apply to tribal actions; under the *Insular Cases*, however, territorial residents received the protection of some 'fundamental' constitutional rights. But tribal sovereignty is also less comprehensive than the power conferred on territorial governments, which are delegated authority to regulate all persons within their boundaries. And territories are plainly outside the borders of US states. (California may not purport to apply its law in Guam.) Reservations, however, may be subject to regulation by the states in which they are located.
>
> (2002: 98)

In addition, the Insular Cases were rulings affirming the Foraker Act, an organic act that provided for the organization of a territorial government in Puerto Rico. More importantly, the district courts created by General Davis and codified in the Foraker Act eventually situated Puerto Rico within the First Circuit Court of Appeals or within the jurisdiction of the United States. Suffice it to say, as I noted in the previous chapter, that Puerto Rico was ascribed a territorial, albeit unincorporated, status. It follows, however unlikely, that a US Congress could incorporate Puerto Rico and grant it admission into the Union as a state on an equal footing to the original thirteen. No Native American tribe, reservation, or domestic dependent nation has ever been ruled as a territory of the United States and placed on a path to become a state of the Union.

So what is the status created by the unincorporated territory? It is a status located somewhere in between a territory and a foreign country. It is a liminal status that enables the US to annex new territories without binding its government to past colonialist or imperialist constitutional precedents. Rather, the new status allows the US government to selectively treat an unincorporated territory as a possession or a part of the United States for constitutional purposes. It is a malleable territorial status that can be ascribed in degrees and invoked to legitimate the arbitrary power of the US global empire. It is a territorial status that enables the US global empire to choose when to treat places like Puerto Rico as a part of the United States or as a separate and unequal possession of the empire. It is a territorial status that enables the US to selectively rule Puerto Rico as a foreign country for constitutional purposes, while simultaneously affirming that it belongs to the United States for international purposes. It is a postcolonial status that enables the US global empire to selectively situate places like

Puerto Rico inside or outside of the United States for constitutional and/or legal purposes.

NOTES

1 Remarks by Senator Foraker of Ohio, against Joint Resolution on the Acquisition of Territories, on 11 January 1899, S.J. Res. 191, 56th Cong., 3rd sess., *Congressional Record* 32, pt. 1: 565.

2 While it is true that the racial narratives invoked by US expansionists during the late 1890s echoed the racial ideologies of the Southern Reconstruction (Woodward 1974: 72–73), it is also true that Puerto Ricans became a sort of alterity for US government officials who were unable to situate the island's residents within the traditional Anglo-American racial categories.

3 For an alternative periodization with additional cases, see Bartholomew H. Sparrow's *The Insular Cases and the Emergence of the American Empire* (2006).

4 See generally *De Lima v. Bidwell,* 182 US 1 (1901); *Goetze v. United States,* 182 US 221 (1901); *Grossman v. United States,* 182 US 221 (1901); *Dooley v. United States,* 182 US 222 (1901); *Armstrong v. United States,* 182 US 243 (1901); *Downes v.* Bidwell, 182 US 244 (1901); Huus *v. New York and Puerto Rico Steamship Company,* 182 US 392 (1901); and *Dooley v. United States,* 182 US 151 (1901); and *Fourteen Diamond Rings v. United States,* 182 US 176 (1901). Some scholars also include two additional cases: *Ex Parte Baez,* 177 US 378 (1900) and *In Re Vidal,* 179 US 126 (1900).

5 See generally *Hawaii v. Mankichi,* 190 US 197 (1903); *González v. Williams,* 192 US 1 (1904); *Kepner v. United States,* 195 US 100 (1904); *Dorr v. United States,* 195 US 138 (1904); *Mendozana v. United States,* 195 US 158 (1904); *Rasmussen v. United States,* 197 US 516 (1905); *Trono v. United States,* 199 US 521 (1905); *Grafton v. United States,* 206 US 333 (1907); *Kent v. Porto Rico,* 207 US 113 (1907); *Kopel v. Bingham,* 211 US 468 (1909); *Dowdell v. United States,* 221 US 325 (1911); *Ochoa v. Hernández,* 230 US 139 (1913); and *Ocampo v. United States,* 234 US 91 (1914).

6 *Balzac v. People of Porto Rico,* 258 US 298 (1922).

7 It is important to note that Chief Justice Fuller equated the word colonialism with what I here describe as imperialism, or more precisely '(m)onarchical and despotic governments unrestrained by written constitutions' (182 US 244, 380). Notwithstanding, my argument is premised on recognizing a conceptual distinction between the words colonialism and imperialism. To this extent, Chief Justice Fuller's conceptualization is consistent with my argument.

Chapter 4

Citizenship and the inclusive exclusion of Puerto Ricans

> Under the Jones Act of 1917, Congress extended statutory US citizenship to the residents of Puerto Rico, but continued the less than equal status of Puerto Rican residents.
>
> (US Congress Representative Don Young [R-AK] 1997: H. Rept. 105–131, 9)

Since 1989, the prevailing view among US law and policymakers is that Puerto Rico is located outside of the United States for citizenship purposes. The US Constitution only confers two types of citizenship, namely a naturalized citizenship (US Constitution, Art. 1, Sect. 8, cl. 4 and 14th Amend., cl. 1) and a *jus soli* or birthright citizenship (US Constitution, 14th Amend., cl. 1). Puerto Rico, and unincorporated territories more generally, lawmakers such as Representative Young argue, are not a *part* of the United States for constitutional purposes and therefore naturalization or birth in Puerto Rico is tantamount to birth or naturalization in a foreign locality. To this extent, persons naturalized or born in Puerto Rico can only acquire a statutory citizenship, or a citizenship created by a congressional statute (legislation) designed to extend access to citizenship in Puerto Rico or a place like it. According to the prevailing interpretations, statutory citizenship designed for Puerto Rico confers a less than equal status on its bearer within the US global empire. This interpretation further suggests that the US global empire has used a hierarchy of less than equal citizenships to rule the residents of unincorporated territories.

Drawing on what Adi Ophir and others (2009) have described as a notion of inclusive exclusion I argue that legal actors used an array of citizenship laws to affirm the inclusion of Puerto Ricans, and the residents of unincorporated territories more generally, within the US global empire, while simultaneously barring them from constitutional equality within the Anglo-American polity. Between 1900 and 1940, Congress enacted a series of laws conferring three types of citizenship on the residents of Puerto Rico, namely a Puerto Rican citizenship (1900–1917), a *jus sanguinis* or derivative form of blood right citizenship (1906–1940), and a statutory form of *jus soli* or birthright citizenship (1940–present). However, these citizenship laws simultaneously established degrees of statutory membership and constitutional exclusion within the Anglo-American polity. The exclusion of Puerto Ricans from access to constitutional membership also affirms the postcolonial nature of these citizenship laws. Even though Puerto Ricans were annexed to the United States, they have been barred from access to a constitutional citizenship, a precondition for equality in the US global empire. More importantly, contemporary US law and policymakers continue to invoke a tautological reading of the latter exclusions to confine Puerto Ricans to a less than equal status within the empire.

THE PUERTO RICAN CITIZENSHIP, 1898–1917

Central to the debates over the annexation of Puerto Rico and the other Spanish territories was the question of the future citizenship status of the island's inhabitants, which were generally represented as 'uncivilized' non-white savages (Mendez Saavedra 1992). Accompanying the development of the US global expansionist tradition was a manifest destiny notion of white Anglo-Saxon exceptionalism (Weston 1972, Gerstle 2001). Legal actors across the ideological spectrum viewed Puerto Ricans, as well as the inhabitants of the other Spanish territories, as a threat to the racial harmony of the United States. Anti-imperialist and imperialists alike feared that granting Puerto Ricans a US citizenship would not only open the door for miscegenation but also lead to the granting of suffrage to racially inferior populations. Yet, while global expansionists reproduced similar narratives of Anglo-Saxon exceptionalism, they were not as concerned with the effects of naturalizing Puerto Ricans upon the annexation of the island. In the end, however, global expansionists capitulated to their imperialist colleagues and did not provide for the collective naturalization of Puerto Ricans in the annexation treaty nor in the ensuing organic act. The failure to include a naturalization provision (individual or collective), or even a promise to do so in the future, represented a departure from past colonialist tradition (Cabranes 1979: 18–21).

As previously noted, the United States annexed Puerto Rico under the terms of the 1898 Treaty of Paris. The citizenship and naturalization provisions for the Spanish subjects inhabiting Puerto Rico at the time of the annexation were outlined in the first clause of Article Nine:

> Spanish subjects, natives of the Peninsula, residing in the territory over which Spain by the present treaty relinquishes or cedes her sovereignty, may remain in such territory or may remove therefrom retaining in either event all their rights of property... In the case they remain in the territory they may preserve their allegiance to the Crown of Spain by making, before a court of record, within a year from the date of the

> exchange of ratifications of this treaty, a declaration of their decision to preserve such allegiance; in default of which declaration they shall be held to have renounced it and to have adopted the nationality of the territory in which they may reside.
>
> (US Congress 1910: S. Doc. 357, 1693)

This clause established two core principles that would define the contours of the Puerto Rican citizenship. The first sentence of this clause recognized a legal distinction between peninsular- and island-born Spanish subjects. Whereas peninsular-born Spanish subjects were permitted to choose to retain their citizenship or acquire the 'nationality' conferred by the United States on Puerto Rico, island- or Puerto Rican-born subjects were barred from retaining their Spanish citizenship. In addition, the Treaty of Paris is the first US annexation treaty that does not contain either a collective naturalization provision or the promise of future naturalization for the island's inhabitants. The Treaty, however, passed the responsibility of determining the citizenship status of the residents of Puerto Rico on to the Congress.

It is important to note that on the question of the citizenship status of the residents of Puerto Rico and the other Spanish territories, anti-imperialist senators debating the ratification of the Treaty felt bound to colonialist precedents. Specifically, anti-imperialists agreed that Puerto Ricans either became citizens once the United States annexed Puerto Rico or that Congress was bound to collectively naturalize the island's inhabitants following the ratification of the Treaty of Paris. Again, Senator Caffery summarized the colonialist argument: 'wherever any territory is acquired by the United States in full sovereignty the citizens thereof become citizens of the United States' (32 Cong. Rec. 433). Anti-imperialist senators, however, for the most part agreed that Puerto Ricans were racially inferior and their incorporation posed a social and political threat to the United States. Thus, anti-imperialists in part rejected the annexation of Puerto Rico and the ratification of the Treaty of Peace for fear of being bound to recognize the equal citizenship status of Puerto Ricans and the other inhabitants of the annexed Spanish territories.

Imperialist and global expansionist senators alike for the most part rejected the argument that the annexation of Puerto Rico automatically or *ipso facto* conferred a US citizenship on the inhabitants of Puerto Rico. They generally agreed that Congress possessed a plenary power to extend or withhold the Birthright Citizenship Clause of the Fourteenth Amendment to Puerto Rico (see for example 32 Cong. Rec. 566). Like the anti-imperialists, however, they believed that Puerto Ricans, and the other non-white inhabitants of the newly annexed islands, were simply uncivilized and racially incapable of assuming the responsibilities of US citizenship (see for example 32 Cong. Rec. 992). To this extent, imperialist and global expansionist senators found common ground in ratifying the Treaty of

Paris, an annexation treaty that essentially barred persons born in Puerto Rico from acquiring a US citizenship.

For the most part, the military argued that Puerto Rico did not become a part of the United States for the purposes of the Fourteenth Amendment upon annexation and opposed the naturalization of Puerto Ricans. The military rejected the anti-imperialist/colonialist argument suggesting that following the ratification of the Treaty of Paris in 11 April 1899 Puerto Rico became a part of the United States for the purposes of the birthright citizenship provision of the Fourteenth Amendment until Congress enacted legislation organizing the island as a territorial part of the United States (US Congress, Magoon 1900: S. Doc. 234). Secretary of War Root invoked prevailing racist narratives of Anglo-American exceptionalism to describe Puerto Ricans as an inferior race incapable of assuming self-responsibility and in constant need of tutelage (Bacon and Brown Scott 1970: 164–165). All the US military governors assigned to the island between the initial occupation and the subsequent enactment of the 1900 Foraker Act echoed Secretary of War Root's racist ideologies (Trías Monge 1981: 68–81; US Congress 1902: H. Doc. 2, 96). Puerto Ricans, according to an array of military actors, were simply unable to grasp the Anglo-American racial and cultural institutions that grew out of the Common Law tradition (1900: S. Doc. 234).

During the military occupation, the Congressional debates over the citizenship and naturalization provision of the 1900 Foraker Act echoed the prevailing ideological debates. Again, as Cabranes has demonstrated, anti-imperialist and imperialist law and policymakers alike invoked racist narratives of Anglo-American exceptionalism to oppose the collective naturalization of Puerto Rico (1979: 26–44). Even anti-imperialist lawmakers who believed that colonialist precedents extended the first sentence or birthright citizenship provision of the Fourteenth Amendment to Puerto Rico following the island's annexation, railed against naturalizing the island's residents. Although global expansionists were not as concerned with the potential racial dangers of naturalizing Puerto Ricans, they could not muster enough support from the imperialist wing of the Republican Party to pass the bill with a collective naturalization provision and Senator Foraker was forced to withdraw the citizenship provision in order to pass the bill (Foraker 1916: 84).

The final version of the 1900 Foraker Act contained a citizenship and naturalization provision that normalized Article Nine of the Treaty of Paris and confined the inhabitants of Puerto Rico to a legal limbo. Not only did this provision depart from all prior and contemporary organic or territorial acts, which included collective naturalization provisions or a promise of future naturalization, but it is also the first time that Congress invents a citizenship status to rule the residents of an annexed territory. To be sure, Section 7 of the Foraker Act established:

> That all inhabitants continuing to reside therein who were Spanish subjects on the eleventh day of April, eighteen hundred and ninety-nine, and then resided in Porto Rico, and their children born subsequent thereto, shall be deemed and held to be citizens of Porto Rico, and as such entitled to the protection of the United States, except such as shall have elected to preserve their allegiance to the Crown of Spain on or before the eleventh day of April, nineteen hundred, in accordance with the provisions of the treaty of peace between the United States and Spain entered into on the eleventh day of April, eighteen hundred and ninety-nine.
>
> (31 Stat. 77, 79)

The Puerto Rican citizenship's recognition of the distinction between peninsular- and island-born inhabitants confined the latter to an anomalous citizenship and immigration status in three ways. First, the establishment of a peninsular/island birth distinction was designed to sever the links between Spanish citizens residing in Puerto Rico and the Spanish crown. This principle essentially eliminated the right to a form of *jus sanguinis* or blood right citizenship within Spanish families confining island-born Spanish subjects to a subordinated status. Second, peninsular-born residents of Puerto Rico were given an opportunity to choose between retaining their Spanish citizenship, acquiring a Puerto Rican citizenship, or acquiring a US citizenship by undergoing the citizenship and naturalization process. In contrast, Puerto Rican citizens were barred from either retaining their Spanish citizenship or acquiring a US citizenship. Under prevailing US immigration and naturalization laws, a person was required to renounce his or her allegiance to a sovereign in order to begin the naturalization process. Whereas peninsular-born subjects could always renounce their allegiance to Spain, Puerto Rican citizens found themselves unable to renounce their allegiance to either Puerto Rico, a non-existent sovereign, or to the United States in order to comply with the law (McGovney 1934). Puerto Ricans found themselves citizens of an unincorporated territory that belonged to, but was not a part of the United States. Puerto Rican citizens became citizens of nowhere.

Even though Justice White's opinion in *Downes* primarily addressed the question of Puerto Rico's territorial status, he made two important statements about the relationship between the citizenship status of Puerto Ricans and the island's unincorporated status. First, Justice White affirmed the prevailing racist narratives of Anglo-American exceptionalism and opposed the naturalization of Puerto Ricans. He described Puerto Rico as an 'alien territory' inhabited by an inferior race of people and suggested that the collective naturalization of Puerto Ricans would 'degrade the whole body of American citizenship' (*Downes*, 182 US 244, 314–315). Justice White embraced the notion that the United States was comprised of both states and territories populated by 'native white inhabitants... endowed with citizenship' (Id. at 320). Second, and perhaps most importantly, Justice White suggested that the collective naturalization of Puerto Ricans would be tantamount to incorporating Puerto Rico (Id. at 332). Drawing on the case of Louisiana, Justice White reasoned that the extension of citizenship to Puerto Rico would be indicative of Congress' intent to incorporate the island as a territory of the United States. As Rivera Ramos has noted, the Court eventually embraced the latter interpretation in *Rassmussen v. United States* [197 US 516 (1905)]. Read together, these arguments suggest that the doctrine of territorial incorporation permitted the annexation of territories without providing for the collective naturalization of the local inhabitants. The doctrine of territorial incorporation permitted the creation of legal constructions like the 'Puerto Rican citizenship' to simultaneously affirm the ownership of the island's inhabitants and their exclusion from membership in the Anglo-American polity, a precondition for equality in the US global empire.

The anomalous status of Puerto Rican citizens presented a number of administrative problems for the nascent global empire. For example, Puerto Rican merchants who were traveling outside of Puerto Rico during the 1898 War were left in a stateless condition without access to travel documents that would enable them to enter the United States. Likewise local merchants with business arrangements outside of the island found their ability to conduct commerce restricted by their anomalous status. Related to these and other debates about the ability of Puerto Rican citizens to travel was the question of what types of duties, taxes, and tariffs applied to Puerto Ricans seeking to repatriate their property to the island. Suffice it to say that between 1900 and 1904, Federal agencies and Congress began to treat Puerto Rican citizens and the residents of other insular areas as non-alien nationals, locating their status somewhere between a citizen and an alien.

In 1904 the Supreme Court normalized the latter interpretation in *Gonzalez v. Williams* (192 US 1). In *Gonzalez* the Court addressed the immigration status of the Puerto Rican citizen without ruling on the constitutionality of this type of membership. The question addressed by this ruling was whether Isabella Gonzalez, a single woman and native of Puerto Rico, was an alien immigrant under the prevailing US immigration and naturalization laws. In 1902, Gonzalez was detained in New York by immigration authorities and barred from entry into the United States on account of her supposed immigration status. She was detained and subjected to deportation proceedings. She sued for a writ of habeas corpus, but a lower court dismissed her case. Gonzalez appealed the dismissal of a writ of habeas corpus requesting an inquiry into her status as a Puerto Rican citizen and its relationship to prevailing US immigration laws. Without questioning the constitutionality of the Foraker Act citizenship, the Supreme Court overturned her detention and citing at least one administrative decision ruled that the Puerto Rican citizenship was tantamount to a non-alien nationality. Accordingly, Puerto Ricans were not alien immigrants or US citizens, but owed allegiance to the United States and could therefore be treated as nationals (Id. at 13).

The Puerto Rican citizenship represented both a departure from past precedents and the creation of a new type of membership consistent with the logic of US global empire. By 1898, under the prevailing colonialist tradition, the inhabitants of annexed territories were collectively naturalized by either an annexation treaty or an organic act. The inhabitants of annexed territories were treated as members of the United States, albeit in most cases subordinated by the territorial status of their residence. Of course, US legal actors consistently invoked racist narratives of Anglo-American exceptionalism to legitimate the departure from past colonialist precedents. In contrast, while the Puerto Rican citizenship affirmed the inclusion of Puerto Ricans within the US global empire as non-alien nationals, it simultaneously barred or excluded Puerto Ricans from access to US citizenship, at least until 1906. To this extent, Puerto Rican citizens were confined to a less than equal status within the US global empire, a status tantamount to that of a non-alien national.

JUS SANGUINIS CITIZENSHIP, 1906–1940

There are two prevailing interpretations of the origins of the extension of US citizenship to Puerto Rico presently. Drawing on the memoirs of Bernardo Vega, historian Lorrin Thomas suggests that Puerto Ricans were unable to acquire a US citizenship until 1917, the year that Congress enacted the Jones Act and collectively naturalized the residents of Puerto Rico (Thomas 2010: 1–2). Vega, an important Puerto Rican activist residing in New York City, recalls how in 1916 while attending a class in public school with German and Hungarian immigrants he engaged in a discussion with a teacher and tried to explain that Puerto Ricans could not acquire a US citizenship because they were unable to comply with prevailing immigration and naturalization laws. More specifically, he argued that in 1916 he was unable to renounce his allegiance to a sovereign country in order to begin the naturalization process (Andreu Iglesias 1984: 27). A second interpretation offered by Judge José A. Cabranes contends that in 1917 Congress gave Puerto Ricans the right to acquire a US citizenship in order to reward their loyalty to the 'American Empire.' Specifically, Cabranes writes: '(i)n granting United States citizenship to the people of Puerto Rico, Congress intended to distinguish between the Puerto Ricans, regarded as worthy or a permanent association with the United States, and the Filipinos who had vigorously and "ungratefully" resisted American rule' (Cabranes 1979: 98–99). Both interpretations are incorrect.

Between 1906 and 1938, Congress enacted a series of laws granting Puerto Ricans the ability to acquire a naturalized citizenship. Congress enacted laws that enabled Puerto Ricans to avail themselves of a US citizenship either by an individual process of naturalization or as a result of a collective naturalization process. Some laws required Puerto Rican citizens to travel to a state or an incorporated territory (Oklahoma, New Mexico, Arizona, Hawai'i, or Alaska), while other laws were extended to Puerto Rico. However, none of these laws changed the territorial status of Puerto Rico, explicitly or implicitly. This meant that persons born in Puerto Rico were not born *in the United States* for citizenship purposes. The citizenship laws developed for Puerto Rico between 1906 and 1938, however, only conferred a right to a *jus sanguinis* (blood right) or derivative forms of parental citizenship.

The 1906 Bureau of Immigration and Naturalization Act (BINA) was the first law to enable the residents of the insular territories, including Puerto Rican citizens, to acquire a US citizenship by establishing a temporary residence in a state or incorporated territory and undergoing an individual process of naturalization (34 Stat. 596). More specifically, Section 30 of the act provided:

> That all the applicable provisions of the naturalization laws of the United States shall apply to and be held to authorize the admission of all persons not citizens who owe permanent allegiance to the United States, and who may become residents of any State or organized Territory of the United States, with the following modifications: The applicant shall not be required to renounce allegiance to any foreign sovereignty; he shall make his declaration of intention to become a citizen of the United States at least two years prior to his admission; and residence within the jurisdiction of the United States, owing such permanent allegiance, shall be regarded as residence within the United States within the meaning of the five year's residency clause of the existing law.
>
> (34 Stat. 596, 607)

Again, it is important to note that although the Federal district court in Puerto Rico had conducted naturalization proceedings for Spanish peninsular-born and other alien residents of the island, Puerto Rican citizens were required to travel to the 'United States' in order to undergo the naturalization process. Available documents from the National Archives and Records Administration (NARA) suggests that most Puerto Rican citizens travelled to New York City to undergo the immigration and naturalization process.

The 1906 BINA also affirmed three basic principles of the nascent global expansionist tradition. First, it affirmed the principle that the Puerto Rican citizenship was not a US citizenship. Puerto Ricans, like other alien immigrants, could only acquire a US citizenship by undergoing the immigration and naturalization process, albeit an amended process. Second, while Puerto Ricans could now acquire a US citizenship, they could only do so by migrating to the United States. Soon after the enactment of the BINA, the US Department of Labor eliminated the power of the Federal district court in Puerto Rico to grant naturalizations forcing all residents of Puerto Rico to travel to a state or an incorporated territory in order to undergo the US naturalization process. On the one hand, island-born Puerto Ricans were now able to acquire a US citizenship through an individual process of naturalization, albeit in a world where Jim Crow laws relegated Latinos to a separate and unequal social status. On the other hand, in order to acquire a US citizenship, island-born Puerto Ricans were required to migrate to a state or incorporated territory and establish a two-year residency, a requirement that was beyond the reach of the masses of working-class Puerto Ricans who could afford to travel and/or wished to live on the island. While the BINA established the possibility of naturalizing Puerto Ricans, and therefore affirming a membership within the Anglo-American polity, it also excluded Puerto Rican citizens residing in the island from the possibility of acquiring a US citizenship. Finally, the BINA affirmed the principle that Puerto Rico, like other insular territories was not located in the United States for immigration and naturalization purposes.

In 1917, Congress enacted legislation providing for the collective naturalization of the residents of Puerto Rico. More specifically, Section 5 of the Jones Act gave the residents of the island a choice between retaining their citizenship or being collectively naturalized. At least 288 persons chose to retain their Puerto Rican citizenship rather than acquiring a US citizenship [*Ex Parte Morales*, 10 PR Fed. 395, 397 (1918); Bothwell González 1979: 2, 310-313]. Unlike Puerto Rican citizens, which were required to choose to retain their status, resident aliens and the children of alien parents were given various time frames to choose to avail themselves of a US citizenship under the terms of Section 5.

Almost immediately after the enactment of the Jones Act, local judges began to issue opinions asserting that the collective naturalization of Puerto Ricans had incorporated or changed the territorial status of the island. They invoked the relevant statements by Justice White in *Downes* and their affirmation in the *Rassmussen* ruling. For example, on 5 April 1917, in *In the Matter of Garffer*, a Federal district court judge ruled that following the enactment of the Jones Act the 'residents in Puerto Rico shall, for naturalization purposes, be considered the same as residents elsewhere in the United States, which for naturalization purposes, therefore, amounts to an incorporation of Porto Rico [sic] in the United States' (9 PR Fed. 544, 546). Likewise in both *In the Matter of Tapia* [9 PR Fed. Rep. 452 (1917)] and *Muratti v. Foote* [25 D.P.R. 568 (1917)] a Federal district court judge and a local municipal judge argued that the collective naturalization provision of the Jones Act was tantamount to the implicit incorporation of Puerto Rico.

However, within six months in the *People of Porto Rico v. Tapia* [245 US 639 (1918)] the Supreme Court reversed the latter rulings without providing an explanation. In *Balzac v. People of Porto Rico*, however, writing for the Court, Chief Justice William H. Taft argued that the collective naturalization provision of the Jones Act was neither an 'express declaration, or an implication so strong as to exclude any other view' that Congress intended to incorporate Puerto Rico [258 US 298, 306 (1922)]. In sum, notwithstanding Justice White's prior statements about the relationship between the collective naturalization of the inhabitants of a territory and its incorporation, the Court established that Section 5 of the Jones Act did not change Puerto Rico's territorial status.

Because the Jones Act did not incorporate Puerto Rico, persons born in the island could only acquire a derivative form of *jus sanguinis* or parental citizenship. According to this logic, Puerto Rico was not located in the United States for the purposes of the Citizenship Clause of the Fourteenth Amendment. Thus persons born in Puerto Rico after the enactment of the Jones Act were born outside of the United States. Since then, persons born in Puerto Rico could acquire a US citizenship either by naturalization or as a result of a derivative form of *jus sanguinis* or parental right. More specifically, at the time only male US citizens could confer a derivative form of *jus sanguinis* citizenship to persons born in the island.

Yet, while the collective naturalization of the residents of Puerto Rico affirmed their membership within the Anglo-American polity, the nature of the citizenship simultaneously reified the legal exclusion of thousands of Puerto Ricans from access to membership within the US global empire. In response, between 1927 and 1938, Congress enacted three corrective laws providing for the collective naturalization of Puerto Ricans and other residents of the island. For example, in 1927, Congress amended [Section 5(a)] citizenship provision of the Jones Act enabling the naturalization of both Puerto Rican citizens who had chosen to retain their status and the children of aliens who did not comply with the time restrictions of Section 5. They were allowed to acquire a US citizenship by making a simple declaration of their interests in accordance with the original language of Section 5.

Also known as Section 5(b), the 1934 amendment provided for the retroactive naturalization of Puerto Ricans who had been outside of the island at the time of the annexation and for women who lost their US citizenship as a result of marriage or coverture. In the first instance, Congress had identified a group of 250 Puerto Ricans who were outside of island prior to the enactment of the Foraker Act and were subsequently unable to acquire a Puerto Rican citizenship. According to a congressional report accompanying the 1934 amendment, these Puerto Ricans became 'a people without a country' and by no fault of their own had become stateless (PR Civil Government Act 1934: H. Rept. 1277, 1). In addition, prior to 1922 the United States embraced the doctrine of coverture, which allowed for the automatic denaturalization of female US citizens who married aliens. Even though Congress began enacting legislation to repudiate the corresponding law and policy in 1922, it did not extend such legislation to Puerto Rico until 1934. It followed that prior to 1934, Puerto Rican women automatically lost their US citizenship as a result of their marriage to an alien and in some instances acquired the citizenship status of their husbands. Because Puerto Rican women acquired a naturalized citizenship, they were unable to reclaim their US citizenship when they widowed or divorced under the prevailing interpretation of the doctrine of coverture. The 1934 amendment extended the 1922 Cable Act to Puerto Rico enabling this class of Puerto Rican women 'to be naturalized' and in most cases reacquire their US citizenship (Bothwell González 1971; Venator-Santiago 2012).

The 1938 amendment [Section 5(c)] provided for the retroactive naturalization of the children of peninsular-born Spanish citizens who chose to remain in Puerto Rico after the annexation. Documents included in an accompanying congressional report explained the problem in the following terms:

> It is estimated there are approximately 6,000 residents of Puerto Rico involved, concerning whose status there appears to have been considerable popular confusion and misunderstanding. They are descendants, born in the island since its cession to the United States, of Spanish subjects who elected on or before April 11, 1900, to retain their allegiance to the Crown of Spain, in accordance with article X [sic] of the treaty of peace which terminated the Spanish–American War.... The descendants of Spanish subjects, who elected to retain their Spanish citizenship, are not citizens of the United States, although born and residing in Puerto Rico, unless naturalized.
>
> (PR Civil Government Act 1938: S. Rept. 1679, 3).

However, like the prior corrective amendments, Section 5c did not change the islands' territorial status. Persons born in Puerto Rico who fell within the crevices of US immigration law could find themselves stateless until Congress enacted further legislation providing for their naturalization.

These and other citizenship laws enacted during the period affirmed a new type of inclusive exclusion. On the one hand, Congress affirmed the inclusion of Puerto Ricans within the US global empire by constantly naturalizing the residents of Puerto Rico. Simultaneously, by not changing the island's territorial status, Congress continued to reify the notion that Puerto Rico was a foreign country for citizenship purposes. Persons born in Puerto Rico to anyone who was not a US citizen (whether they were aware or not of their parent's status) could potentially become stateless until Congress enacted special naturalization legislation addressing the peculiarities of their status. More importantly, the period's citizenship legislation only provided a naturalized citizenship status on Puerto Ricans. From a socio-legal perspective, the residents of this unincorporated territory were ascribed a less than equal citizenship status.

JUS SOLI CITIZENSHIP, 1940–PRESENT

In 1940, Congress enacted legislation conferring on Puerto Ricans a third type of citizenship, namely a birthright or *jus soli* citizenship. The citizenship provisions of the 1940 Nationality Act were in large measure designed to resolve the problems created by the Jones Act citizenship, problems requiring the constant enactment of corrective legislation. The new citizenship law treated Puerto Rico as a part of the United States for citizenship purposes and automatically conferred a *jus soli* or birthright citizenship on all persons born in Puerto Rico. Yet, even though Congress was willing to treat Puerto Rico as an incorporated territory for the purposes of this citizenship law, Congress refused to change the island's territorial status. Congress effectively extended a statutory form of birthright citizenship to Puerto Rico and conferring Puerto Ricans a US native-born status, even though the US global empire continued to selectively rule the island as an unincorporated territory.

In 1933, President Franklin D. Roosevelt issued an executive order convening a committee to review all US immigration and nationality laws and 'to codify the laws into one comprehensive nationality law for submission to the Congress' (US Congress Hearings 1940: 407). The President's Committee included representatives from the Departments of State, Labor, and Justice and was tasked with completing a code by 1935. At the time, US immigration and nationality laws contained 'obsolete, conflicting, unnecessary, and undesirable laws' (US Congress 1940: H. Rept. 2396, 1). The proposed legislation would 'bring together in orderly and systematic form a consolidation or restatement of the laws of the United States upon citizenship, naturalization, and expatriation' in a comprehensive nationality code (Ibid.).

Central to the proposed legislation was a concern with resolving the problems created by birth in foreign countries and unincorporated territories. Both the President's Committee and Congress noted that 'nearly all foreign states' had in recent years completely revised and codified their immigration and nationality laws. At the time, Congress was primarily concerned with the growing number of children of US citizens who were born outside of the United States and acquired a right to *jus soli* citizenship in a foreign country, or more specifically acquired a right to dual nationality and corresponding allegiances. Regarding unincorporated territories, the President's Committee noted two core problems. First, the Committee noted that at the time there were 'no statutory provisions fixing the nationality status of the inhabitants of certain of the outlying possessions of the United States, including American Samoa and Guam' (Hearings 1940: 407). Second, while the Committee recognized that 'the citizenship status of persons born in the United States and the incorporated territories is determined by the Fourteenth Amendment to the Constitution,' the laws governing birth in unincorporated territories were varied (Ibid.). To be sure, while persons born in the US Virgin Islands acquired a right to birthright citizenship since 1927, persons born in Puerto Rico had been acquiring a right to naturalized citizenship since 1906. The proposed nationality code would seek to resolve the problems created by the conflicts between the array of citizenship and nationality laws developed for the insular, outlying or unincorporated territories and US immigration and nationality laws. In 1940, Congress passed the Nationality Act and began to implement it in Puerto Rico on 13 January 1941.

The 1940 Nationality Act treated Puerto Rico as an incorporated territory for the purposes of extending the rule of *jus soli* to the island. This principle was articulated in two core provisions. Section 101(d) established that the term 'United States' when 'used in a geographical sense means the continental United States, Alaska, Hawaii, Puerto Rico, and the Virgin Islands of the United States' (54 Stat. 1137). According to the President's Committee 'birth in Puerto Rico will have the same effect as birth in the continental United States' (Hearings 1940: 415). In addition, Section 202 retroactively extended a right to *jus soli* citizenship to all persons born in Puerto Rico after 11 April 1899. Again, the President's Committee summarized the intent of this section in the following language:

> In other words, this section will, in effect, apply the rule of *jus soli* to Puerto Rico as of the date of its annexation to the United States, treating Puerto Rico for such purposes as an incorporated territory of the United States. It places Puerto Rico on a part with the Virgin Islands with regards to the effect of birth therein since its annexation to the United States.
>
> (Ibid.: 427)

Both provisions treated Puerto Rico as a *part* of the United States or as incorporated territories and differentiated the island from 'outlying possessions' or 'unincorporated territories' for the purposes of extending the rule of *jus soli* citizenship. Since 13 January 1941, all persons born in Puerto Rico acquired a right to a *jus soli* US citizenship.

Within a year, the Puerto Rican Resident Commissioner Bolivar Pagán began to introduce legislation seeking to declare all Puerto Ricans naturalized prior to 1941 native-born US citizens for the purposes of Section 404(c) of the 1940 Nationality Act. Section 404(c) provided for the automatic denaturalization of naturalized citizens who continuously resided in a foreign state for five continuous years (54 Stat. 1170). At the time, Puerto Rican merchants routinely established residence in foreign states like the Dominican Republic and Venezuela in order to operate business endeavors. Notwithstanding prevailing interpretations of the retroactive naturalization of Puerto Ricans under Section 202, Resident Commissioner Pagán feared that Section 404(c) would be used to denaturalize Puerto Rican merchants conducting business in the Caribbean and Latin America more generally. Following the Second World War, in 1948 Congress enacted legislation amending the Nationality Act and declaring all Puerto Ricans who acquired their citizenship as a result of the Jones Act (or the ensuing corrective amendments) native-born citizens for the purposes of Section 404(c). What is important to note, however, is that the legislative history of the 1948 amendment documents that US law and policymakers consistently believed that persons born in Puerto Rico after 1941 were US native-born citizens. The 1948 amendment retroactively affirmed that persons who acquired a naturalized citizenship under the terms of the Jones Act (and its subsequent amendments) were also entitled to a native-born status.

In a sense the extension of the rule of *jus soli* citizenship to Puerto Rico is representative of the postcolonial nature of US global empire. While Congress treated Puerto Rico as an incorporated territory for the purposes of the 1940 Nationality Act, it did not incorporate or change the island's territorial status. Birth in Puerto Rico was tantamount to birth in the United States and Puerto Rican-born citizens acquired a native-born status even though the island remained a foreign country in a domestic or constitutional sense for an array of other purposes. Unlike all territories annexed prior to 1898, Congress has never placed Puerto Rico on a path to statehood. In fact, for more than 60 years, persons born in Puerto Rico acquire a *jus soli* or native-born citizenship status even though they are selectively born outside of the United States for constitutional purposes.

CITIZENSHIP AS CONFINEMENT

During the 1989–1991 Puerto Rican status plebiscitary proceedings, the Congressional Research Service (CRS) submitted a Memorandum on the citizenship status of Puerto Ricans (PRFAA 1992: 81–85). The 1989 CRS Memorandum has since defined the key interpretations embraced by the US global empire of the citizenship status of persons born in Puerto Rico. Two debates illustrate how these interpretations have been used to affirm the inclusive exclusion of Puerto Rican-born US citizens and their less than equal status within the US global empire. One debate suggests that the US global empire has created a hierarchy of *jus soli* citizenships to differentiate between the status of persons born in the United States and persons born in unincorporated territories. A second debate illustrates how these interpretations have been used to confine Puerto Ricans to a less than equal citizenship status.

The 1989 CRS Memorandum responded to a request by Senator Bennett Johnston (D-LA) on whether Congress possessed the constitutional power to expatriate or denaturalize Puerto Rican born citizens should local electors vote in a status plebiscite in favor of independence for the island. The Memorandum began with a discussion of two modalities of acquisition of citizenship in order to establish a distinction between statutory and constitutional citizens. Puerto Ricans, the CRS argued were born outside of the United States and acquired their citizenship as a result of the collective naturalization provision of the 1917 Jones Act. In contrast, the Citizenship Clause of the Fourteenth Amendment conferred a constitutional citizenship on all persons born in the United States. The CRS sought to establish a legal difference between statutory (Jones Act) and constitutional citizens in order to justify Congress' power to enact legislation providing for the denaturalization of persons born in Puerto Rico should Puerto Ricans vote for independence. As noted above, central to the distinction between statutory and constitutional citizens was the location of birth. Only those born inside of the United States could claim a constitutional protection against the collective denaturalization of an act of Congress. The CRS, however, neglected to discuss the language and premises of the 1940 Nationality Act's citizenship provision for Puerto Ricans.

At this point, the CRS Memorandum shifted to a discussion of two constitutional precedents that could be invoked to determine the constitutional status of Puerto Rican born citizens. The CRS begins with a discussion of *Afroyim v. Rusk* [387 US 253 (1967)], a case addressing the power of Congress to enact legislation that revoked the citizenship of naturalized citizens if they participated in a foreign country's elections. Afroyim was born in Poland, but later travelled to the United States and acquired a citizenship by naturalization. He subsequently established residence in Israel and voted in local elections. Drawing on Congressional legislation, the Department of State then revoked his citizenship or denaturalized him. In the case bearing his name, the Supreme Court overturned his denaturalization establishing that his citizenship was constitutional and thus granted him due process rights or protections against arbitrary legislation. The CRS reasoned that if Puerto Rico were located in the United States, the *Afroyim* precedent would protect all Puerto Ricans naturalized by the Jones Act.

The CRS Memorandum then proceeds to discuss *Rogers v. Bellei* [401 US 815 (1971)], which established that Congress held the power for citizens who were not born or naturalized *in* the United States. Mr. Bellei was born and naturalized *outside* of the United States and failed to comply with a prevailing immigration provision requiring him to reside for five continuous years in the United States between the ages of 14 and 28. In *Bellei* the Court concluded that persons born or naturalized outside of the United States are not entitled to a Fourteenth Amendment or constitutional citizenship. It followed that if Puerto Rico was located outside of the United States, persons who acquired their citizenship in the island, either at birth or by naturalization, were not entitled to a constitutional citizenship and the relevant due process protections. Thus, should Puerto Ricans vote to make the island a sovereign or independent country, Congress has the power to enact legislation providing for the expatriation of all Puerto Rican-born citizens.

The CRS Memorandum concludes that Puerto Rico is not located in the United States and Puerto Rican-born citizens are mere statutory citizens without the same constitutional status as persons born *in* the United States. Drawing on a selective interpretation of the Insular Cases, the CRS concludes that 'case law establishes that Puerto Rico, whatever its exact status and relationship to the United States is not itself *in* the United States' (PRFAA 1992: 82). Thus, persons born and/or naturalized in Puerto Rico are merely entitled to a statutory rather than a constitutional citizenship. Because Puerto Rican-born citizens do not acquire a constitutional citizenship, Congress has the power to enact expatriating legislation should a majority of Puerto Ricans vote for independence in a status plebiscite.

Notwithstanding the critiques leveled by Álvarez González in an important article titled 'The Empire Strikes Out' (1990), Federal law and policymakers have since embraced this interpretation. Among the array of responses written by Álvarez González two stand out. First, Álvarez González argues, while Justice White's opinion in *Downes* established that Puerto Rico could be ruled as a foreign locality in a domestic or constitutional sense, he also wrote that Puerto Rico is a possession of the United States in an international sense and is therefore located within its sovereign jurisdiction. Moreover, Álvarez González reminded the CRS that the legislative history of the 1940 Nationality Act situated Puerto Ricans within the United States and imbued island-born citizens with constitutional due process protections. Álvarez González concluded, the *Afroyim* rather than the *Bellei* precedent is applicable to the case of Puerto Rico. Yet, as I noted in the epigraph at the beginning of this chapter, Representative Young embraced the 1989 CRS Memorandum's interpretation to argue that persons born in Puerto Rico acquire a statutory rather than a constitutional citizenship and are therefore less than equal citizens. Likewise, both the Bush and Obama administrations' Presidential Task Forces on the status of Puerto Rico have adopted the 1989 CRS Memorandum interpretation.

The CRS Memorandum's interpretation implicitly suggests that the United States has created a hierarchy of *jus soli* or birthright citizenships. Of course, Álvarez González has noted, the initial CRS Memorandum neglected to discuss the legal history of the 1940 Nationality Act citizenship for Puerto Rico. However, this neglect has not stopped US law and policymakers from embracing the CRS interpretation, an interpretation anchored in the Insular

Cases and the corresponding global expansionist ideology. Thus, if we take this argument seriously, the US global Empire has created a legal hierarchy of birthright citizenships to rule its native-born subjects. Whereas persons born or naturalized *in* the United States (namely the states and districts) acquire a constitutional citizenship at birth, persons born in unincorporated territories acquire a statutory form of birthright citizenship. While Fourteenth Amendment *jus soli* citizens can claim due process protections, statutory citizens, such as Puerto Ricans, can at best claim a less than equal constitutional status. It follows that an immigrant naturalized in the United States can make a constitutional claim to a US citizenship, while a native-born citizen from Puerto Rico cannot. To this extent, as Linda Bosniak's critique (2011: 624) of Ayelet Shachar's *The Birthright Lottery* (2009) suggests, US global empire has used a statutory form of *jus soli* to confine Puerto Ricans to a less than equal citizenship status.

Stated differently, contemporary iterations of the status of Puerto Rican-born citizens affirm their inclusive exclusion within the US global empire. On the one hand, the extension of a *jus soli* citizenship to Puerto Rico affirmed a more inclusive degree of membership within the US global empire tantamount to that of a native-born citizen. Simultaneously, however, the statutory nature affirms the exclusion of Puerto Rican-born citizens from equal membership in the US global empire, a status contingent on the bearer possessing a Fourteenth Amendment or constitutional citizenship. To this extent, the extension of a statutory rather than a Fourteenth Amendment form of birthright citizenship to Puerto Rico served to confine Puerto Ricans to a less than equal status within the US global empire.

Puerto Ricans across the ideological spectrum have also invoked the CRS Memorandum's interpretation of the status of Puerto Rican-born citizens to change their citizenship status in at least two ways. For example, some Puerto Ricans have sought to renounce their US citizenship or self-expatriate in order to acquire a Puerto Rican citizenship. The most recent expression of this attempt began in 1993 when a group of advocates for the independence of Puerto Rico decided to collectively renounce their US citizenship. They hired several notary publics and made public declarations of their intent to self-expatriate and become Puerto Rican citizens. United States' law and policymakers, however, dismissed this act of civil disobedience. Subsequently, Juan Mari Brás, a well-known socialist activist and attorney, travelled to Venezuela and began the process of self-expatriation or renouncing his citizenship under the terms established by the US Department of State. After filing the required forms Mari Brás issued himself a Puerto Rican passport, travelled a bit, and returned to his home in Puerto Rico. On 22 November 1995, the Department of State issued Mari Brás a Certificate of Loss of Nationality, but subsequently withdrew its issuance. The Department of State argued that Mari Brás did not comply with a key element of the process, namely to establish residence in a 'foreign country.'

Puerto Rico, according to the Department of State, was a part of the United States and residence in the island was not tantamount to residence in a foreign country (Mari Brás 2006: 179–287). Puerto Rico, according to the Department of State, is located in the United States for citizenship and immigration purposes. Although other activists have since tried to self-expatriate, the US government has refused to recognize the ability of Puerto Ricans to renounce their US citizenship and subsequently reside in Puerto Rico.

Alternatively, at least one Puerto Rican-born citizen has attempted to acquire a constitutional citizenship by becoming a naturalized citizen. Jennifer Efron was born in Puerto Rico in 1984 and later moved to Florida with her parents where she established a five-year residency. She subsequently applied for naturalization with the Department of Immigration and Naturalization (INS) in order to acquire a constitutional citizenship. The INS rejected her application arguing that she was already a US citizen, albeit a statutory citizen. Efron then sued.

Efron essentially made two arguments. First, drawing on the debates over Representative Young's status plebiscitary legislation for Puerto Rico, Efron argued that if Puerto Rico became an independent country Congress could enact legislation providing for her expatriation. Thus she was seeking a naturalized or constitutional citizenship to protect her status as a US citizen. Second, she argued that the INS' decision to bar her from acquiring a constitutional or irrevocable citizenship effectively violated her Fifth Amendments due process and equal protections. To be sure, the INS was leaving her vulnerable to lose her citizenship. In addition, whereas alien immigrants were able to acquire a constitutional citizenship, Puerto Rican-born statutory citizens were barred from acquiring a constitutional status within the US polity. In the latter instance, Efron concluded, Puerto Ricans were subject to discriminatory policy relegating them to a 'suspect classification' based on 'national origin' or 'race.'

In 1998, a lower district court rejected her arguments as merely speculative. Notwithstanding the fact that prior to 1940 Puerto Ricans were able to acquire a US citizenship by way of naturalization the lower Court judge argued that the case was not ripe and Ms. Efron had not suffered any injury justifying her need to seek a constitutional status. If Puerto Rico became an independent country, then Ms. Efron could pursue her claims. Until then, the Court reasoned, she was merely speculating about a possible injury. After all the 1940 Nationality Act conferred upon her a statutory citizenship with corresponding rights and privileges [*Efron v. United States,* 1 F. Supp. 2d 1468 (1998)]. In 8 November 1999 the Supreme Court affirmed lower court's dismissal of the case without providing an explanation [*Efron v. United States*, 528 US 987 (1999)]. Although the Federal courts acknowledged the statutory nature of the citizenship extended to persons born in Puerto Rico, they were unwilling to grant Puerto Rican-born citizens an opportunity to acquire a constitutional citizenship.

Today, Puerto Rican-born citizens are confined to a less than equal status within the US global empire. Puerto Ricans who reject the inclusive exclusion of US citizenship are barred from renouncing the corresponding status. Likewise, post-1941 Puerto Rican-born citizens who wish to secure a constitutional status within the US global empire are barred from doing so. In the latter case, even though Congress was willing to extend the residents of Puerto Rico a native-born status, the Courts are unwilling to treat this citizenship as tantamount to a Fourteenth Amendment or constitutional citizenship.

THE POSTCOLONIAL CITIZEN?

In *Semi-Citizenship in Democratic Politics*, Elizabeth F. Cohen (2009) states that the citizenship conferred on Puerto Ricans is tantamount to a postcolonial citizenship. Cohen essentially identifies two dimensions of this citizenship. She argues that the postcolonial relationship between Puerto Ricans and presumably the United States engenders 'differences between Puerto Ricans living in Puerto Rico and those who live on the mainland' (2009: 166). Although she does not provide a clear explanation of what she means, elsewhere she claims that while Puerto Ricans are entitled to the same civil rights as other citizens, their access to political rights is 'very complicated' (83). Like most liberal scholars writing about the citizenship status of Puerto Ricans, Cohen simply neglects to incorporate a substantive discussion of the role of US global empire in shaping the contours of the citizenship status of Puerto Ricans. Cohen simply ignores the fact that the United States refuses to extend the Citizenship Clause of the Fourteenth Amendment to Puerto Rico as well as the fact that the Constitution bars the residents of territories from equal civil rights and political participation in the US polity. More importantly, while the first two problems can be resolved by simply using colonialist precedents to rule Puerto Rico, the latter is a fundamental problem of undemocratic constitutions and territorial expansionism.

The citizenship and naturalization policies of the US global expansionist tradition departed from the colonialist tradition in significant ways. Under the colonialist tradition, US law and policy makers included citizenship and naturalization provisions in either the territorial annexation treaty and/or the organic acts used to govern annexed territories. Colonial territories were treated as parts of the United States for citizenship purposes and the Citizenship Clause of the Fourteenth Amendment was operative in these territories. In contrast, the annexation treaties and the initial organic acts used by the global expansionist tradition did not include collective naturalization provisions. Congress subsequently enacted special citizenship and naturalization laws for each of the unincorporated territories. Historically, although some unincorporated territories have been ruled as parts of the United States, with the exception of the US Virgin Islands, no unincorporated territory has been treated as a part of the United States for the purposes of the Citizenship Clause of the Fourteenth Amendment.

In the case of Puerto Rico, the United States has used three citizenship laws to govern the residents of the island. Congress invented a Puerto Rican citizenship tantamount to a non-alien nationality to rule the residents of Puerto Rico between 1900 and 1917. In1906, Congress began to enact legislation enabling Puerto Rican citizens to acquire a naturalized US citizenship. However, because Congress did not incorporate Puerto Rico, only the children of citizens born in the island could acquire this citizenship at birth. In 1940 Congress enacted legislation treating Puerto Rico as a part of the United States for the purposes of extending a right to a *jus soli* or birthright citizenship. Since 1941, all persons born in Puerto Rico acquire citizenship at birth.

My contention, however, is that US citizenship and naturalization laws developed for Puerto Rico both affirmed their inclusive exclusion within the US global empire and confined Puerto Ricans to a less than equal status. While all three citizenship laws affirmed degrees of membership, each law excluded Puerto Rican-born residents of the island from access to a Fourteenth Amendment or constitutional citizenship. Today, the US global empire rules Puerto Rican-born citizens as mere statutory citizens. More importantly, the US government continues to bar Puerto Rican-born citizens from either self-expatriating or acquiring a constitutional citizenship status. To this extent, US law and policymakers continue to rule Puerto Rican-born citizens as less than equal members of the US global empire.

This is an example of a postcolonial citizenship status. Although Congress has historically enacted legislation conferring varying degrees of membership on Puerto Ricans, including the right to a *jus soli* citizenship that confers a native-born status, the US has refused to confer a constitutional status on Puerto Rican-born citizens. Even though Puerto Rican-born citizens can claim a US citizenship at birth, they cannot claim an equal constitutional status within the US global empire. The US global empire has ruled Puerto Ricans under these conditions for more than a century.

Chapter 5

Rights, subjectivity, and the US global empire

The US global empire has also used the doctrine of territorial incorporation to legitimate the creation of a corresponding subjectivity. The basic premises of the new subjectivity were developed between 1898 and 1922 and affirmed the principle that the residents of Puerto Rico could only invoke natural or 'fundamental' constitutional rights and not the full bill of rights. In the years that followed the Second World War, the United States began to grant Puerto Ricans more administrative powers over the governance of the island without changing the island's territorial or constitutional status. This process partially modified the subjectivity of the residents of Puerto Rico. Since 1952, US legal actors have drawn on the doctrine of territorial incorporation to legitimate three competing interpretations of the status of subjects (citizens and aliens alike) residing in Puerto Rico and outside of the United States more generally. Read together, these historical episodes explain the continuities and discontinuities of the US global empire's subjectivities.

THE INSULAR SUBJECTIVITY, 1898–1922

The legal principles shaping the contours of the Puerto Rican subjectivity were developed between 1901 and 1922. The military's territorial law and policy affirmed the plenary power of Congress and the US government more generally to rule the inhabitants of Puerto Rico without constitutional limitations. The residents of Puerto Rico were afforded fundamental rights anchored not on the Constitution, but rather in a natural rights ideology reminiscent of the prevailing narrative of Anglo-American exceptionalism. The 1900 Foraker Act normalized the military's interpretation. In 1901, the Supreme Court tempered that interpretation and clothed it in a constitutional garb. Between 1901 and 1922, Congress and the Court adjusted the doctrine of territorial incorporation to accommodate the rule of US citizens residing in Puerto Rico and other unincorporated territories. However, by 1922 the United States had established the basic legal tenets that would shape the contours of the US global empire's subjectivity.

The 1898 Treaty of Paris affirmed the plenary power of Congress to ascribe a new subjectivity on Puerto Ricans. To be sure, Article Nine gave Congress the plenary authority to determine the future 'civil and political rights of the native inhabitants' of Puerto Rico and the other ceded Spanish territories (1910: S. Doc. 357, 1693). Rather than simply recognizing the automatic extension of the US Constitution's bill of rights to Puerto Rico upon its annexation, the Treaty of Paris established Congress' power to legislate rights for the inhabitants of annexed territories. While anti-imperialist senators denounced this provision as a form of 'tyranny' (32 Cong. Rec. 435), imperialists justified it by appealing to racist narratives of manifest destiny and the inability of inferior races to exercise the right to vote or to understand Common Law rights. Global expansionists such as Senator Foraker argued that while the Constitution did not extend to annexed territories on its own force, when legislating for Puerto Rico and the other newly annexed territories lawmakers would be guided by their oaths to the Constitution's bill of rights (32 Cong. Rec. 567).

The military invoked Article Nine of the Treaty as the source of both Congress' power to legislate over the territories and the rights of the inhabitants. Secretary of War Root unequivocally argued:

> ...that as between the people of the ceded islands and the United States the former are subject to the complete sovereignty of the latter, controlled by no legal limitations except those which may be found in the treaty of cession; that the people of the islands have no right to have them treated as states, or to have them treated as territories previously held by the United States have been treated; or to assert a legal right under the provisions of the Constitution which as established for the people of the United States themselves and to meet the conditions existing upon this continent; or to assert against the United States any legal right whatever not found in the treaty.
>
> (Bacon and Brown Scott 1916/1970: 161)

Secretary Root's argument was not directed at the power of the military to rule as an occupying force. Root's argument referred to the future territorial law and policy for Puerto Rico. Root, like other US law and policymakers, was concerned that Puerto Ricans would invoke constitutional civil rights to challenge or limit the power of the government to rule the island. Again, like other law and policymakers, Secretary Root also applied racist narratives of Anglo-American exceptionalism to explain the inability of Puerto Ricans to grasp or understand Common Law rights.

Ultimately, the military affirmed the extension of natural or fundamental rights to Puerto Ricans. For Secretary Root, natural or fundamental rights essentially entailed granting Puerto Ricans the rights to life, liberty and private property, all protected by due process of law or access to courts of law (Ibid.: 162). In the context of developing a new territorial policy on rights, this meant that Puerto Ricans would acquire basic Common Law rights and retain the Spanish Civil Law institutions that affirmed the prevailing notion of natural or fundamental rights. In his last report submitted to the War Department on 30 June 1900, General Davis summarized his implementation of this logic:

> The criminal and common law of the Saxon would never fit the Porto Rican [sic]. They do not know how to use the privileges they have now of the writ of habeas corpus or the trial by jury, and they not need them. It is easy, with a pure and independent judiciary, to administer the law and protect all in their civil rights.
>
> (1902: H. Doc. 2, 64)

General Davis proposed retaining the Spanish judiciary and creating an appellate Federal district court that could administer or police the local judiciary. To the extent that rights would be available in the Puerto Rican territory, these would primarily protect the inhabitants from being deprived from a right to life, liberty and private property without due process of law or access to a court of law.

Lawmakers debating the Foraker Act embraced the three prevailing political ideologies. Anti-imperialists argued that colonialist precedents treated annexed territories as a part of the United States for constitutional purposes. Although some lawmakers argued that the Constitution's bill of rights extended to Puerto Rico automatically (*ex propio vigore*) upon its annexation, and others sought to incorporate a bill of rights into the Foraker Act itself, all denounced the efforts to grant the US government a plenary authority over Puerto Rico and the failure to recognize the extension of the bill of rights to the island's inhabitants. For anti-imperialists, the Constitution followed the flag to any annexed territory or territory that became a part of the United States sovereignty. Representative Robert Lee Henry (D-TX) summarized the anti-imperialist opposition without mincing words:

> And further, if any American citizen goes to the island of Puerto Rico or these new possessions, this bill denies him the right to invoke the Constitution of the Government which his fathers help found.... But the Government was framed for the benefit of persons and for individual rights, and not to adjust real-estate transactions
>
> (33 Cong. Rec. 2050).

In contrast, imperialists typically rejected the notion that 'barbarians' or non-Anglo-Saxon subjects should have access to the bill of rights, rights that were beyond comprehension to inferior and uncivilized races. Global expansionists adopted the military's interpretation affirming the plenary power of Congress to enact legislation that selectively granted rights to Puerto Ricans. This interpretation would not bind Congress and the government to challenges based on the Constitution's bill of rights.

The 1900 Foraker Act normalized the military's interpretation in two ways. First and foremost, the enacted law did not extend the Constitution's bill of rights to Puerto Rico, nor include a bill of rights for Puerto Ricans. Nowhere was there an indication that Congress was willing to grant Puerto Ricans the same constitutional rights and protections afforded to citizens residing in colonial territories and the states more generally. Instead, the orders issued by General Davis to continue to use a domesticated version of the Spanish municipal judiciary, a version of the courts that could be adjusted to US policy and kept in check by a Federal district court, were codified by Sections 33 and 34 of the Foraker Act (31 Stat. 77, 84). Puerto Rican citizens could only invoke the rights created by the military and those available under the island's Spanish civil code that were consistent with the military's interpretation of the rights that should be available locally.

The ensuing doctrine of territorial incorporation merely tempered the military's interpretation. In the case of *Downes*, the justices wrote opinions that merely contextualized the prevailing ideologies within a constitutional framework. Justice Brown invoked an imperialist interpretation to affirm the military's interpretation. As previously noted, Justice Brown argued that territories were not a part of the definition of the United States and therefore Congress was not bound by the Constitution or more specifically limited by the Territories Clause and its prevailing precedents. He affirmed the plenary power of Congress and the 'American empire' more generally to rule Puerto Rico under the terms of the annexation treaty (182 US 244, 279). On the question of the civil rights of Puerto Ricans, Justice Brown noted that:

> ...it does not follow that in the meantime, a waiting that decision, the people are in the matter of personal rights unprotected by the provisions of our Constitution and subject to the merely arbitrary control of Congress. Even if regarded as aliens, they are entitled to be protected in life, liberty, and property.
>
> (Id. at 283)

Accordingly, Puerto Ricans were entitled to fundamental constitutional or natural rights. Which rights these were, Justice Brown did not say.

In contrast, while Justice White's opinion disagreed with Brown's interpretation of the Territories Clause, they concurred on the question of rights. Unlike Justice Brown's interpretation, Justice White situated the power to rule unincorporated territories in the Territories Clause (Id. at 300). However, unlike the colonialist interpretation adopted by the dissenters, an interpretation that placed the same constitutional limits on the power of

Congress to determine which civil rights would be applicable in the territories as it did in the rest of the United States, Justice White's interpretation expanded the power of Congress under the Territories Clause to determine which civil rights were applicable in an unincorporated territory (Id. at 294). Although bound by the Constitution, Congress could enact legislation that either extended or withheld constitutional rights and other provisions from Puerto Rico so long as these did not violate the fundamental rights of the island's inhabitants. Of course, like Justice Brown, Justice White neglected to define which rights were fundamental. The point, however, is that the doctrine of territorial incorporation expanded the power of Congress under the Territories Clause to choose which constitutional rights and liberties could be extended to or withheld from an unincorporated territory.

As noted in Chapter 3, the Court continued to develop the doctrine of territorial incorporation between 1901 and 1922. During this period, Rivera Ramos has demonstrated, the Court also sought to determine which constitutional rights were applicable in the insular territories, both incorporated and unincorporated. The determination, Rivera Ramos further noted, 'hinged on whether the right in question was considered fundamental' (2007: 91). The Court established that the bill of rights applied to incorporated territories, an interpretation consistent with established colonialist precedents, but not all rights applied to unincorporated territories. Stated differently, while the bill of rights applied to Hawai'i following its incorporation in 1900, not all rights applied to Puerto Rico and the Philippines. Not surprisingly, the Court's determination was consistent with Secretary Root and General Davis' interpretation. Fundamental rights included those rights that protected the due process rights to life, liberty, and property.

The 1917 Jones Act provided for the collective naturalization of Puerto Ricans and included a bill of rights that extended a series of labor and civil rights to the island. The labor rights extended by the Jones Act were only limited to protecting government employees and other workers employed in public works. Ironically, Trías Monge documented, the Jones Act labor rights were actually inferior in scope to those extended to Puerto Rico by the military in 1899 (1981: 2, 89). On the matter of civil rights, Trías Monge further noted, the Jones Act's bill of rights did not extend the rights available in the second, third, seventh, ninth and tenth amendments, rights that were available to US citizens residing in states and incorporated territories (Ibid.). Again, rather than extending the full bill of rights to the newly naturalized US citizens residing in Puerto Rico, Congress chose to extend a limited number of civil and labor rights that affirmed US hegemony in Puerto Rico without empowering US citizens to challenge the US global empire in substantive ways.

As noted in the previous chapter, for jurists in Puerto Rico the collective naturalization provision of the Jones Act resulted in the territorial incorporation of Puerto Rico and the automatic extension of the Constitution's bill of rights to the island. The first round of related legal debates began in the Puerto Rican courts within months of the enactment of the Jones Act. Drawing on the language of Judge White's opinions in both *Downes* and *Rassmussen*, Judges in both Puerto Rican and Federal courts reasoned that Section 5 implicitly incorporated Puerto Rico and local defendants were now entitled to the full protection of the US Constitution's bill of rights. The first case to address this question, *In the Matter of Tapia*, was decided on 21 May 1917 by Judge Peter J. Hamilton in the Federal district court for San Juan. On 16 March 1917, 14 days after the enactment of the Jones Act, Mr. Carlos Tapia was arrested and charged with the crime of 'assault with intent to murder.' Mr. Tapia moved to quash his trial on the grounds that the collective naturalization provision of the Jones Act had incorporated Puerto Rico and his detention violated his civil rights. More specifically, the government had not been indicted by a Grand Jury, a constitutional requirement of the Fifth Amendment. Before this motion was decided in the district court of San Juan, the Federal Court approved Tapia's prior application for a *writ of habeas corpus* and removed the case. Following a lengthy argument over the Court's jurisdiction, Judge Hamilton ruled that the collective naturalization provision of the Jones Act incorporated Puerto Rico and applied the bill of rights 'to those newly made Americans in Puerto Rico as much as to the older American on the Continent' (9 PR Fed. Rep. 452, 494). In a lengthy opinion, Judge Hamilton drew heavily on the colonialist precedents, on the Supreme Court's opinion in *Rassmussen*, and on the Common Law tradition, to argue that Section 5 implicitly incorporated Puerto Rico and the Constitution now applied to the island.

On 13 July 1917, the Puerto Rican Supreme Court reached a similar conclusion in *Muratti v. Foote*. The *Muratti* case, however, entailed a slightly different order of events. To be sure, Mr. José Muratti was accused of second-degree murder prior to the enactment of the Jones Act, but was scheduled for trial after the law was extended to Puerto Rico. Mr. Muratti, like Mr. Tapia, moved to quash his trial because he had not been arraigned by a Grand Jury. Following the trial court's denial of his motion, the Puerto Rican Supreme Court intervened and removed the case. Like the *Tapia* case, the question or issue before the Puerto Rican Supreme Court was whether the US Constitution, and more specifically the Fifth Amendment, was in force in Puerto Rico during Mr. Muratti's trial. The Puerto Rican Supreme Court reversed the trial court's finding and held that the citizenship provision of the Jones Act had in fact incorporated the island. Writing for the Puerto Rican Supreme Court, Justice Adolph G. Wolf essentially reproduced the reasoning used in the *Tapia* opinion and concluded that Mr. Muratti had been deprived of a Fifth Amendment right to a Grand Jury. However, his considerably shorter opinion limited his analysis to precedents established in the *Downes* and *Rassmussen* cases in order to link the collective naturalization of Puerto Ricans to the island's incorporation. Like Judge Hamilton, the Puerto Rican Supreme Court concluded that the collective naturalization of Puerto Ricans had implicitly incorporated Puerto Rico and the Constitution was now in force in the island.

Both cases were subsequently appealed to the US Supreme Court and argued together on 17 and 18 January 1918. Four days later, in *People of Porto Rico v. Muratti* and *People of Porto Rico v. Tapia* [245 US 639 (1918)], a *Per Curiam* or anonymous decision by a majority of the justices, the Supreme Court reversed the local rulings without providing any explanation. Less than six months after a US district court for Puerto Rico and the Puerto Rican Supreme Court upheld the precedents established by the Insular Cases, the Supreme Court had reversed itself without providing any explanation. It would not be until 1922, in *Balzac v. People of Porto Rico,* that the Supreme Court would provide a rationale for its rejection of the *Downes* and *Rassmussen* precedents.[1]

At this point, it is possible to discern one of the two core principles of the global expansionist subjectivity, namely the notion that the status of the unincorporated territory rather than the status of the citizen, can determine the subject's access to rights. Puerto Rico's territorial status mediated the US citizen/resident's access to the bill of rights. Whereas a citizen could theoretically invoke his individual civil rights, a US citizen residing in Puerto Rico, regardless of his race, could only invoke those rights available via the Jones Act or a specific court opinion. The status of Puerto Rico imbued its inhabitants with a less than equal subjectivity. Generally speaking, Congress wielded a power to determine the contours of the unincorporated territorial subjectivity by determining which rights could be withheld or extended to each territory.

In 1922, the Court further established that the Puerto Rican subjectivity was also liminal. In *Balzac v. People of Porto Rico,* the Supreme Court addressed the question of whether the Sixth Amendment's right to trial by jury extended to Puerto Rico. In 1918, Jesús M. Balzac, the editor of the local Puerto Rican newspaper *El Baluarte*, published two pointed editorials attacking governor of Puerto Rico Arthur Yaeger. Balzac was subsequently charged with committing two misdemeanor offenses of criminal libel and prosecuted on two separate occasions. During the local proceedings, Balzac requested a trial by jury arguing that as a US citizen he was entitled to the Sixth Amendment right. The local courts denied his request and he was subsequently convicted, sentenced to five months in a local jail, and fined for the costs of the proceedings. On appeal, both the Puerto Rican and later US Supreme Courts upheld the lower courts' rulings. A unanimous US Supreme Court affirmed the doctrine of territorial incorporation and determined that Congress had not extended the Sixth Amendment right to a trial by jury to the island.

Chief Justice Taft, the author of the opinion, invoked at least eight arguments to justify the Court's holding. However, for the purposes of clarifying my argument I will only discuss three interrelated arguments, namely the affirmation of the power of Congress to withhold the extension of constitutional provisions to Puerto Rico; and the reliance on two racial narratives of Anglo-American exceptionalism. Read together, these rationales explain how the Supreme Court established a second core dimension of the Puerto Rican subjectivity.

Legal scholars generally agree that the Court's interpretation of the constitutional powers of Congress under the Territories Clause consolidated the doctrine of territorial incorporation. The *Balzac* ruling affirmed two core dimensions of this doctrine. First, the Court recognized the power of Congress to determine whether a territory is incorporated or not. Second, Chief Justice Taft also affirmed the power of Congress to select which constitutional provisions it wished to withhold or extend to Puerto Rico. Too be sure, the Chief Justice, a former governor of Cuba and member of the original global expansionist or Large Policy cabal, argued that so long as Congress guaranteed 'certain fundamental personal rights' to the people of Puerto Rico, lawmakers possessed the power to determine which constitutional 'provisions were applicable by way of limitation upon the exercise of executive and legislative power in dealing with new conditions and requirements' (258 US 298, 312). Until the Court determined that the Sixth Amendment right to a trial by jury was either a 'fundamental personal right' or Congress enacted legislation extending this right to Puerto Rico, US citizens residing in Puerto Rico could not claim this constitutional right.

Chief Justice Taft also invoked two racial narratives of Anglo-American exceptionalism to construct a liminal definition of the Jones Act citizenship. One narrative was anchored on a racist depiction of the ability of Puerto Ricans to understand the Common Law jury system, a system that had been in place since the initial occupation in 1898. For example, notwithstanding the fact, as Taft had previously acknowledged in his opinion, that the Puerto Rican Code of Criminal Procedure *granted* 'a jury trial in cases of felony,' the Chief Justice felt compelled to construct a rationale that invoked racial differences in order to withhold access to a trial by jury to Balzac (Id. at 300). According to the Chief Justice, the jury system was an 'Anglo-Saxon' institution developed within the Common Law tradition, a tradition wholly alien to Puerto Ricans who were formed within a Spanish civil law tradition (Id. at 310). Furthermore, Taft argued, Congress had not expressed an intention to 'incorporate in the Union these distant ocean communities of a different origin and language to those of our continental people' (Id. at 311). Accordingly, Puerto Ricans residing in the islands were simply racially incapable of understanding the jury system and therefore they could not claim that the Sixth Amendment right to trial by jury was a fundamental personal right available to US citizens residing in the island. To date, the Supreme Court has not overturned or repudiated this ruling. More than six decades later, the Sixth Amendment's right to trial by jury is not a constitutionally guaranteed right in Puerto Rico.

Chief Justice Taft also invoked a territorial narrative of Anglo-American exceptionalism to affirm the liminal status of both Puerto Rico and its residents in order to legitimate withholding the extension of the right to trial by jury. According to the Chief Justice:

> The citizen of the United States living in Porto Rico cannot there enjoy a right of trial by jury under the federal Constitution, any more than the Porto Rican. *It is locality that is determinative of the application of the Constitution, in such matters as judicial procedure, and not the status of the people who live in it* (emphasis added).
>
> (Id. at 309)

In a subsequent passage, the Chief Justice further noted, once a citizen *moved* to the 'United States proper' s/he would, without having to undergo a naturalization process, enjoy 'all political and other rights' (Id. at 311). The Chief Justice did not clarify how he would reconcile the racial or cultural ability of Puerto Ricans to understand a jury system while residing *in* the United States. However, it stands to reason that the status of the territory imbued the citizen with the ability to gain or lose fundamental constitutional rights like the right to a trial by jury. Presumably, merely touching an incorporated part of the United States would suffice to acquire the protections of the bill of rights not extended to Puerto Rico by Congress. In sum, a Puerto Rican subject could acquire or loose varying degrees of access to the Constitution's civil rights by simply travelling or moving to and from unincorporated territories like Puerto Rico.

In short, the new subjectivity was contingent on the status of the territory. The doctrine of territorial incorporation authorized Congress to create unincorporated territories tantamount to a legal borderland. Congress and the Court were authorized to determine which civil or consttutional rights were extended or withheld from the unincorporated territory, so long as it did not violate the fundamental rights of the subject inhabiting the territory. Both institutions could choose to recognize the extension of the full bill of rights or merely fundamental rights to unincorporated territories. The doctrine of territorial incorporation also affirmed the inclusion of naturalized and native-born Puerto Ricans, while simultaneously excluding these citizens from access to the full bill of rights while residing in Puerto Rico. The unincorporated territorial subjectivity not only established the less than equal membership of Puerto Ricans, but also the unequal access to civil or constitutional rights.

AUTONOMY AND THE REPRODUCTION OF EMPIRE, 1952

Following the Second World War, Congress began to grant Puerto Ricans a greater degree of administrative autonomy over local affairs without changing the island's constitutional or territorial status. The ensuing Puerto Rican administrative apparatus impacted the subjectivity of the island's inhabitants in at least three ways. First, the new Puerto Rican government used its powers to act as a proxy for the US government and reproducing its policies in the island (both anti-democratic and in some cases progressive). Second, the creation of the Commonwealth government affirmed the less than equal status of US citizens residing in Puerto Rico. Congress used this legislative process to both affirm the island's unincorporated status and the corresponding subjectivity ascribed to Puerto Ricans. Third, it is important to note that the Commonwealth government has at times invoked the doctrine of territorial incorporation to legitimate its unconstitutional and anti-democratic laws and policies. Although a messy history, it explains how the US global empire deployed a postcolonial territorial status to reify the less than equal status of subjects residing in Puerto Rico.

Since 1900, Congress has progressively amended the Foraker Act and granted Puerto Ricans more autonomic control over Puerto Rico's governmental institutions without incorporating the island. The initial Foraker Act established an authoritarian system of government for the island enabling the President to assume full control over local public institutions. Under the terms of the Foraker Act, the President appointed a local governor, the judiciary, and an executive council that assumed roles tantamount to that of department heads such as Secretary, Auditor, Attorney General, Commissioner of Education, Treasurer, and Commissioner of the Interior (Mattei Filardi 2012). The Executive Council's powers would also become tantamount to that of a local Senate. Only the lower house of the island's general assembly was controlled by Puerto Ricans and subject to popular elections. The 1917 Jones Act amended the Foraker Act establishing a Senate that was subject to popular elections and ultimately granting Puerto Ricans control over the island's general assembly. Throughout this period and on to the early 1930s, the War Department's Bureau of Insular Affairs managed the local government on behalf of the President. During the mid 1930s, the administration of Puerto Rico's government was mostly transferred to the Department of the Interior. Congress began to transfer administrative authority over the island's local affairs to Puerto Ricans with the appointment of Jesús T. Piñero as Governor of Puerto Rico in 1946. Finally, in 1952 Congress formally authorized Puerto Ricans to adopt a local constitution and assume administrative control over the island's government. However, Congress did not change Puerto Rico's territorial status nor did it cease to retain authority over the island's affairs.

The emergent post-Second World War Puerto Rican government increasingly began to mediate the subjectivity of Puerto Ricans within the US global empire. A year before the enactment of the 1947 Elective Governor Act, the act formally authorizing Puerto Ricans to elect their chief executive, President Harry S. Truman appointed then Resident Commissioner Piñero to become the first Puerto Rican Governor of the island since the US occupation in 1898. Piñero was also one of the key founders of the Puerto Rican *Partido Popular Democratico/Popular Democratic Party* (PPD), a local party promoting permanent territorial autonomy within the US global empire (Acevedo 2005). Jaime Partsch documents that Governor Piñero promptly began to embrace the Truman administration's Cold War policies, including showcasing Puerto Rico as a model for US neocolonial economic dependency in Latin America as well as fostering the US national security agenda (2006: 124–130). In the former case, the US government hoped to use the development of a local infrastructure and the economy more generally in Puerto Rico as an example of what US neocolonialism could accomplish in Latin America, only if Latin American countries were willing to open their doors to the great northern Uncle. The case of Puerto Rico's economic development was important because it demonstrated how an autonomous island could develop a model economy under the US sovereignty. Of course, while it is true that the United States sought to de-emphasize its sovereign domination over the island, the US also did not hide the fact that it owned Puerto Rico.

The latter use of Puerto Rico as a showcase for national security policies resulted in the enactment of totalitarian gag laws and the escalation of the repression of the local nationalist party, the main advocates for Puerto Rican independence at the time. Although the Puerto Rican independence movement was fairly small in scope, the US government had waged an aggressive campaign to eradicate Puerto Rican nationalists since the early 1930s. In 1948, at the behest of Governor Piñero, the Puerto Rican legislature enacted the infamous Law 53, also known as *La Mordaza* (the great gag order), which provided for the complete censure of pro-independence advocacy. More specifically, Law 53 declared a felony 'the promotion, advocation [sic], or preaching willfully or knowingly, of the necessity, desirability or expediency of overthrowing, subverting, or paralyzing the insular government, or any political subdivision thereof by means of force or violence; and the printing, publishing, editing, circulating, selling, distributing, or publicly exhibiting' any subversive materials (Law 53 1948: 170–171). Law 53 enabled both the US global empire and the Puerto Rican government (at times acting as a proxy for the US government) to physically persecute and silence advocates for Puerto Rican independence by criminalizing their very existence (Acosta 1989). Puerto Ricans were essentially relegated to affirming their loyalty to the United States and criminalized for supporting a non-colonial status. To this extent, advocates of territorial autonomy within the United States, a supposed non-colonial territorial status, both reproduced and reified repressive and anti-democratic national security policies of the US global empire.

In 1950, Congress enacted legislation amending the Foraker Act and enabling Puerto Ricans to create a local constitution to administer the island's affairs under an autonomic government. Public Law 600 authorized the creation of a constitutional convention comprised of members from the Puerto Rican political parties and charged with drafting a local constitution. The ensuing Puerto Rican constitution would subsequently be sent to Congress and pending its approval would then be subject to an island-wide referendum. The Foraker Act provisions that were not incorporated into the new constitution became the Puerto Rico Federal Relations Act (Bhana 1975; Trías Monge 1982; Acevedo 2003).

Congressional lawmakers were also clear that neither Public Law 600 nor the ensuing Puerto Rican constitution changed the Federal relationship between Puerto Rico and the United States. In the accompanying Senate Report to Public Law 600, Senator Joseph C. O'Mahoney (D-WY) unequivocally noted:

> The measure would not change Puerto Rico's fundamental political, social, and economic relationship to the United States. Those sections of the Organic Act of Puerto Rico concerning such matters as the applicability of United States laws, customs, internal revenue, Federal judicial jurisdiction in Puerto Rico, representation in the Congress of the United States by a Resident Commissioner, etcetera, would remain in force and effect. Upon enactment of S. 3336, these remaining sections of the organic act would be referred to as the Puerto Rico Federal Relations Act.
>
> (1950: S. Rept. 1720, 3)

Congress also rejected the notion that the Puerto Rican constitution would pave the way for either statehood or independence (Ibid.: 4–5). Suffice it to say that notwithstanding the transfer of administrative authority over local affairs to Puerto Ricans, Congress readily recognized that the Puerto Rican constitution was not intended to change the island's unincorporated territorial status.

In 1951, Puerto Rican lawmakers sent Congress a draft constitution modeled after both international conventions and US state constitutions. Federal lawmakers, however, rejected the proposed constitution on two important grounds, namely because of its affirmation of human rights and its reliance on democracy. The original Puerto Rican constitution included a provision granting the residents of the island a series of social and economic rights and privileges modeled after the United Nations Declaration of Human Rights, an international document approved at the behest of the United States (Trías Monge 1997: 117). For example, as Trías Monge has documented, the infamous Section 20 of the original Puerto Rican constitution 'recognized, among others, but as aspirations or goals, depending on the progressive development of the economy, the right to social protection in the event of unemployment, sickness, old age, or disability; the right to obtain work; the right to an adequate standard of living; and the rights of mothers and children to special care and assistance' (Ibid.). Again, according to Senator O'Mahoney, Section 20 equated 'human rights' to 'constitutional rights' creating confusions and uncertainties that could 'not be remedied by our judicial precedents and constitutional history' (1950: S. Rept.1720, 2). Granting Puerto Ricans human rights was simply too radical.

United States lawmakers also rejected the 'democratic' language and aspirations of the Puerto Rican constitution. More specifically, Senator O'Mahoney's Committee on Interior and Insular Affairs submitted the following objection:

> The committee notes references in the proposed constitution to a 'fully democratic basis' (preamble), 'the democratic system' (preamble), 'democratic heritage' (preamble), 'democratic system of government' (preamble), 'the people in a democracy' (art. II, sec. 19).... The Committee understands that these references are not intended and shall not in any way enlarge, diminish, change or modify the fact that the government under this proposed constitution is intended to be and must be republican in form and substance; that to the extent these references express ideals or aspirations they are understood to be consistent with a government republican in form and substance.
>
> (Ibid.)

Federal lawmakers rejected the Puerto Rican constitution because it affirmed democratic participation rather than the elite form and substance of a republican system of government. United States global empire simply rejected any effort to grant its subjects more human and democratic rights. If Puerto Ricans wished to assume administrative control over their local affairs, they had to reject human rights and democratic self-government and embrace the elitist and anti-democratic form and substance of the US republican system of government. In 1952, following a local referendum where the majority of the population voted in favor of the enactment of the PR constitution, President Harry S. Truman agreed to sign a resolution authorizing the constitution contingent on the elimination of Section 20. The Puerto Rican constitutional convention subsequently relented and removed Section 20 from the final text.

Even after granting Puerto Ricans the right to adopt a local constitution, Congress affirmed the less than equal subjectivity of the residents of Puerto

Rico. Congress, and the US government more generally, barred Puerto Ricans from developing local laws that affirmed the social and economic rights of the residents of the island. Congress barred Puerto Ricans from adopting local legal rights modeled after human rights laws, while simultaneously barring the full extension of the bill of rights to the island. In addition, Congress forbade Puerto Ricans from developing democratic institutions to rule the island. Instead Congress forced Puerto Ricans to adopt an elitist republican system of government, a system of government that undermined both the citizen's access to equal rights and a democratic polity.

Even though the Puerto Rican government began to describe Puerto Rico as a Free Associated State (*Estado Libre Asociado*), loosely translated as a Commonwealth, the United Nations (UN) continued to treat Puerto Rico as an unincorporated territory tantamount to a colony. By 1953, after important negotiations with the United States, the Puerto Rican Governor Luis Muñoz Marín began to work with the President Harry S. Truman and the State Department to submit a letter to the UN requesting that Puerto Rico be removed from the United Nations' list of non-self governing territories. Both Article 73(e) of the United Nations Charter and the 1948 United Nations General Assembly Resolution 222(III) required member empires to report on any constitutional changes in the status of their colonies or non-self governing territories. Following contentious debates and important negotiations in the UN and in the Federal government, the General Assembly agreed to remove Puerto Rico from the list of non-self governing territories under the terms of UNGA Resolution 748(VIII) issued on 27 November 1953 and ceased requiring the United States to report any changes in the island's status. José Trías Monge, one of the architects of the legal dimensions of the Commonwealth constitution and a participant in the UN debates representing Puerto Rico, described the outcomes of the multiple UN votes as recognizing the Puerto Rican Commonwealth's right to exercise self-determination (1983: 59). Ironically, whereas the United States was allowed to cease reporting to the UN Decolonization Committee on the status of Puerto Rico, the US continued to report on the status of its other unincorporated territories, namely the US Virgin Islands, Guam, and American Samoa.

Even though advocates of the Commonwealth argue that Congress recognized the creation of an autonomous territorial status, Federal lawmakers have since debated plebiscitary legislation seeking to change Puerto Rico's territorial status. In fact, since 1898 US lawmakers have introduced upwards of 112 (69 after 1952) status and plebiscitary bills, but have only authorized one plebiscite. The 1967 plebiscite enabled Puerto Ricans to vote on one of three status options, namely independence, statehood, and the Commonwealth. Upwards of 60 percent of the local electors voted for the Commonwealth option. Again, the point is that continued legislative debate over the status and plebiscitary legislation continues to affirm the principle that Puerto Rico remains an unincorporated territory.

The Puerto Rican government has also invoked the doctrine of territorial incorporation to legitimate its authoritarian and anti-democratic powers to police the residents of Puerto Rico. More specifically, at times the Commonwealth government has argued that Puerto Rico's unincorporated territorial status

is tantamount to a borderland or 'intermediate border' for constitutional purposes. In borderland zones US constitutional law becomes more functional, less wooden, or more malleable ultimately granting government agents more power to search persons without the Fourth Amendment's restrictions. For example, in *Torres v. Commonwealth of Puerto Rico* [442 US 465 (1979)], the Commonwealth government invoked Puerto Rico's unincorporated status to legitimate the enactment of a local law authorizing the police to search the luggage of any person travelling to and from Puerto Rico without a warrant or probable cause that the suspect was committing a crime. The Commonwealth government sought to equate the unincorporated territorial status of Puerto Rico to that of an intermediate or international borderland zone for legal purposes and thus avoid the constitutional standards necessary to search persons travelling through Puerto Rico. Writing for the majority in *Torres*, Chief Justice Warren E. Burger summarized the Commonwealth government's interpretation of Puerto Rico's status in the following manner:

> The Commonwealth asserts that these decisions recognize a variety of 'intermediate borders', analogous to the international border of the United States, at which searches are permitted even though normal Fourth Amendment requirements are not satisfied. Puerto Rico then asks us to recognize an 'intermediate border' between the Commonwealth and the rest of the United States. In support of this proposal it points to its unique political status, and to the fact that its borders as an island are in fact international borders with respect to all countries except the United States. Finally, Puerto Rico urges that because of the seriousness of the problems created by an influx of weapons and narcotics, it should have the same freedom to search persons crossing its 'intermediate border' as does the United States with respect to incoming international travelers.
>
> (442 US 465, 472)

Although the Court ultimately rejected the Commonwealth government's interpretation, and extended the Fourth Amendment to Puerto Rico, the Court did not repudiate the doctrine of territorial incorporation nor did it recognize the full extension of the bill of rights to the island. In fact, while the Court recognized the dangers of governing Puerto Rico as a borderland or intermediate border zone it did not go further than simply extending Fourth Amendment protections against warrantless searches and seizures to Puerto Rico.

In sum, Commonwealth status has reproduced and reified a postcolonial subjectivity in at least three ways. Let us recall that the Commonwealth status is premised on the establishment of a permanent autonomous status for Puerto Rico within the US global empire. Autonomy, however, has been limited to relative administrative control over local affairs, subject of course to congressional oversight. Since its inception, the Puerto Rican government has acted as a proxy for US economic and national security interests, criminalizing progressive and at times left-leaning activists in the island. Simultaneously, the US government has barred Puerto Ricans from developing local laws based on human rights and democratic principles, ultimately affirming the less than equal status of the residents of Puerto Rico. In addition, the Commonwealth government has invoked the doctrine of territorial incorporation to legitimate unconstitutional and tyrannical laws and policies that rule the residents of Puerto Rico as unequal US citizens.

TRANSLOCAL PRECEDENTS

Since 1952, US legal actors have used three interpretations of the original doctrine of territorial incorporation to legitimate three distinct and corresponding subjectivities. One of these interpretations is local in scope and has been invoked to legitimate the discriminatory treatment of US citizens residing in Puerto Rico. Two additional interpretations are global in scope, but are almost contradictory. One interpretation draws on the doctrine of territorial incorporation to argue that the bill of rights protects US citizens located outside of the United States from unconstitutional state actions. Alternatively, US legal actors have also invoked the Insular Cases to deprive non-citizens of constitutional protections against Federal action. Each interpretation affirms a different degree of subjectivity within the US global empire.

Presently, the US global empire invokes the doctrine of territorial incorporation to legitimate the discriminatory treatment of US citizens residing in Puerto Rico. The prevailing interpretation suggests that Puerto Rico remains an unincorporated territory and both Congress and the Supreme Court have selectively extended or withheld parts of the bill of rights and the Constitution more generally in a piecemeal fashion. Examples of this interpretation prevail in almost every Federal agency and are routinely documented in government reports. For example in a 1991 United States General Accounting Office (USGAO) report titled *US Insular Areas: Applicability of Relevant Provisions of the US Constitution*, the well known research branch of the US Congress begins by establishing that Puerto Rico is an unincorporated territory governed by the doctrine of territorial incorporation:

> The Constitution does not apply in full to the five insular areas, which are considered 'unincorporated.' Unincorporated areas are under the sovereignty but not considered an integral part of the United States. As mentioned earlier, federal laws explicitly extend certain parts of the Constitution to specific areas. In addition, the Supreme Court long ago decided that 'fundamental' personal rights declared in the Constitution apply to citizens of 'US territories.' Also, the courts have determined that certain other parts of the Constitution apply to individual insular areas, depending on each area's unique relationship with the United States.
>
> (USGAO 1991: 4)

The 1991 USGAO report subsequently examines the applicability by legislation, covenant, military decree or jurisprudence of every provision in the Constitution to the five inhabited US unincorporated territories, namely Puerto Rico, the US Virgin Islands, Guam, American Samoa, and the Northern Mariana Islands. In the case of Puerto Rico, the USGAO unequivocally documents that not all of the bill of rights extend to Puerto Rico. For example, citing the *Balzac* precedent, the USGAO notes that the Sixth Amendment's right to trial by jury does not apply to Puerto Rico (1991: 7). The USGAO report further documents that the US government has only extended the First, Fourth, and Eighth Amendments to Puerto Rico. Only the second sentence of the first clause of the Fourteenth Amendment is applicable to Puerto Rico (Ibid.: 36). Some ambiguities remain regarding the extension of the Second, Third, Fifth, Ninth and the Thirteenth Amendments. Likewise, the report documents other instances where either Congress or the Federal courts have withheld the extension of key provisions of the Constitution to Puerto Rico and the other insular areas. The point, however, is that Federal agencies in every branch of the US government continue to recognize that Puerto Rico is an unincorporated territory and that the bill of rights or the US Constitution has not been extended to Puerto Rico in full.

Given that Congress was willing to confer a native-born citizenship status on Puerto Ricans, the question is why has the US global empire refused to extend the full bill of rights or for that matter all applicable constitutional provisions to Puerto Rico? Why on the one hand affirm the membership of Puerto Ricans, yet simultaneously ascribe an exclusionary subjectivity to the residents of Puerto Rico? One possible answer can be discerned from the Supreme Court's ruling in *Harris v. Santiago Rosario* [446 US 651 (1980)]. In *Harris* the Court addressed the constitutionality of congressional legislation that created discriminatory allocations of Federal grants such as the Aid to Families with Dependent Children (AFDC) to Puerto Rico. Invoking the doctrine of territorial incorporation, a majority of the Court reasoned that Congress could discriminate against Puerto Rico because 'Puerto Rican residents do not contribute to the federal treasury; the cost of treating Puerto Rico as a State under the stature would be high; and greater benefits would disrupt the Puerto Rican economy' (446 US 651, 652). Stated differently, a majority of the Court reasoned that families living in poverty or with limited incomes, that are not likely to pay income taxes in either the mainland or Puerto Rico, residing in Puerto Rico can be treated differently than similarly situated families residing *in* the United States. The Court also reasoned that the proportion of families living in poverty in Puerto Rico is significantly higher than similarly situated families residing *in* the United States. Finally, a majority of the Court reasoned, providing egalitarian access to Federal aid to working-class families in Puerto Rico would harm them because it would give these families resources that would presumably assist them in escaping poverty. Implicit in the latter rationale is the traditional Anglo-American conservative ideology that working class families need to accept their status as a class in the service of the natural elites (Kirk 2001: 8–9). As Justice Thurgood Marshall suggested in his dissent, the Court's rationale authorizes Congress to punish Puerto Ricans for being poor and bars the government from improving the local economy on the grounds that it would be too disruptive (446 US 651, 653). This interpretation enables the US global empire to govern Puerto Rico as a separate and unequal territory and ascribe a less than equal status on the island's inhabitants.

United States legal actors have developed two competing interpretations of the extraterritorial powers of the United States' government over subjects that are based on interpretations of the precedents established by the Insular Cases. One interpretation suggests that the bill of rights extends to citizens outside of the United States. This interpretation is partially anchored on the case of Puerto Rico. Accordingly, since the Second World War Congress has extended the bill of rights to Puerto Rico via legislation or statute. Proponents of this interpretation argue that both the 1947 Elective Governor Act and later the 1960 Puerto Rico Federal Relations (PRFRA) Act (Férnos López-Cepero 2007) unequivocally extended the Constitution's full bill of rights to US citizens residing in Puerto Rico by extending the Privileges and Immunities Clause (US Constitution Art. IV, Sect. 2, cl. 1) to the island. The provision in question first introduced in Section 7 of the 1947 Elective Governor Act, and subsequently reproduced in Section 4 of PRFRA, stated that '(t)he rights, privileges, and immunities of citizens of the United States shall be respected in Puerto Rico to the same extent as though Puerto Rico were a State of the Union and subject to the provisions of the first paragraph of Section 2 of Article IV of the Constitution of the United States.' It followed that US citizens residing in Puerto Rico, a locality selectively situated outside of the United States, were entitled to the full protection of the Constitution's bill of rights. To this extent, Puerto Rican subjects were now entitled to an equal subjectivity within the US global empire, at least in the area of access to civil rights.

In *Reid v. Covert* [354 US 1 (1957)] Supreme Court also invoked the Insular Cases precedents to establish that the Constitution's bill of rights protects US citizens subject to prosecution outside of the United States. In *Reid*, two civilian women were charged and prosecuted in military courts located outside of the United States for murdering their husbands. The question was whether the US government could deny US citizens access to civilian courts and corresponding due process rights. A majority of the Court held that in the absence of a hostile threat, the US government could not deny US citizens access to civilian courts while residing outside of the United States. The US government partially invoked the Insular Cases to argue that at best it was only bound to grant the accused women access to fundamental rights and not the full bill of rights (354 US 1, 5–6). After all the accused women were situated outside of the jurisdiction of the United States. A majority of the Court rejected this interpretation on several grounds. The Court reasoned that the US government was entirely an invention of the Constitution and as such its powers are limited by the Constitution (Id. at 8–9). Invoking a past narrative of Anglo-American exceptionalism, the *Insular Cases*, the Court further argued, 'involved the power of Congress to provide rules and regulations to govern temporarily territories with wholly dissimilar traditions and institutions whereas here the basis for governmental power is American citizenship' (Id. at 14). Without formally repudiating the Insular Cases, the Court dismissed the government's interpretation and established that citizens were fully protected by the Constitution's bill of rights against state actions outside of the United States.

For Puerto Ricans and other residents of unincorporated territories, the *Reid* ruling suggested that the Court abandoned the doctrine of territorial incorporation of 1917. According to the Court's rationale, the Insular Cases' doctrine of territorial incorporation was only applicable to Puerto Rican citizens, a population with a different 'culture' and 'customs' (Id. at 13). It followed that since 1917, the year that Congress provided for the collective naturalization of Puerto Rican citizens, the full bill of rights was applicable to US citizens residing in Puerto Rico. It also meant that at least since 1957, it would be unconstitutional to deny Puerto Ricans the full protection of the bill of rights. The new interpretation suggested that the Insular Cases were a remnant of a bygone era and the US global empire's extraterritorial power was now subject to prevailing constitutional limitations, at least when dealing with US citizens.

Alternatively, in *United States v. Verdugo-Urquidez* [494 US 259 (1990)], the companion case to *United States v. Alvarez-Machain* [504 US 655 (1992)], the Court ruled that the US global empire has the power to kidnap citizens of other nation-states and subsequently prosecute them in the United States without affording them constitutional rights and protections. In 1986, at the behest of the US Drug Enforcement Administration (DEA), the Mexican police captured Rene Martin Verdugo-Urquidez, a Mexican citizen residing in Mexico, and transported him to the US border where he was promptly detained in a US prison. Following Verdugo-Urquidez' arrest, DEA agent Terry Bowen arranged searches of his properties without seeking a warrant. Agent Bowen 'believed that the searches would reveal evidence related to (Verdugo-Urquidez') alleged narcotics trafficking activities and his involvement in the kidnapping and torture-murder of DEA Special Agent Enrique Camarena Salazar' (494 US 259, 262). During the search of Verdugo-Urquidez' residence in Mexico, the DEA found a 'tally-sheet' that supposedly documented his drug trafficking activities. Verdugo-Urquidez was subsequently charged and prosecuted. During his trial, Verdugo-Urquidez invoked a Fourth Amendment right to suppress the evidence collected by the US government in the warrantless search of his home in Mexico. The district court granted Verdugo-Urquidez' request and ruled that the DEA's search violated the Fourth Amendment of the US Constitution. The Ninth Circuit court of appeals affirmed the lower Court's decision, but a majority of the Supreme Court subsequently overturned the decision.

The central constitutional question was whether Verdugo-Urquidez, a Mexican citizen residing in Mexico, could claim a Fourth Amendment constitutional right against the actions of US government officials. A majority of the Court said no, the Constitution's bill of rights does not protect non-resident aliens subject to US government actions outside of the United States. The Supreme Court used several rationales to justify its holding, including an interpretation of the precedents established by the Insular Cases. For example, writing for the Court, Chief Justice William Rehnquist reasoned that Verdugo-Urquidez was not part of 'the people' of the United States and therefore could not claim constitutional protections that were written for members of the US polity. He also reasoned that Verdugo-Urquidez had committed crimes outside of the United States and the Constitution did not extend extraterritorially or outside of the United States. In addition, Chief Justice Rehnquist invoked three precedents from the Insular Cases to limit the extension of the bill of rights outside of the United States. He began by arguing that the 'global view' of the application of the Constitution taken by the lower courts was contrary to the precedents established in the Insular Cases, 'which held that not every constitutional provision applies to governmental activity even where the United States has sovereign power' (Id. at 268). Drawing on the doctrine of territorial incorporation, the Chief Justice continued to argue that the Constitution does not extend to unincorporated territories, or territories 'not clearly destined for statehood,' without congressional legislation (Id.). Stated differently, given that Mexico was not a territory destined to become a state of the Union, the Constitution did not extend to this territory on its own force and without congressional legislation. Finally, Rehnquist reasoned, given that only 'fundamental constitutional rights are guaranteed to the inhabitants of those territories' the United States is not bound to 'endorse the view that every constitutional provision applies wherever the United States Government exercises its power' (Id. at 268–269). In sum, non-resident aliens could be charged and prosecuted for breaking a US law outside the United States and could not claim constitutional protections against the actions of US government officials. The Insular Cases granted the US global empire a plenary or absolute power over some aliens who broke US laws, regardless of where they committed the crime.

BORDERLAND SUBJECTIVITIES

In sum, the doctrine of territorial incorporation created a new subjectivity situated somewhere in between the colonialist and imperialist traditions. By 1898, the colonialist tradition established that US citizens residing in annexed territories were entitled to the full protection of the Constitution's bill of rights. In contrast, the imperialist tradition either granted Congress a power to enact legislation extending (and withholding) civil rights to occupied territories or simply granted the US government a plenary power to rule an occupied territory without constitutional limitations. The doctrine of territorial incorporation granted the inhabitants of annexed unincorporated territories 'fundamental' civil rights. While not entitled to the full protection of the bill of rights, the subject inhabiting an unincorporated territory was also not bereft of rights, at least in theory. While the US government did not guarantee the full application of the bill of rights in unincorporated territories, it also placed fundamental constitutional limitations on the power of the US global empire's ability to rule in these localities. This latter compromise still enabled the US global empire to exercise hegemony over the subjects of unincorporated territories.

At the time of this writing US legal actors have used the Insular Cases to legitimate three interpretations of the power of the US global empire over subjects (citizens and aliens alike) residing in unincorporated territories and/or outside of the United States. The traditional interpretation suggests that Congress and the Supreme Court have the power to withhold or extend constitutional rights to unincorporated territories so long as the corresponding actions do not violate the fundamental rights of the subject. In *Reid*, however, the Court established that the Insular Cases were no longer relevant, and the Constitution placed limitations on the extraterritorial powers of the US government over citizens. In *Verdugo-Urquidez*, rather than invoking imperialist precedents, the Supreme Court drew on the Insular Cases to legitimate the US government's plenary power over aliens who violate US laws outside of the United States. As I will discuss in subsequent chapters, the US global empire selectively invokes each of these interpretations to legitimate its extraterritorial laws and policies.

NOTE

1 *Balzac v. People of Porto Rico,* 258 US 298 (1922). It is important to note that Gettys suggests that the state department treated Puerto Rico as an incorporated territory between 1917 and 1922 and granted persons born in the island a US citizenship status (1934: 155).

Chapter 6

Unincorporated camps

Guantánamo Bay and the war on terror

> There are *places* which are not land or territory; and there was at least one such place where slavery had flourished in its most horrible form, where above all other places it needed to be wiped out and destroyed – a place with no certainty to be described as a territory of the United States or as 'within the United States;' and yet a place most certainly subject to the jurisdiction of the United States.
>
> (Selden Bacon, 'Territory and the Constitution', 1901: 101)

Following the events of 11 September 2001, the Bush administration declared a global war on terror with little or no definition of the geographical scope of the war. Unlike more conventional wars defined by national boundaries separating warring countries, the global war on terror was open ended. In *The Dark Side*, Jane Mayer recounts how within days of the 11 September attacks, White House Counsel Alberto Gonzalez approached members of Congress seeking authorization for the Bush administration to go to war against the perpetrators of the attacks and 'demanded that Congress expand the President's war authority...to target not just those terrorists who could be linked to the September 11 attacks, but anyone whom the President deemed a terrorist' (2008: 44–45). Notwithstanding considerable haggling and compromises between lawmakers and the White House, Congress subsequently enacted the 2001 Authorization for Use of Military Force Act (AUMF) granting the Bush administration the power to 'use all necessary and appropriate force against those nations, organizations, or persons he determines planned, authorized, committed, or aided the terrorist attacks that occurred on 11 September 2001, or harbored such organizations or persons, in order to prevent any future acts of international terrorism against the United States by such nations, organizations or persons' [Section 2(a)]. The resulting language not only enabled the Bush administration to finance a post-Cold War military-industrial-complex, but also wage a global war to re-assert the preeminence of the US global empire.

The subsequent creation of torture, intelligence gathering, and detention camps in the US Naval installation located in Guantánamo Bay, Cuba (Rose

2004; Meeropol 2005; Begg and Brittain 2006; The Constitution Project 2013) not only became one of the key global signatures of the United States' war on terror, but also served as the testing ground for the corresponding constitutional interpretations. Guantánamo and its camps became symbols of the lengths to which the United States would go to assert its hegemonic power (Margulies 2006; Olshansky 2007). The Guantánamo camps asserted the power of the US global empire to carve a territorial 'legal black hole' amidst a saturated real estate market of civil and human rights laws. Moreover, the legal debates over the policies used to manage the torture, intelligence gathering, and detention camps as well as the ensuing outcomes of these debates provide one of the clearest descriptions of the legal dimensions of US global empire.

Prevailing debates over the legal status of Guantánamo, as well as the broader legal narrative of the war on terror, have privileged a liberal narrative of rights obscuring how competing logics of territorial expansionism have framed the constitutional interpretations embraced by the US government. Notwithstanding the contributions of Taylor Saito (2007) and Raustiala (2009), critics of US law and policy have traditionally focused on whether the Federal government has the power to withhold or extend civil rights and privileges to its detainees or whether it has violated international laws protecting human rights of subjects detained in the Guantánamo Bay camps. This line of reasoning shaped the dominant critiques of the Bush administration. In *Enemy Aliens,* David Cole summarized the basic argument:

> ...trading non-national's basic human rights not only disserves our long-term interest, but is wrong as a constitutional and normative matter. The constitutional argument is a trump card; even if one were to disagree with the first two points, and to conclude that it serves the citizenry's interests to deny foreign citizens basic human rights it is not a choice we should allow ourselves to make in a constitutional democracy.
>
> (2003: 226)

Likewise, in *Democracy Detained,* Barbara Olshansky, the Director Counsel for the Guantánamo Global Justice Initiative argued:

> Denied not only constitutional protections, but all international law protections as well, the men detained at Guantánamo were immediately subjected to interrogation under extreme conditions that included physical and psychological torture and abuse. How and were these individuals stripped of their dignity and human rights? From the Bush administration's perspective, the calculus was quite simple: they had been deemed 'enemy combatants.' ... The designation carries with

> it a prescribed set of confinement conditions that deprive so-called 'enemy combatants' of all of their human rights.
>
> (2007: 86)

This analysis emphasized a political reading of the Bush administration's legal interpretations that privileged a liberal narrative about the direct access of individuals to the rights (constitutional and human rights) administered by the state, without considering how 'locality' or the territorial status of Guantánamo mediated this access. Even though Olshansky and other cause lawyers and activists recognized the relationship between the Bush administration's war on terror policies and the expansion of US empire, the territorialization of law was absent from the analysis. This of course is not to dismiss or diminish the importance of legal strategies that are confined to a court apparatus. These strategies are important and have real consequences on the lives of detainees. However, this analysis obscures the centrality of the Bush administration's reliance on US territorial jurisprudence.

My contention is that the Bush administration and its congressional allies partially relied on an imperialist interpretation of US territorial law in order to both curtail challenges anchored on a rights discourse and to legitimate the so-called imperial presidency. However, I further contend, a majority of Supreme Court justices relied on the precedents established by the Third View or doctrine of territorial incorporation to temper the Bush administration and Congress' imperialist interpretation. The Court relied on a reading of the Insular Cases and *Downes* more specifically to place some limits on the power of the President and his interpretation of the status of detainees and Guantánamo. Rather than some 'new paradigm' of power, the resulting constitutional interpretation of the powers of the United States to conduct a war on terror, I argue, is a continuation of the century-old logic used to rule unincorporated territories. To this extent, the constitutional justification of the Guantánamo camps, and to a large extent the war on terror policies more generally, are an iteration or continuation of the logic the US global empire established between 1898 and 1901.

LEGALIZING THE GUANTÁNAMO CAMPS

Although the US government began to detain suspected terrorists and other so-called 'enemy combatants' soon after the events of 11 September, by January 2002 the Bush administration had built a torture, intelligence gathering, and detention camp in Guantánamo Bay for the burgeoning numbers of detained enemies. More than a decade later, it is pretty clear that the Bush administration and its collaborators serving in Congress sought to construct a camp in a territorial space or locality outside of the 'reach of any law' (Mayer 2008: 146). More specifically, as John Yoo explains in *War by Other Means,* the Bush Administration eventually settled on using the US naval station located in Guantánamo Bay because they believed that the 'federal courts probably wouldn't consider Gitmo as falling within their habeas jurisdiction, which had in any event been understood to run only within the territorial United States or to American citizens abroad' (2006: 142–143). Central to this logic was an imperialist interpretation of the definition of the United States, which excluded leased territories. At the same time, Guantánamo was also under the sovereign control of the United States and free from any other nation's influence, including Cuba's.

The United States leased Guantánamo Bay, Cuba following the 1898 War and has since exercised complete control over the territory's affairs. As previously noted, the United States expelled the Spanish regime from Cuba during the 1898 Spanish–American War and retained control over the island until it was able to create a puppet government that could assume local control. In 1901, Congress enacted the Platt Amendment granting the United States 'a right to intervene' in Cuban affairs anytime that the 'life, property, and individual liberty' of its citizens and corporations was threatened by domestic or international forces. By 1903, the US government had secured a treaty with the US controlled Cuban government authorizing the lease of lands to create several coaling and naval stations, including Guantánamo Bay. While Article Three of the 1903 treaty recognized that the Republic of Cuba retained ultimate sovereignty over Guantánamo, it also established that 'during the period of the occupation by the United States of said areas under the terms of this agreement the United States shall exercise complete jurisdiction and control over and within said areas' [6 Bevans 1114 (1903)]. In 1934, again under the aegis of a United States controlled regime, Cuba signed a treaty affirming the lease agreement for Guantánamo Bay, but stipulated that both contracting parties (Republic of Cuba and the US) were required to agree before the lease could be dissolved. In essence, the Cuban legislation and treaties affirmed the permanent occupation of the United States over Guantánamo Bay and placed the selected territory under the permanent jurisdiction of the US (Article Three).

Even though leased territories remain under the sovereignty of the lessor, the United States has ruled leased territories as 'possessions' tantamount to unincorporated territories. In *Vermilya-Brown Co., Inc. v. Connell* [335 US 377 (1898)] the Supreme Court addressed the question of the status of leased territories for the purposes of extending Federal or national legislation. In this particular case, the question raised was whether the 1838 Fair Labor Standards Act covered employees of US contractors working in a military base located in Bermuda, a British colonial dependency. A majority of the Court drew upon the basic principles of the doctrine of territorial incorporation to affirm the extension of the latter legislation to the leased territory in Bermuda. In the process, the Court established that Guantánamo Bay was leased under the same terms as Bermuda (Id. at 383). More importantly, the Court ruled that the Territories Clause authorized Congress to rule Bermuda and Guantánamo Bay, like Puerto Rico, Guam, the Guano islands, Samoa, and the Virgin Islands, as possessions for the purposes of extending Federal legislation (Id. at 388). Stated differently, for legal purposes, since 1938 the United States has ruled Guantánamo Bay, Cuba as an unincorporated territory. To this extent, any analysis of the status of detainees in the Guantánamo Bay camps should consider the legal impact of treating this locality as an unincorporated territory.

Progressive or cause lawyers and other activists began to challenge the creation of the camps in Guantánamo immediately after the Bush administration opened the infamous Camp X-Ray (Olshansky 2002; Cole 2003; Meeropol 2005). The earliest legal challenge was brought in January 2002 by a coalition of progressive clergy, lawyers and professors on behalf of some detainees and seeking a statutory *writ of habeas corpus* (28 USC §2241) to compel Federal courts to render a judgment on the legality of the Guantánamo camps. Even though the case was dismissed for lack of jurisdiction, it set the stage for subsequent litigation seeking *habeas corpus* relief. Notwithstanding the number of legal challenges that were brought to the courts since 2002, scholars generally agree that three cases defined the Supreme Court's interpretation of the legal and constitutional status of the US camps in Guantánamo Bay, namely *Rasul v. Bush* [542 US 466 (2004)], *Hamdan v. Rumsfeld* [548 US 557 (2006)], and *Boumediene v. Bush* [553 US 723 (2008)]. The legal histories of these opinions demonstrate how both the Bush administration and the Supreme Court invoked competing interpretations of the Insular Cases and the precedents established by the rulings relevant to Puerto Rico to authorize the torture, interrogation, and detention camps in Guantánamo Bay.

RASUL V. BUSH (2004)

The case of *Rasul v. Bush* combined a number of *habeas corpus* petitions lodged by two British, two Australian, and twelve Kuwaiti citizens detained in Guantánamo Bay for two years (2002–2004). The detainees were held without being charged, informed of what rights were available to them, provided access to counsel or courts, or recourse to any legal process. Based on the available transcripts, it is not clear that the US armed forces possessed any evidence that these detainees were collaborating with the 'enemy.' They appear to have been in the wrong place at the wrong time. Most if not all were turned over to the US armed forces by members of the notorious Northern Alliance, an anti-Taliban coalition that included international drug dealers and other criminal organizations operating in Afghanistan. Most if not all were also tortured by US forces during their detentions (Meeropol 2005; Begg and Brittain 2006). All the detainees were seeking access to a statutory *writ of habeas corpus* (28 USC §2241) in order to challenge their detention by compelling the US government to reveal why they were holding them in the first place.

In the legal brief submitted by the Bush administration, Solicitor General Theodore Olson essentially argued that Rasul and the other detainees were enemy combatants held outside of the United States for legal purposes and therefore not entitled to *habeas corpus* relief. Solicitor General Olson, however, developed at least two mutually constitutive rationales, namely one emphasizing the individual status of Rasul and the other detainees and one focusing on the territorial status of Guantánamo. On the question of the individual status of Rasul and the other detainees, citing the precedents established by *Johnson v. Eisentrager* [339 US 763 (1950)], Solicitor General Olson in part argued that US courts lacked 'jurisdiction over claims filed on behalf of Guantánamo detainees because they are aliens with no connection to the United States' (Rasul Brief for Respondents 2004: 12). In addition, citing the Supreme Court's decision in *United States v. Verdugo-Urquidez* [494 US 259 (1990)], Olson reasoned that enemy combatants held outside of the United States were not entitled to constitutional rights such as Fifth Amendment protections and privileges such as the *writ of habeas corpus* normally available to citizens or aliens with a connection to the United States (Rasul Brief for Respondents 2004: 14). To be sure, because 'enemy combatants' were 'aliens' captured outside of the United States, they possessed no connection or ties to the United States and were therefore outside of the scope of the civil rights protections afforded by the Constitution. Or so the US government argued.

Solicitor General Olson's brief also adopted an imperialist interpretation of Guantánamo Bay's territorial status in order to situate the camps outside of the reach of both constitutional and international law. The Solicitor General argued that 'leased US military installations abroad are outside the sovereign territory of the United States... yet indisputably within the control of US armed forces' (Rasul Brief for Respondents 2004: 39). Thus, because the Constitution was limited to the territorial boundaries of the United States, it did not afford rights and protections to 'aliens' detained outside of the United States. International law or more specifically the International Covenant on Civil and Political Rights (ICCPR), Olson further argued, 'is inapplicable to conduct by the United States outside its sovereign territory' (Ibid.: 49). In sum, because Guantánamo was located outside the United States, neither the constitution nor international law could regulate US policies and practices in the camps. Guantánamo was relegated to a space located somewhere between the constitutional borders of the United States and those of international law. According to this interpretation, the camps were located in what Agamben has described as a 'state of exception.'

The Bush administration also rejected progressive allusions to the Insular Cases. To be sure, as previously noted, one of the key premises of the doctrine of territorial incorporation is that although Congress may withhold or extend constitutional rights to an unincorporated territory, some fundamental rights apply to these localities. Over time, Congress and the Court have extended the Fourth and Fifth Amendments to places like Puerto Rico. Olson responded in two ways. First, he argued that Guantánamo was not an incorporated territory because in *United States v. Spelar* [338 US 217 (1949)] the Supreme Court established that the Federal Tort Claims Act did not extend to a military base in Newfoundland (Rasul Brief for Respondents 2004: 39). Second, he proceeded to distinguish Guantánamo from the other unincorporated territories such as Puerto Rico, Guam and the Panama Canal Zone by arguing that that over time Congress and the Courts had extended the rights and privileges in question to these unincorporated territories (Ibid.: 39–42). Of course, Olson neglected to acknowledge that the doctrine of territorial incorporation gave Congress a functional power to cherry-pick which Federal laws and constitutional provisions could be withheld or extended to particular territories. Or stated differently, just because the Federal Torts Claims Act did not extend to a military base in Canada does not mean that the principle to govern the military bases is not informed by the doctrine of territorial incorporation. If anything, a critical reading of the *Spelar* precedent actually affirms the doctrine of territorial incorporation.

Giorgio Agamben's use of Carl Schmitt's notion of the state of exception ([1931] 2003) to describe Guantánamo is helpful, but also misleading (2003: 2–3). In fact, as Agamben suggests, the Bush administration invoked a state of emergency in order to create a 'zone of indistinction' where the military norms could be normalized into law and the access to constitutional rights of the detainees suspended. To paraphrase Agamben, the Bush administration described the camps located at Guantánamo as 'being outside' of the sovereignty of the United States and therefore outside of the law, and yet 'belonging' or under the control of the US military (2003: 35). Solicitor General Olson and the Bush administration more generally asked the Supreme Court to grant the President the power to normalize a state of emergency, here understood as a perpetual continuation of the war on terror, and create a state of exception where suspected enemies could be held outside of the law and subject to the will of their guards. Detainees or enemy aliens need not be charged, granted any rights (constitutional or international), they could be tortured, and simply held in perpetuity, all within the 'edifice of the law' (Zizek 2004: 158).

Agamben's interpretation, however, is problematic on political and conceptual terms. First, Agamben's argument only explains Congress and the Bush administration's laws and policies, while neglecting the Supreme Court's interpretation. The Court rejected congressional laws suspending the detainees' access to the *writ* and ultimately tempered the Bush administration's policies. To the extent that the Court is the final arbiter of the Constitution in the United States, its opinions matter when seeking to understand US law and policy. More importantly, while the Bush administration repeatedly either skirted around the Court's pronouncements or as Vice-President Richard Cheney argued, repeatedly sought to adjust its policies to the Court's interpretations (2011: 359–363), it also sought the constitutional legitimacy that this branch of government could provide. To this extent, Agamben's interpretation only describes part of the story, the story of the Bush administration's efforts to create torture and detention camps situated in a state of exception.

Second, Agamben's interpretation is anchored on a liberal narrative of civil rights that ignores the relevance of US territorial law and policy, or as Mark Rifkin argues, is divorced 'from territoriality' (Svirsky and Bignall eds 2012: 79). Agamben's discussion of the suspension of the *writ of habeas corpus* draws on doctrinal jurisprudence of the Suspension Clause of the Constitution (US Constitution, Art. I, Sect. 9, cl. 2), which is traditionally anchored on US civil war cases. The civil war cases essentially authorized President Abraham Lincoln to use military commissions during the civil war to prosecute civilians charged with aiding and abetting the South. Acting under the authority of President Lincoln's invocation of a state of emergency, the military suspended the *writ of habeas corpus* in the United States during the war and used military commissions to prosecute conspirators aiding and abetting the South, even when there were civilian courts available to judge conspirators. Read in this context, President Bush's policies are a mere continuation of a longstanding practice to suspend the *writ* during a state of emergency (for example war). However, any reading of the actual legal briefs and related jurisprudence unequivocally shows how the Bush administration invoked an imperialist interpretation of the territorial status of Guantánamo to legitimate the creation of a state of exception. For the Bush administration the camps at Guantánamo were situated in a locality tantamount to an occupied territory, a territory ruled by the military as a foreign location or a location situated outside of the sovereignty of the United States for constitutional purposes. To compare the status of a citizen whose access to the *writ of habeas corpus* was temporarily suspended while *in* the United States to the experience of an 'alien' or 'enemy combatant' whose access to the *writ* was permanently suspended while detained in an 'occupied' territory is misleading. Ironically, even the Supreme Court recognized the problem with this type of analysis. Of course, the analysis is more complicated given the competing interpretations of the powers of the US government over 'territories' and the corresponding subjectivity of alien enemy combatants detained in these territories. However the point is that the available evidence, documented in the corresponding legal texts, demonstrates that the subjectivity of the detainees held in the Guantánamo camps is inextricably linked to the territorial status of Guantánamo Bay, Cuba.

The brief for Rasul essentially made two arguments challenging the Bush administration. First, the Bush administration could not construct a 'law free zone' or 'legal limbo' where government agents operated without legal restraints. This reading is consistent with the notion that the US possesses a plenary power to treat Guantánamo as an occupied territory situated outside of the jurisdiction of the United States. Second, Rasul and the other detainees should be granted access to the *writ of habeas corpus* as a matter of justice. The bulk of the Rasul brief challenges every interpretation offered by the Solicitor General's briefs and explains how the legal authorities cited are inapplicable to the Guantánamo case at hand. However, it is important to note that the Rasul brief expressly cites the Insular Cases on two important footnotes and implicitly throughout. In the first footnote, discussion of the *Balzac* precedent, the attorneys for Rasul argue that the Due Process clause extends extraterritorially to unincorporated territories like Guantánamo and places restraints on the 'Executive, when he acts with respect to an alien outside the United States' (Rasul Brief for Petitioners 2004: 19, fn 20). In the second footnote, the Rasul brief cites cases like *Downes* to describe Guantánamo as an unincorporated territory and to establish that some fundamental rights extend to the camps (Rasul Brief for Petitioners 2004: 46, fn 47). Rather than arguing for the extension of the full bill of rights, the Rasul lawyers merely invoked prevailing precedents to gain their clients access to due process rights and the *writ*. The choice to reify the doctrine of territorial incorporation was of course pragmatic. It asked the Court to merely enforce an interpretation that would recognize the extension of rights to the detainees held in Cuba.

Subsequently, a six–three majority of Supreme Court justices sided with Rasul and the other petitioners and held that a statutory *writ to habeas corpus* (28 USC §2241) extended to Guantánamo. The majority actually embraced the Rasul brief's critique of the Bush administration's narrow interpretation of precedents. The Court also used this opportunity to assert its power of judicial review tempering the so-called imperial presidency or the pretentions by the Executive Branch to run Guantánamo without checks and balances from the judiciary. However, while the so-called liberal majority of justices issued a fairly narrow opinion establishing that the statutory form of *habeas corpus* was operative in Guantánamo, they neglected to challenge the very existence of the camps in the first place. In fact, the majority appeared to affirm the notion that the US could rule Guantánamo as an unincorporated territory selectively withholding or extending rights and privileges to the camps. More importantly, the *Rasul* opinion did not challenge the ability of the President to construct and manage a torture, intelligence gathering, and detention camp in a non-contiguous unincorporated territory.

Within a year, Congress enacted the 2005 Detainee Treatment Act (DTA) seeking to bar the extension of the *writ of habeas corpus* to Guantánamo. More specifically, the DTA amended the original statute conferring a *writ of habeas corpus* (28 USC §2241) by restricting the ability of the courts to hear *habeas* petitions and other challenges raised by detainees. To be sure, Section 1005(e) established that:

> ...no court, justice, or judge shall have jurisdiction to hear and or consider (1) an application for a writ of habeas corpus filed by or on behalf of an alien detained by the Department of Defense at Guantánamo Bay, Cuba; or (2) any other action against the United States or its agents relating to any aspect of the detention by the Department of Defense of an alien at Guantánamo Bay, Cuba.
>
> (119 Stat. 2739, 2741–2742)

This restriction sought to curtail the ability of the courts to engage in the judicial review of the Bush administration's policies and the Executive branch more generally. Again, a majority of lawmakers was willing to grant the President an unchecked power to wage a war against terror without regard to the human or civil rights of the administration's detainees, many whom were found to be innocent or whom were never charged of committing a crime.

HAMDAN V. RUMSFELD (2006)

In *Hamdan* the Court essentially examined whether the military commissions created by the Bush administration to prosecute detainees were lawful within the Uniform Code of Military Justice (UCMJ) and Common Article 3 of the Geneva Conventions. A military commission, Gary D. Solis notes, is essentially 'a wartime military trial with less stringent rules of procedure and rules of evidence found in courts-martial' and civilian courts more generally (Fidell and Sullivan 2002: 196). Military commissions have been employed in the United States since the founding, but the laws authorizing them have been modified over time. For example, the Supreme Court has in the past established that citizen civilians cannot be tried in a military commission when a civil court is functioning. Moreover, the 1949 Geneva Convention excludes 'prisoners of war' from being tried in military commissions and requires a prosecuting nation to try them in the same tribunals used for military personnel (Ibid.: 197–198). The military commissions created by the Bush administration in the aftermath of the 11 September events were especially controversial because they did 'not provide for appeal of the verdict or sentence' and the President or the Secretary of Defense retained the final power to review the sentences (Ibid.: 201). Suffice it to say that the Bush administration's military commissions effectively subordinated detainees to the rules created by the President and barred the courts from reviewing the process.

In November 2001, Afghan militia captured Salim Ahmed Hamdan, a Yemeni national and Osama Bin Laden's former chauffeur, during hostilities between the United States and the Taliban. He was subsequently transferred to a US military facility and in June 2002 to Guantánamo Bay. A year later, Hamdan was charged with 'one count of conspiracy "to commit... offenses triable by military commission"' (548 US 557, 566). The charges applied retroactively to Hamdan for having served as a driver to Osama Bin Laden between 1996 and 2001. More importantly, as the Justice John Paul Stevens wrote, '(t)here is no allegation that Hamdan had any command responsibilities, played any leadership role, or participated in the planning of any activity' (Id. at 570). Hamdan was simply a driver for the leader of a terrorist organization. At best, as the Bush administration argued, Hamdan had the potential to become a dangerous individual.

Hamdan argued that the Geneva Convention required the United States to try him under the same military tribunals available to US soldiers rather than President Bush's military commissions. He also argued that the charge of 'conspiracy to commit a crime' was not a 'violation of the laws of war.' Finally, he contended that the procedures adopted by the military commissions to try him 'violate the most basic tenets of military and international law, including the principle that a defendant must be permitted to see and hear evidence against him' (548 US 557, 567). On a broader scale, Hamdan's petition also challenged the legality of the Detainee Treatment Act's efforts to curtail the ability of detainees to challenge the Bush administration and Congress' war and terror policies.

Paul D. Clement, the new US Solicitor General, centered his response on the individual legal status of Hamdan. For example, among other things, Clement argued that Hamdan was an alien held outside of the US and therefore not entitled to the rights and privileges available to citizens and aliens with ties to the US (Hamdan Brief for Respondents 2004: 8). He argued that as an enemy combatant and member of Al-Qaeda Hamdan was not entitled to a prisoner of war status and therefore to the Geneva Convention protections (Ibid.: 6–7). Additionally, Clement challenged any interference by the courts that would undermine the ability of the President to conduct a war. In sum, the key debates emphasized questions about the legal status of Hamdan's body and the source of law to prosecute him.

Again a majority of the justices, primarily comprised of the so-called liberal block of the Court, sided with the progressive argument and struck down the prevailing military commissions. The majority reasoned that the President did not make a sufficiently compelling argument that Hamdan was so dangerous that he needed to be tried by a military commission, or a procedure that deviated from the procedures outlined in the Uniform Code of Military Justice. Writing for the majority, Justice Stevens concluded that 'the procedures adopted to try Hamdan deviate from those governing courts-martial in ways not justified by any "evident practical need"' (548 US

557, 634). It followed that the DTA provisions limiting Hamdan's access to basic procedural rights and privileges were unjustified and violated Common Article 3 of the Geneva Convention.

However, while the Court tempered the Bush administration's efforts to preserve its ability to torture detainees in the Guantánamo camps, it neglected to create the conditions that would have barred torture. The brief by Neal K. Katyal, the Counsel of Record for Hamdan, documented instances of torture in Guantánamo and framed the need to extend the Common Article 3 of the Geneva Convention against this backdrop. For example, citing a *New York Times* article by Neil Lewis, Katyal wrote:

> While all the detainees were threatened with harsh tactics if they did not cooperate, about one in six were eventually subjected to those procedures, one former interrogator estimated. The interrogator said that when the interrogators arrived they were told they had great flexibility in extracting information from detainees because the Geneva conventions did not apply at the base.
>
> (Hamdan Brief for Petitioner 2006: 2)

Notwithstanding the unwillingness of the media, including the *New York Times*, to use the word 'torture' to describe what was colloquially known as 'harsh or enhanced interrogations', by the time that Hamdan reached the Court there was little doubt that the US government was torturing detainees in Guantánamo. To this extent it is possible to read the Court's ruling as a tacit effort to temper the Bush administration's policies in Guantánamo. A more convincing, and certainly more democratic, position would have been to use this opportunity to declare that the bill of rights extended to Guantánamo like it should extend to all territories under the sovereignty of the United States. Certainly a court that can claim a power of judicial review can also establish that the Constitution follows the flag.

In his memoirs, former Vice-President Dick Cheney explains how after the *Hamdan* ruling the Bush administration began to develop a 'new legal underpinning' in order to enable the Central Intelligence Agency (CIA) to continue using 'enhanced interrogations' in its global war on terror (Cheney and Cheney 2011: 361). According to the Vice-President:

> The president decided to make aspects of the program public in order to save it. He announced he would bring the terrorists currently in CIA custody to Guantánamo for trial, and he submitted legislation that would provide congressional approval for military commissions and clarify the kinds of questioning that would be allowed under the Detainee Treatment Act.
>
> (Ibid.)

Within months Congress enacted the 2006 Military Commissions Act (MCA), which barred all courts, justices, and judges from hearing any pending or future *habeas corpus* proceedings (120 Stat. 2600, 2635–2636). The MCA also amended the Uniform Code of Military Conduct enabling sympathetic soldiers to carry out the war on terror without fear of being accused of committing war crimes. The Bush administration and Congress' response was to affirm the plenary and absolute powers of the 'imperial presidency' by curtailing the ability of the judiciary to exercise judicial review. The Bush administration and its lawmakers used congressional legislation to affirm the creation of a camp where constitutional and international rights could be suspended.

BOUMEDIENE v. BUSH (2008)

Lackdar Boumediene and his five co-petitioners emigrated from Algeria to Bosnia and Herzegovina during the 1990s. On 11 September 2001, all were peacefully residing in Bosnia and none were engaged in hostile activities against the United States or its allies. In October 2001, the Bosnian police arrested Boumediene and the other five petitioners, 'under pressure from US officials, who threatened to cease diplomatic relations with Bosnia if Petitioners were not arrested.' United States officials alleged that Boumediene and the other Algerians were plotting to attack the US Embassy in Sarajevo. By 17 January 2002, the Supreme Court of the Federation of Bosnia and Herzegovina ordered the release of Boumediene and his co-petitioners after a three-month investigation (with the collaboration of US officials and Interpol) failed to provide any evidence to support the charges and accusations leveled by the US government. On the same day, the Human Rights Chamber of Bosnia and Herzegovina issued an order barring the removal of Boumediene and his co-petitioners from Bosnian territory. Within hours, however, US military officials, with the support of Bosnian police officers, managed to kidnap Boumediene and his co-petitioners and subsequently removed them to the Guantánamo Bay camps. In Guantánamo, they were accused of being members of Al-Qaeda (Boumediene Brief for Petitioners 2007: 1–3).

While they were filing petitions for a *habeas corpus* hearing, Congress passed the 2006 Military Commissions Act and the Bush administration sought to dismiss their petition. Boumediene and his co-petitioners asked two basic questions. First, they inquired whether the MCA could strip them of their ability to file a *habeas corpus* petition. Second, they asked whether the Bush administration possessed the power to detain them indefinitely and without access to *habeas corpus* proceedings. Their Supreme Court brief raised a wide array of arguments ranging from questioning whether the MCA was tantamount to a constitutional suspension of the *writ of habeas corpus* to questions about the historical scope or application of *habeas corpus* privileges to aliens. At the end of the brief, however, Boumediene's brief also alluded to the Insular Cases and the doctrine of territorial incorporation more generally in order to invoke a constitutional privilege to a *habeas corpus* proceeding. Specifically, they argued that the Insular Cases established a guarantee of the extension of natural or 'fundamental' rights to unincorporated territories (Boumediene Brief for Petitioners 2007: 45). It followed that even aliens held in an unincorporated territory could invoke the basic or fundamental privilege of a *writ of habeas corpus*, or so they reasoned.

The Bush administration made two sets of arguments. First, they argued that the Military Commissions Act provided adequate alternative procedures to a constitutional *writ of habeas corpus*. Second, revisiting the constitutional arguments that the administration made in *Rasul*, Solicitor General Clement argued that aliens detained in Guantánamo were not entitled to a constitutional privilege of *habeas corpus*. Accordingly, Guantánamo was located outside of the geographical borders of the United States and prevailing case law such as *Eisentrager* and *Verdugo-Urquidez* barred aliens with no connections to the US from accessing Federal courts or civil rights such as the Fourth Amendment. Central to the Bush administration's logic was the notion that Guantánamo is located *outside* of the United States for constitutional purposes.

In addition, the Solicitor General sought to dismiss the relevance of the doctrine of territorial incorporation on at least three instances. First, citing *Downes* and other territorial jurisprudence, Solicitor General Clement argued that constitutional civil rights were not operative on their own force (*ex propio vigore*) and were extended to the territories via legislation (Boumediene Brief for Respondents 2007: 18 fn 5). Congress had not extended the bill of rights or any constitutional rights for that matter to Guantánamo, or so the Bush administration reasoned. Clement also argued that the Insular Cases' doctrine of territorial incorporation only applied to 'ceded' (annexed) territories and not to leased territories like Guantánamo Bay. While it was true that the US controlled the territory in question, Cuba never ceded Guantánamo to the United States and thus retained ultimate sovereignty over the area (Ibid.: 69–70). Stated differently, the Bush administration equated Guantánamo to an *occupied* rather than an *annexed* territory. Finally, the Solicitor General concluded that the Insular Cases established that Congress did not have to 'implement all constitutional guarantees' in the territories (Ibid.: 71). To this extent, the United States was not bound to recognize the extension of all civil rights in Guantánamo. Suffice it to say that the Bush administration's revisiting of *Rasul* affirmed an imperialist interpretation of the territorial status of Guantánamo for constitutional purposes.

In *Boumediene v. Bush*, the Court again sought to temper the Bush administration and Congress' Guantánamo laws and policies, but this time it invoked the Constitution. Whereas in *Rasul* the justices relied on statutes to temper the administration's interpretation, and in *Hamdan* on international law grounds, in *Boumediene* the Court drew on the constitutional law to invalidate some dimensions of the Guantánamo laws policies. Writing for a 5–4 majority of the Court, Justice Anthony Kennedy held that Boumediene and others detained in Guantánamo held a constitutional privilege of *habeas corpus* and the procedures contained in the Detainee Treatment Act (DTA) to review the status of the detainees were 'not an adequate and effective substitute for habeas corpus.' It followed that the Military Commissions Act, which drew on the DTA, operated 'as an unconstitutional suspension of the writ' (*Boumediene*, 553 US 723, 732–733). Justice Kennedy then proceeded to offer an array of rationales that included a discussion of the history of the *writ of habeas corpus* in the United States and in England, as well as a refutation of the Bush administration's precedents, including a refutation of the cited territorial jurisprudence.

Central to Justice Kennedy's reasoning were several misleading interpretations of US territorial law and policy addressing the extension of constitutional rights to unincorporated territories. Justice Kennedy invoked a 'functional approach' to ascribe Guantánamo an unincorporated territorial status and justify the application of the century-old doctrine of territorial incorporation to the camps. He misleadingly argued that the United States began to develop a distinction between incorporated and unincorporated territories in 1898, following the acquisition of Puerto Rico and the other non-contiguous Spanish territories (553 US 723, 756). The ensuing doctrine of territorial incorporation established that the Constitution applied in full in incorporated territories 'surely destined for statehood, but only in part in unincorporated territories' (Id., at 757). Of course, as previously noted, Puerto Rico and the other Spanish territories were not the first non-contiguous territories annexed by the United States. In fact, the United States annexed Alaska in 1867 and the Republic of Hawai'i by 1893 and subsequently enacted statehood legislation providing for their admission into the Union. Notwithstanding, Justice Kennedy's point was that the non-contiguous nature of Puerto Rico influenced the US government's decision to develop a new territorial doctrine.

Justice Kennedy again misleadingly described the development of the doctrine of territorial incorporation as an effort to protect the legal cultures of the newly annexed unincorporated territories. Justice Kennedy wrote:

> Prior to their cession to the United States, the former Spanish colonies operated under a civil-law system, without experience in the various aspects of the Anglo-American legal tradition, for instance the use of grand and petit juries.... The Court thus was reluctant to risk the uncertainty and instability that could result from a rule that displaced altogether the existing legal systems in these newly acquired territories.
> (Id., at 757)

In support of this interpretation, Justice Kennedy used a racist rationale to legitimate cultural sensitivity of his interpretation of the doctrine of territorial incorporation. Justice Kennedy cited the following passage in Justice Brown's majority opinion in *Downes*:

> It is obvious that in the annexation of outlying and distant possessions grave questions will arise from differences in race, habits, laws, and customs of the people, and from differences of soil, climate, and production, which may require action on the part of Congress that would be quite unnecessary in the annexation of contiguous territory inhabited only by people of the same race, or by scattered bodies of native Indians.
>
> (*Id.*)

Stated differently, according to Justice Kennedy the decision to ascribe an unincorporated territorial status on Puerto Rico (and on the other unincorporated territories), as well as its decision to limit the extension of constitutional rights to mere fundamental or personal rights, was a function of the Court's desire to protect the islands from 'uncertainty and instability.' Moreover, even though Justice Kennedy cites Justice Brown's racist reasoning in *Downes* in order to justify the separate and unequal treatment of Puerto Ricans, he framed his reasoning within a narrative of cultural sensitivity, an effort to protect the subjects of US global empire from the dangers of annexation.

Justice Kennedy's functional approach affirmed the notion that the US government could develop particular or distinct laws and policies for each unincorporated territory so long as the fundamental rights of the inhabitants were protected. The United States was neither bound to recognize the extension of the full bill of rights to an unincorporated territory, nor was it bound to afford all unincorporated territories the same constitutional rights and privileges. Thus, while over time the United States could extend the full bill of rights to Puerto Rico, it need not do so to other unincorporated territories like American Samoa or Guantánamo Bay. So long as the US guaranteed the fundamental or personal rights of the inhabitants of unincorporated territories it could develop different laws and policies to rule each territory differently, perhaps being sensitive to the cultural nuances of each locality.

Justice Kennedy used this argument to reject Congress and the Bush administration's laws and policies for the war on terror detainees without binding the latter to treat Guantánamo as a constitutional part (incorporated territory) of the United States. To be sure, citing the Court's ruling on *Murphy v. Ramsey* [114 US 15, 44 (1885)], a ruling addressing a dispute in the territory of Utah, Justice Kennedy wrote:

> The necessary implication of the argument is that by surrendering formal sovereignty over any unincorporated territory to a third party (Cuba), while at the same time entering into a lease that grants total control over the territory back to the United States, it would be possible for the political branches to govern without legal constraint. Our basic charter cannot be contracted away like this. The Constitution grants Congress and the President the power to acquire, dispose of, and govern territory, not the power to decide when and where its terms apply. Even when the United States acts outside its borders, its powers are not 'absolute and unlimited' but are subject 'to such restrictions as are expressed in the Constitution'.
>
> (553 US 723, 765)

Again, like the latter arguments, Justice Kennedy used a precedent addressing the status of an 'incorporated' territory to defend his functional approach, an interpretation developed for unincorporated territories. The point is that rather than invoking a colonialist interpretation of US territorial jurisprudence to reject Congress and the Bush administration's imperialist interpretation of the status of Guantánamo Bay, Justice Kennedy invoked the doctrine of territorial incorporation as an alternative. For constitutional purposes, Guantánamo Bay occupied a borderland space located somewhere between an annexed colonial territory and an occupied locality.

It is worth noting that the dissent essentially supported the Bush administration's imperialist reading of the status of Guantánamo, but did not reject the doctrine of territorial incorporation. Writing for one of the dissents in *Boumediene*, Justice Scalia used two arguments to challenge Justice Kennedy's 'functional approach' and differentiate Guantánamo from other *annexed* unincorporated territories like Puerto Rico. Justice Scalia argued that Guantánamo was not under or part of the sovereignty of the United States. It followed that the Constitution did not ensure the privilege of the *writ of habeas corpus* to aliens detained in a territory located outside of the sovereignty of the United States (Id., at 835). In addition, Justice Scalia further argued, the Insular Cases addressed the status of territories annexed or acquired under the authority of the Territories Clause. To this extent, annexed territories, ceded to the United States by a treaty, became a part of the sovereignty of the United States. Guantánamo was merely leased from Cuba and had not become a part of the United States for the purposes of the doctrine of territorial incorporation, or so Justice Scalia reasoned (Id., at 839). In his dissent, Justice Scalia affirmed both the imperialist and the global expansionist interpretation.

In sum, the Court's ruling in *Boumediene* tempered the Congress and the Bush administration's laws and policies for Guantánamo. With the support of Congress, the Bush administration used an imperialist interpretation to legitimate the laws and policies governing the Guantánamo Bay camps. Rather than administering Guantánamo as an unincorporated territory, a position consistent with the Insular Cases and the *Vermilya-Brown* precedents, lawmakers and the administration governed Guantánamo Bay as an occupied territory selectively situated outside of the United States for both international law and constitutional purposes. Likewise, this imperialist iteration affirmed the US government's plenary power to bar access to fundamental constitutional rights to the detainees. This power, the Bush administration argued, was purely under the purview of the Executive branch and should be exempt from traditional constitutional restrictions. Likewise, alien enemy combatants should not be granted any rights that will limit the Commander-in-Chief's ability to manage the camps. Congress and the Bush administration sought to govern Guantánamo in what Carl Schmitt and later Giorgio Agamben described as a 'state of exception.'

In contrast, a majority of Supreme Court justices embraced a 'progressive' or 'liberal' interpretation of the doctrine of territorial incorporation to establish that Guantánamo Bay is an unincorporated territory and the detainees held in the camps are thus entitled to some fundamental rights. While the Court recognized Congress' power to enact legislation enabling the Bush administration to rule the military camps in Guantánamo, it also recognized that detainees were entitled to 'fundamental' constitutional rights limiting the government's power. Again, while the Court could have invoked the *Reid* precedent to dismiss the doctrine of territorial incorporation as a product of a bygone racist era, the Court chose to affirm a century-old doctrine that enabled the US global empire to continue to manage camps in Guantánamo, albeit tempered by the Court's interpretation. The Court's affirmation of the doctrine of territorial incorporation reified the ability of the US global empire to selectively rule territories within its power as separate and unequal localities where subjects can be treated as less than equal persons or human beings.

AFTER GUANTÁNAMO?

In January 2009, President Barack H. Obama issued Executive Order No. 13492 directing the closure of the detention camps located in Guantánamo Bay, Cuba. Detainees would subsequently be transferred to US Federal facilities, where they would be held pending future determination of their status. An array of Federal facilities ranging from military prisons to Federal ADX super prisons were available to hold the detainees remaining in custody. Likewise, Guantánamo held, and still holds, an array of detainees ranging from innocent subjects to high valued detainees captured throughout the world. Soon after, Congress began to enact a series of measures 'limiting or prohibiting the use of appropriated funds to transfer

Guantánamo Bay detainees to the United States' (USGAO 2012: 1). Although the President could have circumvented this type of financial regulation, the political price he would have to pay far out weighted the cost of sustaining the territorial symbol of the US global empire, even for a Nobel Peace Prize-winning President.

Since then, President Obama has revisited his campaign promises to liberal constituencies demanding the closure of Guantánamo and is now an advocate of the indefinite incarceration of detainees, regardless of their innocence or guilt. Take for example the Obama administration's position in *Janko v. Obama* [Civil Case No. 051310 (2009)]. Abdulrahim Abdul Razak Al Ginco (AKA Janko), a Syrian national who arrived in Afghanistan in 2000, was taken into custody on January 2002 in Kandahar, Afghanistan and subsequently held in the Guantánamo Bay camps since then. According to the official transcripts, the US government concedes that soon after arriving in Afghanistan, Janko 'was not only imprisoned, but tortured by al Qaeda into making a false "confession" that he was a US spy, and imprisoned thereafter by the Taliban for over eighteen months at the infamous Sarpusa prison in Kandahar' (*Janko* 2009: 7). Notwithstanding, the Obama administration argued for the indefinite detention of Janko in Guantánamo. Since then, the Obama administration also signed into law the 2013 National Defense Authorization Act, which authorized the indefinite detention of persons presently held in the Guantánamo Bay camps. By 23 March 2013, the Pentagon had requested an additional $49 million dollars to build permanent camps in Guantánamo Bay that could house the current population of detainees indefinitely. The Guantánamo Bay camps have become a fixture of the US global empire. Despite the terrible reputation amassed by the injustices committed against human beings housed in these camps, both Republican and Democratic Presidents have used operated them as a territorial site for the permanent incarceration of the Guantánamo detainees, regardless of their innocence or guilt. At present, the Supreme Court's affirmation of the doctrine of territorial incorporation provides sufficient constitutional legitimacy to enable President Obama and Congress to normalize the camps.

CONTINUITIES AND DISCONTINUITIES

The Supreme Court's Guantánamo Bay rulings affirm a century-old doctrine of territorial incorporation developed to grant constitutional legitimacy to a new type of US expansionism, global in scope. The Court treated Guantánamo Bay as an unincorporated territory selectively situated outside of the United States. While it affirmed the authority of Congress and the President to respectively rule and manage the territory, it also placed some limits on the government's powers by recognizing the fundamental rights of the camps' detainees. The corresponding Court's rulings merely tempered Congress' and the President's powers over Guantánamo, while simultaneously affirming the global authority of US empire. To this extent, the Guantánamo cases represent a more extreme application of the doctrine of territorial incorporation. Unfortunately, the precedents established by these cases have also been used to legitimate other anti-democratic policies adopted as part of the global war on terror.

Chapter 7

The extraterritorial subjectivities of US global empire

An epilogue?

> Under these statutes consuls could and did make criminal laws, initiate charges, arrest alleged offenders, try them, and after conviction take away their liberty or their life sometimes at the American consulate. Such a blending of executive, legislative, and judicial powers in one person or even in one branch of the Government is ordinarily regarded as the very acme of absolutism.
>
> (*Reid v. Covert* 1957)

> If we expect aliens to obey our laws, aliens should be able to expect that we will obey our Constitution when we investigate, prosecute, and punish them....Foreign nationals investigated and prosecuted for alleged violations of United States criminal laws are just as vulnerable to oppressive government behavior as are United States citizens investigated and prosecuted for the same alleged violations.
>
> (Justices William J. Brennan and Thurgood Marshall, dissenting opinion, *United States v. Verdugo-Urquidez* 1990)

The US global empire has also invoked the precedents established by *Downes* and the other Insular Cases to legitimate the legal construction of extraterritorial subjectivities. United States law and policymakers are treating extraterritorial spaces as tantamount to legal borderlands located somewhere in between the sovereign borders of the United States and the international arena. In these extraterritorial spaces the constitution may apply in part or not at all. Federal agents and their proxies are regulated by degrees of constitutional limitations contingent on the status of their subjects. Citizens and non-citizens alike deemed subjects in these extraterritorial spaces are either granted some constitutional protections or none at all. The US global empire kidnaps, tortures, interrogates, incarcerates and assassinates subjects in these extraterritorial spaces with unequal access to rights and justice. Ironically, US law and policymakers often invoke constitutional jurisprudence to justify their tyrannical policies and practices towards individual subjects in these extraterritorial spaces.

THE JURISPRUDENCE OF EXTRATERRITORIAL SUBJECTIVITY

Since 1901, the US global empire has invoked at least three core Supreme Court rulings to legitimate the legal construction of extraterritorial subjectivities. The three rulings are partially anchored on competing interpretations of the precedents established by the Insular Cases. These precedents have created baseline interpretations of the US global empire's extraterritorial subjectivity. Ironically, the Court has used the Insular Cases to affirm the extraterritorial regulation of US agents, and well as to both curtail or extend civil rights to citizens and aliens alike outside of the United States. All have been invoked in one way or another in the more recent iterations of the US war on terror.

The US Supreme Court's ruling in *Johnson v. Eisentrager* [339 US 763 (1950)] is probably the most invoked or cited of the three opinions. In *Eisentrager* the Court addressed the question of whether convicted non-resident enemy aliens held in a US controlled facility outside of the United States could gain access to Federal courts via the use of a *writ of habeas corpus*. The German spies were previously captured in China, convicted by a military commission after the war, and subsequently held in a United States facility located in US *occupied* Germany. The Court held that the Constitution did not grant enemy aliens access to US courts.

Central to this holding were two important interpretations of the status of enemy aliens. First, the Court linked access to civil rights to a hierarchy of subjectivities. Writing for the Court, Justice Robert H. Jackson reasoned:

> The alien, to whom the United States has been traditionally hospitable, has been accorded a generous and ascending scale of rights as he increases his identity with our society. Mere lawful presence in the country creates an implied assurance of safe conduct and gives him certain rights; they become more extensive and secure when he makes preliminary declaration of intention to become a citizen, and they expand to those of full citizenship upon naturalization.
>
> (339 US 763,770)

The farther the alien was from attaining citizenship, the less access to rights she possessed. Second, the trial and incarceration situated the enemy combatants outside of the jurisdictions of Federal courts (Id. at 778).

Eisentrager also invoked the doctrine of territorial incorporation in two important ways. The majority invoked the *Downes* precedent to argue against granting the full bill of rights to enemy elements such as 'guerrilla fighters' and 'warewolves' located outside of the United States (Id. at 784). In contrast, the dissent argued that while 'no one would suggest' that the United States should 'apply every constitutional provision of the Bill of Rights in controlling temporarily occupied countries', that did not mean that the 'Constitution is wholly inapplicable in foreign territories that we occupy and govern' (Id. at 796–797). In the latter case, the dissenting Justice Hugo Black recognized that *Downes* granted some fundamental rights to aliens detained outside of the US. Notwithstanding that *Eisentrager* used *Downes*, a ruling addressing the status of *annexed* territories, to establish a new standard for *occupied* territories, what is important to note is that the logic of US global empire framed debates over the subjectivity of aliens held in occupied territories outside of the United States.

In some ways, the Court's interpretation in *Eisentrager* normalized the application of the doctrine of territorial incorporation to *occupied* spaces. Rather than anchoring its interpretation on *Fleming*, the precedent used to legitimize the selective extension of the constitution to occupied territories, the Court invoked *Downes*, a precedent used to rule *annexed* territories. To this extent, *Eisentrager* blurred the lines between occupied and annexed territories enabling the US global empire to apply the doctrine of territorial incorporation in either type of territory.

Alternatively, as previously noted, in *Reid v. Covert* [354 US 1 (1957)], the Court held that the bill of rights placed limitations on the government's actions outside of the United States. In this instance, the military sought to prosecute two civilian women in military courts for murdering their military spouses while outside of the United States. Both women were also US citizens. Writing for the majority, Justice Black reasoned:

> At the beginning we reject the idea that when the United States acts against citizens abroad it can do so free of the Bill of Rights. The United States is entirely a creature of the Constitution. Its power and authority have no other source. It can only act in accordance with all the limitations imposed by the Constitution. When the Government reaches out to punish a citizen who is abroad, the shield which the Bill of Rights and other parts of the Constitution provide to protect his life and liberty should not be stripped away just because he happens to be in another land. This is not a novel concept. To the contrary, it is as old as government. It was recognized long before Paul successfully invoked his right as a Roman citizen to be tried in strict accordance with Roman law.
>
> (354 US 1, 5–6)

Again, as previously noted, the Court established that the bill of rights placed constitutional limitations on government actions against citizens *outside* of the United States. This interpretation rejected the precedents established by the Insular Cases (Id., at 9) dismissing their relevance a 'temporary' measure to govern 'territories with wholly dissimilar traditions and institutions' (Id., at 14). Of course, at the end of the day the US global empire has to abide by its own legal precedents in order for these to have any meaningful relevance.

Finally, in *United States v. Verdugo-Urquidez* (1990), the Court cited the Insular Cases to limit the reach of the Constitution outside of the United States. As noted before, in *Verdugo-Urquidez*, the Court examined whether a foreign national accused of violating US laws while residing in a foreign country and subsequently kidnapped and prosecuted in US courts could request the protections afforded by the Fourth Amendment. A majority of the Supreme Court held that the Fourth Amendment did not extend outside of the United States to a non-resident alien nor could did it place limits on the actions of government agents outside of the United States.

As previously noted, a majority opinion cited the precedents established by the Insular Cases as one of the key rationales justifying its holding. Writing for the majority, Chief Justice William H. Rehnquist argued:

> The global view taken by the Court of Appeals of the application of the Constitution is also contrary to this Court's decisions in the *Insular Cases*, which held that not every constitutional provision applies to governmental activity even where the United States has sovereign power… And certainly, it is not open to us in light of the *Insular Cases* to endorse the view that every constitutional provision applies wherever the United States Government exercises its power.
>
> (Id., at 268–269)

Notwithstanding the Supreme Court's prior precedents established in *Torres v. Commonwealth of Puerto Rico*, which extended the Fourth Amendment to an unincorporated territory, or *Reid v. Covert*, placing constitutional limits on government actions outside of the US, the Court used an imperialist interpretation of the Insular Cases to suggest that the Fourth Amendment was not available outside of the United States. The majority's rationale empowered US government agents to police non-resident aliens anywhere in the globe without fear that the bill of rights would hamper their ability to kidnap and prosecute subjects violating US laws outside of the United States. Moreover, although the ruling did not expressly revoke the *Reid v. Covert* precedent, it certainly opened the door to undermine the power of the latter precedent by freeing the government from constitutional restrictions or limitations. Chief Justice Rehnquist's rationale expanded the scope of the *Insular Cases* from unincorporated territories to the world, treating the world as a sort of no-man's borderland.

THE BOUNDS OF THE RULE OF LAW

In *Democracy in America*, Alexis de Tocqueville wrote:

> There is hardly a political question in the United States which does not sooner or later turn into a judicial one. Consequently the language of everyday party-political controversy has to be borrowed from legal phraseology and conceptions.... (I)t infiltrates through society right down to the lowest ranks, till finally the whole of society have contracted some of the ways and tastes of the magistrate.
>
> (Mayer ed. 1969/2000: 270)

De Tocqueville not only sought to explain the mores of US political culture, but how politicians, most of whom were conservative lawyers by profession, sought to affirm their aristocratic ideologies in the United States and counter the democratic impulses of the people. As was the case in 1898, today advocates of US global empire seek to legalize or rather 'constitutionalize' their policies. Both the Bush and Obama administrations have justified their war on terror policies by invoking their legality. Both Presidents Bush and Obama have argued that their war on terror policies are consistent with the rule of law in the United States.

Notwithstanding, contemporary liberal critics of the United States' war on terror policies continue to argue that these policies violate the rule of law. Underlying this critique is a premise that the United States is bound to guarantee subjects and citizens alike equal access to just legal rights and protections. Some critics invoke the US Constitution and its bill of rights as the fundamental source of law protecting subjects and citizens alike from government abuses. Others look to international conventions or rather human rights as a source of legal protections (Honigsberg 2009; Mokhtari 2009; Sarat and Hussein 2010).

The Liberal interpretation of the relationship between the US Constitution and the subjects of the war on terror can further be divided in two strands. A more theoretical strand focuses on how US laws and policies violate the rule of law. Since 11 September 2001 two strands of this critique have developed in the United States. One strand argues that the United States conducts its war on terror outside of the rule of law. Invoking Carl Schmidt's notion of the state of exception and Michel Foucault's notion of biopolitics, critics such as Giorgio Agamben argue that in the aftermath of the 11 September attacks the US government sought to normalize a state of emergency in order to suspend the law (the bill of rights, *writ of habeas corpus*, and other constitutional checks and balances on the President's power) and adopt policies (including the creation of detention camps) that would be unmitigated by the rule of law. The ensuing policies, Agamben writes, enabled the creation of a state of exception where subjects were relegated to a status of 'bare life' (1998; 2003). Their lives were subject to the will of their guards. In a more direct manner, Judith Butler writes:

> In the name of a security alert and national emergency, the law is effectively suspended in both its national and international forms. And with the suspension of law comes a new exercise of state sovereignty, one that not only takes place *outside* the law, but through an elaboration of administrative bureaucracies in which officials now not only decide who will be tried, and who will be detained, but also have ultimate say over whether someone may be detained indefinitely or not (emphasis added).
>
> (2004: 51)

This strand of analysis, however, only explains the Bush administration's interpretation of the law, andneglects to engage the Supreme Court's rendition of the power of the United States to conduct a war on terror. Let us recall that the Supreme Court consistently tempered the Bush administration's interpretations and instead required the US government to develop laws and policies consistent with a broader notion of US global empire. Stated differently what Agamben and Butler are criticizing is the narrative of the 'imperial presidency' or an interpretation put forward by the Bush administration granting the President plenary powers to conduct the so-called war on terror.

While I do not take issue with Agamben or Butler's critique of the Bush administration it is important to note the limits of their critique, namely that it focuses on the interpretations of the President and to some degree the Republican controlled lap-dog Congress, which provided the President with a necessary legal cover to carry out its abuses. This strand of critique also obscures the differences between poorly regulated policies such as renditions and detention policies that were regulated by the Supreme Court. In the latter case the 'final' interpretation was largely tempered by the liberal wing of the Supreme Court, which drew on the doctrine of territorial incorporation, the underlying logic of US global empire, to temper the Bush administration's policies. The point, however, is that while the Supreme Court has tempered the Bush and Obama administration's excesses, the Court has not declared the overall war on terror policies unconstitutional. Suffice it to say that the US global empire's use of the doctrine of territorial incorporation continues to affirm the ability of the US government to conduct its indefinite war on terror.

A second strand of critique, mostly argued by progressive attorneys and other activists, equates the rule of law to the extension of equal access to civil and/or human rights. Attorneys, scholars, and activists alike have defended at least three complementary critiques. First, progressives denounce policies that bar subjects of the US war on terror access to equal constitutional or civil rights and protections (*habeas corpus*), which are available in Article Three or constitutional courts of law. The argument essentially establishes that the rule of law would grant subjects of the war on terror access to US courts of law, to an attorney, and generally to all the civil and procedural rights available to persons accused of committing a crime (including an act of terror) in the United States. Progressives also equate international conventions (for example Third Common Article of the Geneva Conventions) and human rights laws to the rule of law criticizing efforts by the US government to deny these rights and protections to subjects of US imperialism. For example, as previously noted, the typical critique contends that the Bush administration's efforts to classify any detained person as an 'enemy combatant', and the refusal to treat detainees as 'prisoners of war' undermines the international rule of law. A third interpretation proposes using human rights norms to interpret the US bill of rights (Cole 2003: 211–233) or argues for consistent interpretations of both legal sources (Scarry 2010). Again, without disagreeing with the substance of the critique, in all of its iterations, this argument obscures the role that the doctrine of territorial incorporation plays in defining the parameters of the rule of law in the United States. The explanatory nature of the progressive critique simply fails to account for the constitutionality of the US global empire.

Official United States' extraterritorial policy on the rule of law is partially anchored on competing iterations of the Insular Cases' doctrine of territorial incorporation. Liberal legalists, including the liberal majority of justices in the Supreme Court, have invoked the notion that the United States can withhold the full extension of the bill of rights to detainees and localities within the purview of the US global empire. Instead, the Court has determined that detained subjects can be entitled to some fundamental civil or constitutional rights and protections. The debate is not about whether some rights may extend, but rather about which rights and protections are fundamental and which are not. For more than a century, the jurisprudence sustaining the US global empire has justified the selective extension of rights and protections to unincorporated territories or other localities situated *outside* of the United States. Stated differently, the rule of law in the United States affirms the selective extension and withholding of laws to unincorporated territories and other localities under the purview of the US global empire. Focusing the critique of the rule of law on the imperial presidency's policies or an idyllic notion of a liberal sovereign nation obscures and neglects the enduring legacy of the doctrine of territorial incorporation and its more recent iterations. The prevailing anti-democratic, demeaning, and inegalitarian laws and policies of the US war on terror are actually anchored on the rule of law, or more specifically on the century-old precedents used to legitimate the US global empire.

KIDNAPPING

The United States' government reliance on 'forcible abductions' or 'kidnappings' is also anchored on the US global empire's legal logic. In *United States v. Alvarez-Machain* [504 US 655 (1992)], the companion case to *Verdugo-Urquidez*, a majority of the Court affirmed the power of the Federal government to forcibly kidnap a Mexican national suspected of engaging in criminal activities while residing in Mexico. In 1985, Enrique Camarena-Salazar, a US agent of the Drug Enforcement Administration, was captured, tortured over a two-day period, and later murdered *in* Mexico. The DEA accused Humberto Alvarez-Machain, a Mexican physician, of prolonging Camarena-Salazar's 'life in order to extend the interrogation and torture' (Id. at 657). In 1990, a US Federal court indicted Alvarez-Machain for his role in the torture and murder of Camarena-Salazar and after failing to persuade the Mexican government to extradite Alvarez-Machain hired several bounty hunters to forcibly abduct or kidnap him. Soon after, the DEA contracted José Francisco Sosa to kidnap Alvarez-Machain and remove him to El Paso, Texas, where he was arrested by Federal officers and subsequently tried for his alleged role in the murder of agent Camarena-Salazar. Lower District and Appeals Courts, however, ruled against the DEA and ordered Alvarez-Machain's release and repatriation to Mexico.

On appeal, the Supreme Court affirmed the Federal government's power to kidnap Alvarez-Machain despite the existence of an extradition treaty between Mexico and the United States. The 1978 Extradition Treaty between the United States and Mexico established a mechanism for the extradition of citizens accused of committing certain crimes. A majority of the Court, however, reasoned that the treaty said 'nothing about the obligation of the United States and Mexico to refrain from forcible abductions of people from the territory of the other nation, or the consequences under the Treaty if such an abduction occurs' (Id. at 663). The majority of the Court invoked a gap or silence in the Treaty's language to affirm the power of US agents to sidestep the extradition process and kidnap Alvarez-Machain without affording him basic due process protections or legal rights more generally. Accordingly, a Mexican national accused of committing a crime outside of the United States, albeit a crime that impacts Federal agents, could now be kidnapped and prosecuted in US Federal courts.

In *Alvarez-Machain,* the Court affirmed three of the core precedents framing the logic of the US war on terror policies and US global empire more generally. First, a majority of the Court established that the Constitution does not bind the actions of the Federal government or its agents outside of the United States. Federal agents can engage in bounty hunting and forcibly abduct or kidnap foreign nationals accused of violating US laws in foreign countries, even if the crimes that they are being accused of committing are not crimes in their home countries (for example conspiracies). Second, while foreign nationals can be kidnapped and subsequently prosecuted in the US, they are not afforded the legal rights available to a person residing in the United States. Finally, a majority of the Court affirmed the power of the US government to adopt unilateral interpretations of bilateral extradition treaties. In sum, *Alvarez-Machain* affirmed the US global empire's plenary power to police the world without the traditional constitutional or treaty restrictions that would normally govern domestic political acts.

EXTRAORDINARY RENDITIONS

The legal concept of rendition has been used to describe the transfer of a subject suspected of committing a crime from one jurisdiction to another. In the United States, domestic transfers generally occurred between states of the Union. In international terms, renditions refer to the transfer of persons from one country to another. Typically, the United States has used a process of deportation or in some cases it has relied on extradition treaties. According to Michael John Garcia, a legislative attorney for the Congressional Research Service, President Ronald Reagan first authorized renditions of suspected terrorists in 1986 and since the 1990s the United States has used this measure as a regular part of its counterterrorism measures (CRS 2009: 4). The concepts of irregular, extraordinary and/or extrajudicial renditions, however, were coined to describe the Bush administration's transfer of non-citizen detainees suspected of engaging in terrorist activities to countries where they could be tortured in order to gain actionable intelligence.

In *The Dark Side* (2008), Jane Mayer documents that following the events of 11 September 2001 the Bush administration authorized the Central Intelligence Agency (CIA) to use renditions in order to gather actionable intelligence from suspected terrorists. Mayer notes, the CIA used renditions to carve a space 'outside the realm of the law' in order to interrogate detainees without constitutional or international constraints (2008: 110–111). More specifically, the CIA sought to torture detainees without the limits placed by civil and human rights laws. Mayer further points out that the CIA used third countries that had not signed international human rights conventions or in some cases employed 'merchant marine vessels' (Ibid.: 146–147). The main objective of renditions, however, was to secure a location that could operate in a 'state of exception' enabling interrogators to torture detainees without fear of legal consequences.

Garcia's analysis of the legal debates informing the use of renditions, however, suggests that the doctrine of territorial incorporation shaped the contours of extraordinary renditions in two important ways. First, citing the *Verdugo-Urquidez* precedent, Garcia notes 'noncitizens who have not entered the United States have historically been recognized as receiving few, if any, constitutional protections (though noncitizens in foreign territory under the *de facto* control of the United States, such as Guantánamo Bay, Cuba, may be owed greater protections than other noncitizens abroad)' (CRS 2009: 4). In other words, the rendition of aliens or suspected detainees to an unincorporated territory could in fact imbue a detainee with some fundamental rights. Second, Garcia argues, the United States has generally taken the position that human rights treaty provisions such as Article 3 of the *Convention Against Torture* (CAT) generally apply to persons located within the United States. Article 3 of the CAT bars a country from sending a person to another country where the person may be subject to torture. However, Garcia further contends, 'it could still be argued that the express provisions of CAT Article 3 do not apply to extraordinary renditions occurring *outside* of the United States' (CRS 2009: 14). Given that unincorporated territories are selectively located outside of the United States, Garcia's analysis suggests, it is possible to argue that Federal agents could stage a rendition from an unincorporated territory without fear of violating international human rights laws.

CITIZEN ENEMY COMBATANTS

As previously noted, the United States has typically ascribed the status of enemy combatants to spies or other suspected members of a foreign military force. Ascribing an individual the status of enemy combatant enables the US government to prosecute detainees in special military tribunals and/or commissions rather than in a constitutional court. Military tribunals and/or commissions typically grant accused subjects fewer civil rights and protections than constitutional courts. More importantly, the procedure for prosecution and subsequent detention of enemy combatants has las long been part of US military law and policy, typically invoked during a time of war (CRS 2005; CRS 2010). To this extent, debates over the detention of enemy combatants are anchored on military law rather than US territorial law and policy.

For the most part, enemy combatants tend to be non-citizens captured outside of the United States. However, following the events of 11 September the Bush administration captured several US citizens and sought to detain them in military brigs or holding facilities. Although most citizens were captured outside of the United States, in at least one instance Federal agents captured a US citizen in the United States. Also known as the Puerto Rican Al-Qaeda or Abdullah Al Muhajir, José Padilla was arrested at Chicago O'Hare International Airport on 8 May 2012 and initially held as a material witness of the 11 September events. Soon after propagandists within the Bush administration began to accuse Padilla of being an Al-Qaeda operative intent on making 'dirty bombs' to destroy US cities. Padilla was detained in a South Carolina naval station and held without charges, access to an attorney, and generally *incommunicado*. The Federal government held Padilla, a US citizen, without charging him for the better part of four years.

Although military law precedents rather than US territorial law and policy govern the legal status of enemy combatants, several scholars have established at least two social connections between the case of Padilla and the US global empire's war on terror policies. One argument suggests that Padilla's prosecution and subsequent detention was racialized (Cole 2003; Negrón-Muntaner 2007: 256–259). Scholars compare the prosecution of John Phillip Walker Lindh, dubbed the 'American Taliban,' with Padilla's experience. Lindh, the son of wealthy white or Anglo-American citizens, was captured in Afghanistan armed and fighting against US forces and subsequently repatriated to the United States. Within months of his capture, Lindh was able to acquire legal representation and was subsequently tried in a US court. In contrast, Padilla, the son of 'brown' Puerto Rican migrants was tortured and detained for more than three years as well as denied the basic civil liberties afforded to Lindh. Unlike Lindh, Padilla was captured on US soil without having committed any crime and with no evidence that he was going to commit a crime. While Lindh reached a plea agreement admitting that he provided services to the Taliban, Padilla was convicted of a conspiracy to commit a crime against the United States. Stated differently, US global empire's white man's burden is premised on double standards that afford white Anglo-American terrorists equal civil and criminal rights, while submitting Puerto Rican enemy combatants to a separate and unequal double standard.

Frances Negrón-Muntaner also links the case of Padilla to the history of Puerto Rican nationalism (2007: 258). To be sure, Puerto Rican nationalists have a longstanding tradition of waging war against the US annexation of the island. During the 1930s, nationalists under the leadership of Pedro Albizu Campos fought against US government officials for the independence of Puerto Rico. In 1954, four Puerto Rican nationalists fired into the chamber of the US House of Representatives during public hearings relating to immigration legislation in protest of the United States' continued colonization of the island. More recently, Puerto Rican Maoists generally known as 'Los Macheteros' waged low-intensity attacks on the United States and at least in one occasion robbed a Wells Fargo Bank. When captured, as the case of Oscar López Rivera demonstrates, members of Los Macheteros as well as members of other separatist organizations were prosecuted as seditionists and given extreme sentences designed to banish them from society for life (Nieves Falcón 2013). Suffice it to say that the Padilla case evoked parallels between the forms of terrorism espoused by Al-Qaeda and the Puerto Rican nationalists, which targeted the United States' government.

TORTURE

Western legal conceptions of torture, Darius Rejali suggests, have been concerned with the state's use of violence to elicit the truth (2009: 36–37). Torture, by definition, entailed the infliction of pain and suffering on the body of the detained subject. Legal actors used torture to uncover truths and evidence about a crime. Military uses of torture focused on intelligence and information gathering. Presently, the United Nations Convention Against Torture defines torture as:

> ...any act by which severe pain or suffering, whether physical or mental, is intentionally inflicted on a person for such purposes as obtaining from him or a third person information or a confession, punishing him for an act he or a third person has committed or is suspected of having committed, or intimidation or coercing him or a third person, or for any reason based on discrimination of any kind when such pain or suffering is inflicted by or at the instigation of or with the consent or acquiescence of a public official or any person acting in an official capacity.
>
> (UNCAT, Art. 1, cl. 1)

Although the United States ratified the UNCAT, members of the Bush administration all but confessed that the United States used torture in its war against terrorism. Publicly available declassified memorandums document the arguments used by members of the Bush administration to construct legal justifications for the use of torture to gather intelligence (for example Greenberg and Dratel 2005; Jaffer and Singh 2007). In *War by Other Means*, John Yoo recounted how various members of the Bush administration invoked concepts like 'coerced interrogations' to legitimate what the rest of the world has consistently defined as torture (2006: 191). Even former Vice-President Dick Cheney admitted in his memoirs that the Bush administration used 'enhanced interrogations' while lamenting President Obama's return to the pre-11 September regulations (2011: 362–363). There can be no doubt that the United States relied on torture to gather intelligence to wage an ineffective but grandiose war on terrorism.

In a 2002 memorandum to the US Department of Defense's legal counsel addressing the possible legal constraints applicable to the 'interrogations' of subjects captured in Afghanistan, then Assistant Attorney General Jay S. Bybee invoked the *Verdugo-Urquidez* precedent in two distinct ways (Greenberg and Dratel 2005: 144–171). Central to the early debates was a concern that captured subjects tortured and subsequently detained in a US facility would successfully challenge the Bush administration in a US court of law. The first question relating to this problem was whether US officials were required to read Fourth Amendment 'Miranda' warnings to captured detainees subject to torture (Ibid.: 145). So-called 'Miranda' warnings informed persons subject to interrogation of their Sixth Amendment right to an attorney and a Fourth Amendment protection against being compelled in any criminal case to be a witness against himself [sic]. In US law, failure to inform a detained person of these rights could result in a dismissal of the 'evidence' or information gathered during an interrogation for the purposes of a trial. In *Verdugo-Urquidez*, Bybee argued, the Supreme Court had established that the Fourth Amendment did not extend to aliens accused of committing crimes *outside* of the United States (Ibid.: 145—146). It followed both that US officials did not have to 'Mirandize' detainees and the Fourth Amendment more generally did not extend to non-citizens tortured outside of the United States.

Second and more generally, Bybee further reasoned, the *Verdugo-Urquidez* precedent established that non-citizens detained outside of the United States were not entitled to constitutional rights. Bybee wrote 'with respect to trials of foreign nationals conducted outside of the US territory, our conclusion is additionally supported by the well established fact that the Fifth Amendment does not confer rights upon aliens outside the sovereign territory of the United States' (Ibid.: 148). This latter argument, however, opened the door to a more totalitarian interpretation. To be sure, the United States ratified the UN Convention Against Torture with the understanding that it would use prevailing domestic interpretations of the Fifth, Eighth, and/or Fourteenth Amendments of the Constitution to interpret the scope of the CAT definitions of torture. To the extent that Bybee's reasoning extended to international obligations, it followed that US agents torturing captured detainees outside of the United States would not be prosecuted in US courts for violating the CAT provisions. United States agents were free to torture suspects detained outside of the US without fear of prosecution.

DRONES

The United States drone program is the embodiment of US global empire. The United States has been using unmanned aerial vehicles, also known as drones or remote controlled aircrafts, to both wage war on and police the global South by other means. United States' soldiers and other Federal agents can use satellite technology to control drones anywhere around the world and conduct extrajudicial killings of suspects without having to deploy any personnel. More importantly, given their size and maintenance requirements, the United States government can launch drones from non-descript locations anywhere around the world without having to rely on expensive military installations. Drones can carry an assortment of weapons including the infamous hellfire missiles. Drones have been employed to provide surveillance, to attack enemy targets, to fight pirates, and in recent years to conduct extrajudicial executions primarily in the global South. In a sense, the US drone program is the newest iteration of the pursuit of global naval supremacy, albeit in its pursuit of global 'airborne' supremacy.

Legal arguments for the use of drones in extrajudicial executions also contain references to precedents affirming the logic of US global empire. In February 2013, amidst the public hearings for the nomination of John Brennan to head the Central Intelligence Agency, a Department of Justice White Paper was leaked to the media describing the legal framework of the drone program's extrajudicial executions of US citizens. In the name of national self defense, the 16-page White Paper established three basic criteria for the extrajudicial executions of US citizens anywhere outside of the sovereign US territory, namely that: 1) citizens pose an imminent threat to US national security; 2) United States forces are unable to capture the citizen during the 'relevant window of opportunity'; and 3) the use of lethal operations complies with fundamental law-of-war principles (USDOJ White Paper 2013: 7–8). Justifying this reasoning is a 'functional' argument establishing that the United States does not have the operational capabilities (or is willing to spend the resources to develop the necessary rapid response strike force) to capture a terrorist before s/he escapes or disappears. None of the subjects, however, are given an opportunity to contest the intelligence report that identifies them as targets before being subjected to extrajudicial assassinations. This is especially alarming because anyone familiar with the US ideological intelligence apparatus will readily note how prone or willing US agents are to collect any intelligence that conforms to the prevailing political agenda of the US global empire.

The USDOJ White Paper invokes an antilogy to legitimate the extrajudicial killings of citizens outside of the geographical boundaries of the United States. Citing *Reid v. Covert* and *US v. Verdugo-Urquidez*, the memo argues that DOJ 'assumes that the rights afforded by Fifth Amendment's Due Process Clause as well as the Fourth Amendment, attach to a US citizen even while he is abroad.' The next sentence, however, argues that the 'US citizenship of a leader of al-Qa'ida or its associated forces, however, does not give that person constitutional immunity from attack' (USDOJ White Paper 2013: 5). Stated differently, while on the one hand citizens subject to US policies outside of the geographical boundaries of the United States, perhaps in a legal borderland, on the other hand they can be subject to extrajudicial assassination without warning or without being able to exercise their due process rights.

The question is whether the functional approach theory of the doctrine of territorial incorporation laid out in *Boumediene* influences the determination to execute a citizen without providing him or her with due process rights. A liberal interpretation of the *Covert* and the *Boumediene* precedents suggests that the government cannot act without constitutional limitations outside of the United States. At the same time, the Obama administration's argument suggests that there may be exceptions, namely based on the practical circumstances on the ground. Putting aside the debates over the need to stop a terrorist in 'hot pursuit,' the Obama administration argues that in some circumstances the only way to stop a potential threat is by executing the potential perpetrator. Under these circumstances, the USDOJ White Paper finds sanctuary in the logic of the Insular Cases, namely because under certain circumstances it might be practicable to assassinate a potential enemy even if the subject has not or is not committing an aggression against the United States. Suffice it to say that the doctrine of territorial incorporation's emphasis on drawing ontological borders and creating extraterritorial zones enables the United States global empire to construct an argument consistent with the Court's interpretation.

FOREIGN INTELLIGENCE SURVEILLANCE ACT

The 1978 Foreign Intelligence Surveillance Act (FISA) authorizes the Attorney General and the Director of National Intelligence to wire tap or monitor the communications of 'foreign powers or agents of a foreign power' located outside of the United States. Under the terms of the FISA, government agents seeking to monitor the conversations of subjects were required to obtain approval or a warrant from a semi-secret Foreign Intelligence Surveillance Court (FISC). However, following the events of 11 September, the Bush administration authorized the National Security Agency (NSA) to monitor telephone and email conversations of persons suspected of either being or aiding a terrorist organization without a 'warrant.' Central to the latter authorization is granting the NSA a power to monitor the conversations of US citizens and non-citizens alike without demonstrating probable cause to collect information, a pre-condition of the Fourth Amendment. In 2008, Congress amended the FISA in two important ways:

> First, it eliminated the requirement that the Government describe to the court each specific target and identify each facility at which its surveillance would be directed, thus permitting surveillance on a programmatic, not necessarily individualized, basis. Second, it eliminated the requirement that a target be a 'foreign power or an agent of a foreign power.' Third, it diminished the court's authority to supervise, instance-specific privacy – intrusion minimization procedures (though the government still must use court-approved general minimization procedures).
>
> [Breyer, dissenting opinion in Clapper v. Amnesty International USA, 568 US __ (2013)]

The President was enabled to monitor conversations of suspected enemies of the United States with minimal if any checks and balances from the judiciary.

Subsequently, Amnesty International USA sued the Federal government challenging the authority of the President to monitor telephone and email communications between Amnesty attorneys and their clients, some of which were located outside of the United States. In *Clapper v. Amnesty International USA* (2013) a majority of the Supreme Court dismissed Amnesty's lawsuit on arguing that Amnesty had not demonstrated a concrete injury resulting from the FISA surveillance. According to Judge Samuel Alito, Amnesty was only speculating whether the Federal government was monitoring their attorneys' communications and whether the information gathered would be used to harm their clients. Judge Alito also made reference to the impact that the *Verdugo-Urquidez* precedent could have on a potential case suggesting that '(a)lthough the foreign client might not have a viable Fourth Amendment claim, it is possible that the monitoring of the target's conversations with his or her attorney would provide grounds for a claim of standing on the part of the attorney' [568 US (2013)]. It is true that at the time Edward Snowden, Glenn Greenwald, and Laura Poitras had not revealed the extent of the NSA's surveillance programs, but given the ongoing public support of President Obama's oversight of the NSA, it is not clear that documenting this information would have made a difference in the Supreme Court's rulings. In sum, not only are subjects (aliens and citizens alike) communicating from a place located outside (as well as inside) of the United States subject to government monitoring, but they also have no recourse to challenge a Federal agent's representation of the communication in question. Given the United States global empire's proclivity to use forcible kidnappings, renditions, detentions, torture, and extrajudicial assassinations, FISA surveillance can indeed determine a subject's life or death.

EXTRATERRITORIAL BORDERLANDS

The US global empire's extraterritorial law and policy seeks to create a sort of legal borderland to regulate the extension or withholding of rights. Central to the legal construction of extraterritorial spaces is the idea that the US global empire can create artificial borders that help limit the scope or reach of the law (constitutional, national, and/or international) and create a borderland space where subjects deemed enemies of the US global empire can be kidnapped, tortured, interrogated, incarcerated, and even assassinated. The ensuing subjectivity is territorialized in an extraterritorial borderland. For more than a century, the Insular Cases have provided the necessary jurisprudence enabling United States' government officials to legitimate tyrannical and anti-democratic practices. The precedents established by the Insular Cases have enabled advocates of US global empire to treat extraterritorial spaces as separate and unequal localities where subjects can be ruled as less than equal persons or human beings.

Chapter 8

Conclusion

The United States began to conceptualize itself as a postcolonial global empire following the Spanish War of 1898. Previously, United States' expansionism was in part premised on the annexation of new territories that were colonized and subsequently organized into new states of the Union. Alternatively, the United States occupied territories for mere strategic military or economic purposes. In 1898, the United States began to *annex* territories without intending to colonize them or admit them into the Union as states. Moreover, unlike prior forms of US expansionism, post-1898 expansionism sought to strategically annex new territories throughout the world, which could in turn house naval bases and military installations more generally.

United States' global expansionism is further premised on ascribing a borderland status of annexed territories. Prior to 1898, territories annexed for colonialist purposes were treated like constitutional parts of the definition of the United States. In contrast, territories subject to imperialist occupation were generally situated outside of the United States for constitutional purposes. In some instances, however, the Supreme Court authorized Congress to enact legislation selectively treating occupied territories as part of the United States for international purposes. The global expansionist tradition combined elements from the latter traditions enabling US law and policymakers to selectively rule annexed territories as foreign localities for domestic or constitutional purposes. Stated differently unincorporated territories were ascribed a borderland status enabling the US global empire to situate these localities somewhere between an annexed and an occupied territory for constitutional purposes.

United States global empire has traditionally invoked the Territories Clause as a source of constitutional legitimacy. Like the colonialist tradition, advocates of US global expansionism sought to anchor the power to the United States to rule annexed territories on the Territories Clause. However, unlike the colonialist tradition, US global expansionism has invoked a more expansive interpretation of the Territories Clause, one that grants the US government hegemonic powers to develop local policies to exploit and subordinate both acquired territories and their inhabitants. In contrast, the imperialist tradition has been rooted in an array of constitutional provisions other than the Territories Clause. Mooring its power on the Territories Clause not only enables US global empire to differentiate itself from other expansionist traditions, but also to hide behind the rhetoric of the rule of law. In other words, the United States global empire tautologically claims to follow the rule of law, laws and policies constructed to legitimate its own difference from other expansionist traditions.

United States global empire developed corresponding citizenship and nationality laws and policies to affirm the inclusive exclusion of the inhabitants of unincorporated territories. By 1898, territories were treated as constitutional parts of the United States for the purposes of conferring citizenship. To be sure, birth in a territory was tantamount to birth in the United States. In contrast, occupied territories were treated as foreign countries located outside of the United States for citizenship purposes. The US global expansionist tradition has used citizenship laws that affirm varying degrees of membership within the polity, while for the most part excluding citizens and persons from a constitutional citizenship, a precondition for more egalitarian treatment within the US global empire. What is important to note, however, is that even citizens who can claim a statutory form of birthright citizenship are ascribed a separate and unequal status within the US global empire.

In addition, the US global empire adopted the extension of personal or fundamental civil rights to unincorporated territories. Again, prior to 1898, the inhabitants of colonial territories could claim the same constitutional civil rights protections as those residing in a state of the Union. In contrast, the Federal government reserved the right to impose a state of exception on occupied territories because these were located outside of the United States. The Insular Cases adopted a sort of in-between position limiting the extension of civil rights to unincorporated territories to fundamental or personal rights. Of course, the definition of the scope of personal or 'fundamental' rights remains obscure and is subject to a functional approach. Nonetheless, unincorporated territories are not subject to the same standards as occupied territories.

A hundred years later, the United States government continues to invoke the global expansionist precedents to shape the contours of its war on terror. For example, leased territories like Guantánamo Bay housing torture and detention camps are ruled as unincorporated territories selectively situated in a borderland space between the United States and Cuban sovereignties. Likewise, the US global empire invokes imperialist interpretations of the Insular Cases to legitimate an array of policies targeting enemy aliens. To this extent, the contemporary war on terror represents both a continuation and the expansion of a century-old tradition of United States' global expansionism.

IS IT POSSIBLE TO DEMOCRATIZE THE US GLOBAL EMPIRE?

Liberal scholars Robert Dahl (2003) and Sanford Levinson (2006) demonstrate that the US Constitution is an undemocratic legal text. Dahl emphasizes the undemocratic nature of the US electoral system, a system that among other things places the power to elect the President in the hands of the Electoral College rather than the vote of the people; provides for a Senate that grants disproportionate powers to states with small populations over those with larger numbers of residents; and tolerates unfair and disproportionate gerrymandering. Levinson expands the analysis to emphasize how the US Constitution enables more authoritarian rule of the President and provides for the creation of a hierarchy of citizenships. Although their analysis leaves the reader wondering if it is simply not better to throw away the US Constitution and write a new document premised on fostering more democracy, both scholars also offer suggestions for correcting the undemocratic dimensions of this legal text.

In the preceding pages I have emphasized two different dimensions of the undemocratic nature of the Constitution, namely one that highlights the borderland status of unincorporated territories and one that underlines the separate and unequal status of the subjects inhabiting these localities within the US global empire. Since 1898, unincorporated territories have been selectively ruled as foreign possessions in a domestic or constitutional sense. The subjects inhabiting (or detained in) these localities are selectively barred from equal access to constitutional civil rights. Even undocumented aliens residing in the United States have access to more civil rights, including the right to a constitutional citizenship as well as a constitutional right to trial by jury, than native-born citizens residing in Puerto Rico or for that matter any unincorporated territory. But, is it possible to adopt a more democratic interpretation of the status of territories and their subjects? At least five alternative answers have been posed.

In the case of Puerto Rico the most obvious answer is that the granting of independence could provide access to the most democratic alternative (Berríos Martínez *et al.* 2010). To be sure, independence could enable Puerto Ricans to craft a democratic constitution that addresses the undemocratic limitations of the US Constitution. As previously noted, the debates over the 1952 Puerto Rican Constitution highlight a historical willingness of Puerto Ricans to embrace a democratic constitution that is informed by human and democratic rights. This willingness is part of the political culture of the island. Of course, at present Puerto Rican electors have not chosen to pursue this option. Moreover, any move to make Puerto Rico a sovereign nation-state would require the cooperation of the US global empire, certainly during a transitionary period and beyond. There is no evidence that the US global empire is committed to supporting the development of democratic regimes, quite the opposite.

A second option would entail pursuing some sort of enhanced autonomic or semi-sovereign option in the form of an associated republic or something of this nature (Rigau and García-Passalacqua 1987). This approach essentially entails granting a greater measure of sovereignty to the governments of the four unincorporated governments (Puerto Rico, American Samoa, US Virgin Islands, and Guam) akin to that of Micronesia. The unincorporated territories would be treated as associated republics (or some version of this model) and would negotiate their relationships to the United States through the State Department rather than through Congress. Constitutionally, this would entail re-defining the notion of a territory that is 'foreign in a domestic sense' to authorize a new type of relationship. To the extent that the residents of these 'republics' would possess sovereign control over local affairs it is possible to argue that they would be able to develop a more democratic system of government. Certainly in the case of Puerto Rico, as previously noted, there is a strand of the autonomic or so-called Commonwealth Party that has embraced more democratic constitutions than that of the United States.

A third alternative is to return to the colonialist model and treat all annexed, leased, or occupied territories as parts of the United States for constitutional purposes. This would entail rejecting the differentiation between an incorporated and an unincorporated territory, a distinction that is not present in the Constitution of the United States. It would also entail guaranteeing that all constitutional rights not locally inapplicable would be extended to any territory within the sovereign domain of the United States. Obviously, under this model territories would not possess the same political power that states possess, but at least in the area of civil rights, it would be possible to guarantee that all inhabitants of US territories would have access to the same civil rights as the residents of the United States. Again, this option only guarantees access to civil rights and possibly some political rights. It does not resolve the larger political problems caused by the status of territories in a state-centered federal system or for that matter the problems caused by an undemocratic constitution.

A fourth alternative is to revisit Justice Kennedy's functional approach and establish a constitutional baseline for all territories belonging to the United States (annexed, leased and/or occupied). This would entail recognizing that all inhabitants of US territories are entitled to the equal protection of the law, including equal access to a constitutional citizenship. In keeping with the logic of this approach, the assumption is that the Constitution applies *ex propio vigore* or on its own force in the territories and that all persons inhabiting a US territory should be entitled to equal protection of the law. However, unlike US colonialism, in the case of territories with local governments, the functional approach would recognize a variety of electoral systems and institutional forms of government that cater to the particular context of the territory in question. Again, this approach does not question the undemocratic relationship of power between territories and the US government or the undemocratic Constitution of the United States.

In recent years, some liberal scholars who identify with a so-called 'radical democracy' theory, postmodern theory, and other more trendy cultural debates, argued for the extension of statehood to Puerto Rico in order to promote statehood for Puerto Rico (Negrón-Muntaner and Grosfoguel 1997). In particular Ramón Grosfoguel, writing from the perspective of a radical democrat, argues for the colonial incorporation of Puerto Rico as an alternative to 'neocolonialism' and as a way to gain access to:

> ...annual transfers of billions of dollars of social capital from the metropolitan state to the modern colony (e.g. food stamps, health, education, and unemployment benefits), constitutional recognition of metropolitan citizenship and democratic/civil rights, the possibility of migration without the risks of illegality, and the extension of Fordist social relations that incorporated the colonial people to metropolitan standards of mass consumption.
>
> (Ibid.: 66)

Statehood would essentially provide Puerto Ricans with a political seat at the Federal table, equal constitutional protections, and access to the same financial benefits available to US citizens residing in the United States.[1] Of course, this radical democratic stance does not question the undemocratic nature of the US Constitution, nor does it question the implications of becoming a part of the US global empire. In any event, it reifies the traditional tolerance by liberals of US exceptionalism. The point, however, is to note that this is an alternative argument that is part of a broader conversation about addressing the separate and unequal status of Puerto Ricans within the US global empire.

NOTE

1 The impact on congressional reapportionment of seats essentially makes it politically impossible for Puerto Rico to become a state of the United States. Traditionally, Puerto Ricans, like US-based Latino/as more generally, vote for the Democratic Party. Granting statehood to Puerto Rico would entail granting the island two Senators and five Representatives, all of which would identify with the Democratic Party. Notwithstanding, a more important question is whether statehood would improve the Puerto Rican economy in a meaningful way. Based on the latest report by the US General Accounting Office (2014), there is little evidence that admitting Puerto Rico as a new state would improve the island's finances in a meaningful way, especially given the disastrous impact of two dozen years of failed privatization initiatives.

Bibliography

PRIMARY SOURCES

Laws and statutes

1789 Northwest Ordinance, 1st Cong., 1st sess. *United States Statutes at Large* 1 (1789): 50.

1887 General Allotment Act (Dawes Act), *United States Statutes at Large* 24 (1887): 388.

1897 Dingley Act, Chapter 11, 55th Cong., 1st sess., *United States Statutes at Large* 30 (1897): 151.

1898 Treaty of Paris 55th Cong., 3rd sess., *United States Statutes at Large* 30 (1898): 1754.

1898 Teller Amendment, 55th Cong., 2nd sess., *United States Statutes at Large* 30 (1898): 738.

1900 Foraker Act, Chapter 191, 56th Cong., 1st sess., *United States Statutes at Large* 31 (1900): 77.

1900 Government for the Territory of Hawaii Act, Chapter 339, 56th Cong., 1st sess., *United States Statutes at Large* 31 (1900): 141.

1901 Army Appropriations Act (Platt Amendment), 56th Cong., 2nd sess., *United States Statutes at Large* 31 (1901): 895.

1906 Bureau of Immigration and Naturalization Act, Public Law 338, 59th Cong., 1st sess., *United States Statutes at Large* 34 (1906): 596.

1917 Jones Act, Public Law 368, Chapter 368, 64th Cong., 2nd sess., *United States Statutes at Large* 39 (1917): 951.

1922 Cable Act, Public Law 346, Chapter 411, 67th Cong., 2nd sess. (1922): 1021.

1927 Puerto Rico Civil Government Act (Section 5a), Public Law 797, Chapter 503, 69th Cong., 2nd sess., *United States Statutes at Large* 44 (1927): 1418.

1934 Puerto Rico Civil Government Act (Section 5b), Public Law 477, Chapter 845, 73rd Cong., 2nd sess., *United States Statutes at Large* 48 (1934): 1245.

1938 Puerto Rico Civil Government Act (Section 5c), Public Law 521, Chapter 225, 75th Cong., 3rd sess., *United States Statutes at Large* 52 (1938): 377.

1940 Nationality Act, Public Law 853, Chapter 876, 76th Cong., 3rd sess., *United States Statutes at Large* 54 (1940): 1137.

1947 Elective Governor Act, Public Law 361, Chapter 489, 80th Cong., 1st sess. (1947): 770.

1950 Puerto Rico Organization of Constitutional Government Act, Public Law 600, Chapter 446, *United States Statutes at Large* 64 (1950): 319.

1978 Foreign Intelligence Surveillance Act, Public Law 95–511 *United States Statutes at Large* 92 (1978): 1783.

1984 Convention Against Torture and Other Cruel, Inhuman or Degrading Treatment or Punishment (Available at www.ohchr.org/EN/ProfessionalInterest/Pages/CAT.aspx) (Accessed 21 October 2014).

2001 Authorization for Use of Military Force Act, 107th Cong., *United States Statutes at Large* 115 (2001): 224.

2005 Detainee Treatment Act, *United States Statutes at Large* 119 (2005): 2739.

2006 Military Commissions Act, *United States Statutes at Large* 120 (2006): 2600.

2013 National Defense Authorization Act, 112th Cong. (Available at http://thomas.loc.gov/home/thomas.php) (Accessed on 21 October 2014).

An Act To Authorize Protection to be given to Citizens of the United States Who May Discover Deposits of Guano (Guano Islands Act), 34th Cong., 1st sess., *United States Statutes at Large* 11 (1856): 119.

An Act To Authorize the Secretary of the Interior to Issue Certificates of Citizenship to Indians (1924 Indian Citizenship Act), 68th Cong., 1st sess., *United States Statutes at Large* 43 (1924): 253.

Executive Order No. 13492, Review and Disposition of Individuals Detained at the Guantánamo Bay Naval Base and Closure of Detention Facilities, 74 Fed. Reg. 4897 (22 January 2009).

Lease of Lands for Coaling and Naval Stations (1903 Guantánamo Bay Lease Treaty), Treaty Series 418, Bevans 6 (1968): 113.

Ley Número 53, Sixteenth Legislature of Puerto Rico, 10 June 1948.

Plebiscitary Commission (Authorizing 1967 Plebiscite), Public Law 88–271, 88th Cong., 2nd sess., *United States Statutes at Large* 78 (1964): 17.

Puerto Rico, H.J. Res. 430, Public Law 447, Chapter 567, *United States Statutes at Large* 66 (1952), 327.

Treaty Between the United States of American and Cuba Defining their Relations (1934), *United States Statutes at Large* 48 (1934): 1682.

United Nations General Assembly, *Charter of the United Nations*, Article XI, § 73 (1945).

United States Congress (1878) Revised Statutes of the United States, 1873–1874, 43rd Cong., 1st sess., Washington: Government Printing Office.

United States Congress. House of Representatives. Hearings Before the Committee on Immigration and Naturalization, House of Representatives, To Revise and Codify the Nationality Laws of the United States into a Comprehensive Nationality Code, 76th Cong., 1st sess. (1940).

Government and official reports

Congressional Research Service (1985) *Admission of States Into the Union After the Original Thirteen: A Brief History and Analysis of the Statehood Process*, prepared by Sheridan, P.B., 85–765 GOV, Washington, D.C.: Government Printing Office.

Congressional Research Service (2005) *Detention of American Citizens as Enemy Combatants*, prepared by Jennifer K. Elsea, RL31724, Washington, D.C.: Government Printing Office.

Congressional Research Service (2009) *Renditions: Constraints Imposed by Laws of Torture*, prepared by Michael Jones Garcia, RL32890, Washington, D.C.: Government Printing Office.

Congressional Research Service (2010) *Judicial Activity Concerning Enemy Combatant Detainees: Major Court Rulings*, prepared by Jennifer K. Elsea and Michael Jones Garcia, R41156, Washington, D.C.: Government Printing Office.

Department of Justice (2013) *White Paper: Lawfulness of a Lethal Operation Directed Against a US Citizen Who Is a Senior Operational Leader of Al-Qa'ida or an Associated Force*. Online. Available at: http://msnbcmedia.msn.com/i/msnbc/sections/news/020413_DOJ_White_Paper.pdf (accessed 1 March 2013).

Kavass, I.I. and Sprudz, A. (eds) (edn 1903) Charles E. Magoon: Reports on the Law of Civil Government in Territory Subject to Military Occupation by the Military Forces of the United States, Bureau of Insular Affairs, United States Department of War, Washington, D.C.: Government Printing Office.

Puerto Rico Federal Affairs Administration (1992) Puerto Rico: Political Status Referendum, 1989–1991, Volume 2: Reports and Studies on The Puerto Rico Political Status and Related Issues, Washington, D.C.: PRFAA.

Remarks by Representative Bell from Colorado, speaking against the ratification of 1898 *Treaty of Paris*, on 24 January 1899, 55th Cong., 3rd sess., *Congressional Record* 32, part 1: 992.

Remarks by Representative McClellan of New York, Speaking against the enactment of the 1900 *Foraker Act*, on 22 February 1900, 56th Cong., 1st sess. *Congressional Record* 33, 2063–64.

Remarks by Senator Caffery of Louisiana, speaking against the ratification of the 1898 *Treaty of Paris*, on 6 January 1899, 55th Cong., 3rd sess., *Congressional Record* 32, part 1: 433.

Remarks by Senator Caffery of Louisiana, speaking against the ratification of the 1898 *Treaty of Paris* on 6 January 1899, 55th Cong., 3rd sess., *Congressional Record* 32, part 1: 436.

Remarks by Senator Foraker of Ohio, speaking for the ratification of 1898 *Treaty of Paris*, on 11 January 1899, 55th Cong., 3rd sess., *Congressional Record* 32, part 1: 567.

Remarks by Senator Spooner of Wisconsin, speaking for the ratification of the 1898 *Treaty of Paris*, on 2 February 1899, 55th Cong., 3rd sess., *Congressional Record* 32, part 2: 1384.

Remarks by Senator Spooner of Wisconsin, speaking for the ratification of 1898 *Treaty of Paris* on 2 February 1899, 55th Cong., 3rd sess., *Congressional Record* 32, part 2: 1385–86.

United States Congress. House of Representatives. *Colonization of the Free People of Color*, 19th Cong., 2nd sess. (1827): H. Rept. 101.

United States Congress. House of Representatives. *Admission of Utah Into the Union*, 42nd Cong., 2nd sess. (1872): Misc. Doc. 165.

United States Congress. House of Representatives. To Regulate The Trade of Puerto Rico and for Other Purposes, 56th Cong., 1st sess. (1900): H. Rept. 249.

United States Congress. House of Representatives. Report of the Military Governor of Porto Rico on Civil Affairs, Part 13 located in US War Department, Annual Reports of the War Department for the Fiscal Year Ended June 30, 1900, 56th Cong., 2nd sess., (1902): H. Doc. 2.

United States Congress. House of Representatives. Laws, Ordinances, Decrees, and Military Orders Having Force of Law Effective in Porto Rico May 1, 1900, 60th Cong., 2nd sess., (1909): H. Doc. 1484.
United States Congress. House of Representatives. Amend Act to Provide A Civil Government for Puerto Rico, 73rd Cong., 2nd sess., (1934): H. Rept. 1277.
United States Congress. House of Representatives. Nationality Act of 1940, 76th Cong., 3rd sess. (1940): H. Rept. 2396.
United States Congress. House of Representatives. United States–Puerto Rico Political Status Act, 104th Cong., 2nd sess., (1996): H. Rept. 104–713, Part 1.
United States Congress. House of Representatives. United States–Puerto Rico Political Status Act, 105th Cong., 1st sess., (1997): H. Rept. 105–131, Part 1.
United States Congress. Senate. Treaties, Conventions, International Acts, Protocols and Agreements Between the United States of America and Other Powers, 1776–1909, 61st Cong., 2nd sess., (1910): S. Doc. 357.
United States Congress. Senate. Correcting United States Citizenship Status of Certain Persons Born in Puerto Rico, 75th Cong., 3rd sess., (1938): S. Rept. 1679.
United States Congress. Senate. Providing for the Organization of a Constitutional Government by the People of Puerto Rico, 81st Cong., 2nd sess., (1950): S. Rept. 1720.
United States Congress. Senate. Report on the Legal Status of the Territory and Inhabitants of the Islands Acquired by the United States During the War with Spain, Considered with Reference to the Territorial Boundaries, the Constitution and the Laws of the United States, by Charles H. Magoon, 56th Cong., 1st sess., (1900): S. Doc. 234.
United States General Accounting Office (1991) US Insular Areas: Applicability of Relevant Provisions of the US Constitution, GAO/HRD-91-18, Washington, D.C.: Government Printing Office.
United States General Accounting Office (2004) *Treaty of Guadalupe Hidalgo: Findings and Possible Options Regarding Longstanding Community Land Grant Claims in New Mexico,* GAO-04-59, Washington, D.C.: Government Printing Office.
United States General Accounting Office (2012) *Guantánamo Bay Detainees: Facilities and Factors for Consideration if Detainees Were brought to the United States,* GAO-13-31, Washington, D.C.: Government Printing Office.
United States General Accounting Office (2014) *Puerto Rico: Information on How Statehood Would Affect Selected Federal Programs and Revenue Sources,* GAO-14–31, Washington, D.C.: Government Printing Office.
United States War Department (1899) *Report of Brig. Gen. Geo. W. Davis, U.S.V. on Civil Affairs of Puerto Rico,* Rept. No. 186123, Washington, D.C.: Government Printing Office.

SECONDARY SOURCES

Acevedo, H.L. (ed.) (2003) *La Generación del 40 y la Convención Constituyente,* Rio Piedras: Universidad Interamericana de Puerto Rico.
Acevedo, H.L. (ed.) (2005) *Jesús T. Piñero, El hombre, el político, el gobernador,* Colombia: Quebecor World Bogotá.
Ackerman, B. (1991) *We the People: Foundations,* vol. 1, London: The Belknap Press of Harvard University Press.

Acosta, I. (1989) *La Mordaza: Puerto Rico, 1948–1957*, Rio Piedras: Editorial Edil, Inc.

Adams, E.B. (1898) 'The Causes and Results of Our War with Spain From a Legal Stand-Point', 8(3): 119–133.

Agamben, G. (1998) *Homo Sacer: Sovereign Power and Bare Life*, trans. Daniel Heller-Roazen, Stanford, CA: Stanford University Press.

Agamben, G. (2003) *State of Exception*, trans. Kevin Attell, Chicago, IL: The University of Chicago Press.

Aleinikoff, T.A. (2002) *Semblances of Sovereignty, The Constitution, the State, and American Citizenship*, Cambridge, MA: Harvard University Press.

Alvarez, A. (1924) *The Monroe Doctrine, Its Importance in the International Life of the States of the New World*, New York: Oxford University Press.

Álvarez González, J.J. (1990) 'The Empire Strikes Out: Congressional Ruminations on the Citizenship Status of Puerto Ricans', *Harvard Journal on Legislation* 27: 309–366.

Álvarez González, J.J. (2009) *Derecho constitucional de Puerto Rico y relaciones constitucionales con los Estados Unidos, Casos y materiales*, Bogotá: Editorial Temis, S.A.

Andreu Iglesias, C. (ed.) (1977, 2nd edn 1984) *Memoirs of Bernardo Vega: A Contribution to the History of the Puerto Rican Community in New York*, New York: Monthly Review Press.

Andrews, C.C. (ed.) (1856) *Official Opinions of The Attorneys General of the United States, Advising the President and Heads of Departments in Relation to their Official Duties, and Expounding the Constitution, Treaties, With Foreign Governments and with Indian Tribes, and the Public Laws of the Country*, Washington: Robert Farnham.

Arendt, H. (1948; 9th edn 2004) *The Origins of Totalitarianism*, New York: Schocken Press.

Bacon, R. and Brown Scott, J. (eds) (1916; 2nd edn 1970) *The Military and Colonial Policy of the United States, Addresses and Reports by Elihu Root*, New York: AMS Press.

Bacon, S. (1901) 'Territory and the Constitution', *Yale Law Journal* 10(3): 99–117.

Baldwin, S.E. (1899) 'The Constitutional Questions Incident to the Acquisition and Government by the United States Island Territory', *Harvard Law Review* 12: 393–416.

Beach, J.K. (1899) 'Constitutional Expansion', *Yale Law Journal* 8(5): 225–34.

Becker, C. (1900) 'Law and Practice of the United States in the Acquisition of Government of Dependent Territory', *Annals of the American Academy of Political Science* 16: 60–76.

Begg, M. and Brittain, V. (2006) *Enemy Combatant: My Imprisonment at Guantánamo, Bagram, and Kandahar*, New York: The New Press.

Bensel, R.F. (1990) *Yankee Leviathan: The Origins of Central State Authority in America, 1859–1877*, New York: Cambridge University Press.

Berríos Martínez, R., Martín García, F. and Catalá Oliveras, F. (2010) *Puerto Rico: Nación independiente imperativo del Siglo XXI*, San Juan: Editora Corripio.

Bhana, S. (1975) *The United States Development of the Puerto Rican Status Question, 1936–1968*, Lawrence, KS: The University of Kansas Press.

Bickel, A.M. (1973) 'Citizenship in the American Constitution', *Arizona Law Review* 15: 369–387.

Bosley, W.B. (1900) 'The Constitutional Requirement of Uniformity in Duties, Imposts and Excises', *Yale Law Journal* 9(4): 64–169.

Bosniak, L. (2011) 'Citizenship in an Unequal World: A Discussion of *The Birthright Lottery: Citizenship and Global Inequality*', *Perspectives on Politics* 9(3): 621–624.

Bothwell González, R.B. (1971) *Trasfondo Constitucional de Puerto Rico: Primera Parte, 1887–1974,* Rio Piedras: Editorial Universitaria.

Bothwell González, R.B. (ed.) (1979) *Puerto Rico: Cien años de lucha politica,* 5 vols, Rio Piedras: Editorial Universitaria.

Boydston, J. (2005) 'Locating Settle Colonies in the Postcolonial Imaginary', *American Quarterly* 57(4): 1123–1229.

Brady, D.W. (1988) *Critical Elections and Congressional Policymaking*, Stanford, CA: Stanford University Press.

Brown, E.S. (1918; edn 2000) *The Constitutional History of the Louisiana Purchase*, Washington, D.C.: Beard Books.

Bruff, H.H. (2009) *Bad Advice: Bush's Lawyers in the War on Terror*, Lawrence: University Press of Kansas.

Burgess, J.W. (1899) 'How May the United States Govern its Extra-Continental Territory?' *Political Science Quarterly* 14(1): 1–18.

Butler, J. (2004) *Precarious Life: The Powers of Mourning and Violence*, New York: Verso.

Cabranes, J.A. (1979) *Citizenship and the American Empire: Notes on the Legislative History of the United States Citizenship of Puerto Ricans*, New Haven, CT: Yale University Press.

Callinicos, A. (2009) *Imperialism and Global Political Economy*, Cambridge: Polity.

Cheney, D. and Cheney, L. (2011) *In My Life, A Personal and Political Memoir*, New York: Threshold Editions.

Cohen, E.F. (2009) *Semi-Citizenship in Democratic Politics*, New York: Cambridge University Press.

Cole, D. (2003) *Enemy Aliens and Constitutional Freedoms in the War on Terrorism*, New York: The New Press.

Costigan, G.P. (1899) 'The Third View of the Status of Our New Possessions', *Yale Law Journal* 9(3): 124–133.

Dahl, R.A. (2003) *How Democratic Is the American Constitution?* Second Edition, New Haven, CT: Yale Nota Bene.

Delgado Cintrón, C. (1988) *Derecho y colonialismo: La trayectoria historica del derecho puertoriqueño*, Rio Piedras: Edil.

Deloria Jr., V. and Wilkins D.E. (1999) *Tribes, Treaties and Constitutional Tribulations*, Austin, TX: University of Texas Press.

Dudley, M.K. and Agard, K.K. (1993) *A Call for Hawaiian Sovereignty*, Honolulu: Na Kane O Ka Malo Press.

Duffy Burnett, C. (2006) 'The Edges of Empire and the Limits of Sovereignty: American Guano Islands', in M.L. Dudziak, and L. Volpp (eds) *Legal Borderlands: Law and the Construction of American Borders*, Baltimore: The Johns Hopkins University Press.

Duffy Burnett, C. and Marshall, B. (eds) (2001) *Foreign in a Domestic Sense: Puerto Rico, American Expansion, and the Constitution,* Durham, NH: Duke University Press.

Farrand, M. (1896) *The Legislation of Congress for the Government of the Organized Territories of the United States, 1789–1895,* Newark, NJ: Wm. A. Baker.

Farrand, M. (1905) 'The Indian Boundary Line', *The American Historical Review,* 10: 782–791.

Farrand, M. (1913) *The Framing of the Constitution of the United States,* New Haven, CT: Yale University Press.

Férnos López-Cepero, A. (ed.) (2007) *Documentos Históricos Constitucionales de Puerto Rico,* San Juan: Ediciones Situm.

Fidell E.R. and Sullivan D.H. (2002) *Evolving Military Justice,* Annapolis: Naval Institute Press.

Fisher, H.N. (1899) *Principles of Colonial Government: Adapted to the Present Needs of Cuba and Porto Rico, and of the Philippines,* Boston, MA: L.C. Page and Company.

Fletcher, L.E. and Stover, E. (2008) *Guantánamo and its Aftermath: US Detention and Interrogation Practices and Their Impact on Former Detainees,* Berkeley, CA: Human Rights Center and International Human Rights Law Clinic.

Flack, H.E. (1908) *The Adoption of the Fourteenth Amendment,* Baltimore, MD: Johns Hopkins Press.

Foraker, J.B. (2nd edn 1916) *Notes on a Busy Life,* vol. 2, Cincinnati, OH: Steward and Kidd Company.

Friedrich, C.J. (1950) 'Military Government and Dictatorship', *Annals of the American Academy of Political Science* 267: 1–7.

Fuller, P. (1901) 'Some Constitutional Questions Suggested by Recent Acquisitions', *Columbia Law Review* 1 (2): 108–109.

Gardiner, C.A. (1899) 'Our Right to Acquire and Hold Foreign Territory', *The American Law Review* 33: 161–187.

Gerstle, G. (2001) *American Crucible: Race and Nation in the Twentieth Century,* Princeton, NJ: Princeton University Press.

Getches, D.H., Wilkinson, C.F., and Williams, Jr., R.-A. (eds) (1979; 4th edn 1998) *Cases and Materials on Federal Indian Law,* St. Paul, MN: West Group.

Gettys, L. (1934) *The Law of Citizenship in the United States,* Chicago, IL: The University of Chicago Press.

Gould, L.J. (1969) *La ley Foraker, raíces de las política colonial de los Estados Unidos,* Río Piedras: Editorial U.P.R.

Greenberg, K.J. and Dratel, J.L. (eds) (2005) *The Torture Papers, The Road to Abu Ghraib,* New York: Cambridge University Press.

Grupo de Investigadores Puertorriqueños (eds) (1984) *Breakthrough From Colonialism: An Interdisciplinary Study of Statehood.* 2 vols, Río Piedras: Editorial de la Universidad de Puerto Rico.

Haney López, I.F. (1996) *White by Law, The Legal Construction of Race,* New York: New York University Press.

Hardt, M. and Negri A. (2000) *Empire,* Cambridge, MA: Harvard University Press.

Harlow, N. (1982) *California Conquered: The Annexation of a Mexican Province, 1846–1850,* Berkeley, CA: University of California Press.

Hobsbawm, E.J. (1989) *History of Civilization: The Age of Empire, 1875–1914,* vol. 3, New York: Vintage Books.

Hobsbawm, E.J. (2008) *On Empire: America, War, and Global Supremacy*, New York: The New Press.

Honigsberg, P.J. (2009) *Our Nation Unhinged: The Human Consequences of the War on Terror*, Berkeley, CA: University of California Press.

Horsman, R. (1981) *Race and Manifest Destiny, The Origins of American Racial Anglo-Saxonism*, Cambridge, MA: Harvard University Press.

Jaffer, J. and Singh, A. (2007) *Administration of Torture, A Documentary Record From Washington to Abu Ghraib and Beyond*, New York: Columbia University Press.

King, W.L. (1950) *Melville Weston Fuller: Chief Justice of the United States, 1888–1910*, New York: The MacMillan Company.

Kirk, R. (1953, 7th edn 2001) *The Conservative Mind: From Burke to Eliot*, Washington, D.C.: Regnery Publishing, Inc.

LaFeber, W. (1986) 'The 'Lion in the Path': The U.S. Emergence as a World Power', *Political Science Quarterly* 101: 705–718.

Langdell, C.C. (1899) 'The Status of Our New Territories', *Harvard Law Review*, 12: 365–392.

Lawson, G. and Seidman, G. (2004) *The Constitution of Empire: Territorial Expansion and American Legal History*, New Haven, CT: Yale University Press.

Levinson, S. (2006) *Our Undemocratic Constitution: Where the Constitution Goes Wrong (and How the People Can Correct It)*, New York: Oxford University Press.

Levinson, S. and Sparrow, B. (eds) (2005) *The Louisiana Purchase and American Expansion, 1803–1898*, Lanham: Rowman & Littlefield Publishers, Inc.

López Baralt, J. (1999) *The Policy of the United States Towards its Territories with Special Reference to Puerto Rico*, Rio Piedras: Editorial de la Universidad de Puerto Rico.

Lowell, A.L. (1899) 'The Status of Our New Possessions – *A Third View*', *Harvard Law Review* 13: 155–176.

Mahan, A.T. (1898) *The Interest of America in Sea Power, Present and Future*, Boston, MA: Little, Brown and Company.

Margulies, J. (2006) *Guantánamo and the Abuse of Presidential Power*, New York: Simon and Shuster.

Margulies, J. (2006) *Memorias de un ciudadano*, Colombia: Editorial Barco de Papel.

Mattei Filardi, L. (2012) *La sombra del imperio: Los inicios del consejo ejecutivo en Puerto Rico, 1900–1904*, San Juan: Isla Negra Editores.

Mayer, J. (2008) *The Dark Side: The Inside Story of How The War on Terror Turned Into a War on American Ideals*, New York: Doubleday.

Mayer, J.P. (ed.) (1969 edn 2000), *Alexis de Tocqueville: Democracy in America*, trans. George Lawrence, New York: Perennial Classics.

McCarthy, N.M., Poole, K.T. and Rosenthal, H. (1998; rev 1999) 'Congress and the Territorial Expansion of the United States', unpublished paper, Stanford-University of California-San Diego conference on the History of Congress.

McGovney, D.O. (1911) 'American Citizenship, Part II: Unincorporated Peoples and Peoples Incorporated With Less Than Full Privileges', *Columbia Law Review* 11(4): 326–347.

McGovney, D.O. (1934) 'Our Non-Citizen Nationals, Who Are They?' *California Law Review* 22: 593–635.

Meeropol, R. (ed.) (2005) *America's Disappeared: Secret Imprisonment, Detainees, and the 'War on Terror'*, New York: Seven Stories Press.

Mendez Saavedra, M. (1992) *1898: La guerra hispanoamericana en caricaturas/ The Spanish American War in Cartoons*, San Juan: Comisión Puertorriqueña para la celebración del Quinto Centenario del Descubrimiento de América y Puerto Rico.

Mokhtari, S. (2009) *After Abu Ghraib: Exploring Human Rights in America and the Middle East*, New York: Cambridge University Press.

Morse, A.P. (1900) 'Status of Inhabitants of Territory Acquired by Discovery, Purchase, Cession, or Conquest, According to the Usage of the United States', *The American Law Register* 48(6): 332–339.

Nazario Velasco, R. (1999) *Discurso legal y orden poscolonial: Los abogados de Puerto Rico ante el 1898*, Hato Rey: Publicaciones Puertorriqueñas, Inc.

Negrón-Muntaner, F. (ed.) (2007) *None of the Above: Puerto Ricans in the Global Era*, New York: Palgrave.

Negrón-Muntaner, F. and Grosfoguel, R. (eds) (1997) *Puerto Rican Jam: Essays on Culture and Politics*, Minneapolis, MN: University of Minnesota Press.

Neuman, G.L. (2009) 'The Extraterritorial Constitution after *Boumediene v. Bush*', *Southern California Law Review* 82: 259–290.

Nieves Falcón, L. (ed.) (2013) *Oscar López Rivera: Between Torture and Resistance*, New York: PM Press.

Norgren, J. (1996) *The Cherokee Cases, The Confrontation of Law and Politics*, New York: McGraw-Hill, Inc.

Olshansky, B. (2002) *Secret Trials and Executions: Military Tribunals and the Threat to Democracy*, New York: Seven Stories Press.

Olshansky, B. (2007) *Democracy Detained: Secret Unconstitutional Practices in the US War on Terror*, New York: Seven Stories Press.

Onuf, P.S. (1987) *Statehood and Union, A Brief History of the Northwest Ordinance*, Bloomington, IN: Indiana University Press.

Ophir, A., Givoni, M. and Hanafi, S. (eds) (2009) *The Power of Inclusive Exclusion, Anatomy of Israeli Rule in the Occupied Palestinian Territories*, New York: Zone Books.

Partsch, J. (2006) *Jesús T. Piñero: El exiliado en su patria*, San Juan: Ediciones Huracán.

Prucha, F.P. (1994) *American Indian Treaties, The History of a Political Anomaly*, Berkeley, CA: University of California Press.

Randolph, C.F. (1898) 'Constitutional Aspects of Annexation', *Harvard Law Review* 12: 291–315.

Raustiala, K. (2009) *Does the Constitution Follow the Flag? The Evolution of Territoriality in American Law*, New York: Oxford University Press.

Reichstein, A.V. (1989) *The Rise of the Lone Star: The Making of Texas*, College Station, TX: Texas A&M University Press.

Rejali, D. (2007) *Torture and Democracy*, Princeton, NJ: Princeton University Press.

Rigau M.A. and García-Passalacqua, J.M. (eds) (1987) *Republica Asociada y Libre Asociación: Documentación de un Debate*, San Juan: Editorial Atlantico, Inc.

Rivera Ramos, E. (2007) *American Colonialism in Puerto Rico: The Judicial and Social Legacy*, Princeton, NJ: Markus Wiener Publishers.

Rodríguez Beruff, J. (2007) *Strategy as Politics: Puerto Rico on the Eve of the Second World War*, Río Piedras: La Editorial.

Rodríguez Torres, J.F. (2011) *Isla de Pinos, Presidio y Paraiso*. San Juan.

Rose, D. (2004) *Guantánamo: The War on Human Rights*, New York: The New Press.

Rossiter, C. (1948, 2nd edn 2004) *Constitutional Dictatorship, Crisis Government in the Modern Democracies*, New Brunswick, NJ: Transaction Publishers.

Russell, T.H. (1900) 'Results of Expansion', *Yale Law Journal* 9(6): 239–245.

Sarat, A. and Hussain, N. (eds) (2010) *When Governments Break the Law: The Rule of Law and the Prosecution of the Bush Administration*, New York: New York University Press.

Scarry, E. (2010) *Rule of Law, Misrule of Men*, Cambridge, MA: MIT Press.

Schmitt, C. (1926; edn 1988) *The Crisis of Parliamentary Democracy*, trans. Ellen Kennedy, Cambridge, MA: MIT Press.

Schmitt, C. (1931; edn 2003) *La Dictadura: Desde los comienzo del pensamiento moderno de la soberanía hasta la lucha de clases proletaria*, trans. José Díaz García, Madrid: Alianza Editorial.

Schmitt, C. (1950; edn 2002) *El Nomos de la tierra en el derecho de gentes del <Ius publicum europaeum>*, trans. D. Schilling Thou, Granada: Editorial Comares, S.L.

Schoultz, L. (1998) *Beneath the United States, A History of US Policy Toward Latin America*, Cambridge, MA: Harvard University Press.

Shachar, A. (2009) *The Birthright Lottery: Citizenship and Global Inequality*, Cambridge, MA: Harvard University Press.

Shattuck, P.T. and Norgren, J. (1991) *Partial Justice, Federal Indian Law in a Liberal Constitutional System*, Providence: BERG.

Shipman, P.R. (1900) 'Webster on the Territories', *Yale Law Journal* 9(5): 185–206.

Shulman, M.R. (1995) *Navalism and the Emergence of American Sea Power: 1882–1893*, Annapolis: Naval Institute Press.

Sizemore, M.R. (2013) 'When are the People?: Temporality, Popular Sovereignty, and the US Settler State', *South Central Review* 30(1): 3–31.

Skaggs, J.M. (1994) *The Great Guano Rush, Entrepreneurs and American Oversees Expansion*, New York: St. Martin's Press.

Skorownek, S. (1982, edn 1990) *Building A New American State: The Expansion of National Administrative Capacities, 1877–1920*, New York: Cambridge University Press.

Sparrow, B.H. (2006) *The Insular Cases and the Emergence of the American Empire*, Lawrence, KS: University Press of Kansas.

Sumner, W.G. (1899) 'The Conquest of the United States by Spain', *Yale Lw Journal* 8(4): 168–93.

Svirsky, M. and Bignall, S. (eds) (2012) *Agamben and Colonialism*, Edinburgh: Edinburgh University Press.

Taylor, Jr., R.M. (ed.) (1987) *The Northwest Ordinance: 1787, A Bicentennial Handbook*, Indianapolis: Indiana Historical Society.

Taylor Saito, N. (2007) *From Chinese Exclusion to Guantánamo Bay, Plenary Power and the Prerogative State*, Boulder, CO: University of Colorado Press.

Thayer, J.B. (1899) 'Our New Possessions', *Harvard Law Review*, 12: 464–85.

The Constitution Project (2013) *The Report of the Constitution Project's Task Force on Detainee Treatment*, Washington, D.C.: The Constitution Project.

Thomas, L. (2010) *Puerto Rican Citizen: History and Political Identity in Twentieth-Century New York City*, Chicago, IL: The University of Chicago Press.

Thompson, L. (2010) *Imperial Archipelago: Representation and Rule in the Insular Territories Under U.S. Dominion After 1898*, Honolulu, HI: University of Hawai'i Press.

Thorpe, F.N. (ed.) (1909) *The Federal and State Constitutions, Colonial Charters, and Other Organic Laws, States, Territories, and Colonies Now or Heretofore Forming the United States of America*, 7 vols, Washington, D.C.: Government Printing Office.

Torruella, J.R. (1988) *The Supreme Court and Puerto Rico, The Doctrine of Separate and Unequal*, Río Piedras: Editorial de la Universidad de Puerto Rico.

Torruella, J.R. (2007) *Global Intrigues, The Era of the Spanish-American War and the Rise of the United States to World Power*, Río Piedras: Editorial de la Universidad de Puerto Rico.

Trask, D.F. (1981; 2nd edn 1996) *The War With Spain in 1898*, Lincoln, NE: University of Nebraska Press.

Trías Monge, J. (1980), *Historia constitucional de Puerto Rico*, vol. 1, Río Piedras: Editorial Universitaria.

Trías Monge, J. (1981) *Historia constitucional de Puerto Rico*, vol. 2, Río Piedras: Editorial Universitaria.

Trías Monge, J. (1982) *Historia constitucional de Puerto Rico*, vol. 3, Río Piedras: Editorial Universitaria.

Trías Monge, J. (1991) *El choque de dos culturas juridicas en Puerto Rico, el caso de la responsabilidad civil extracontractual*, Austin, TX: Equity Publishing Company.

Trías Monge, J. (1997) *Puerto Rico: The Trials of the Oldest Colony in the World*, New Haven, CT: Yale University Press.

Trinklein, M.J. (2010) *Lost States: True Stories of Texlahoma, Transylvania, and Other States that Never Made It*, Philadelphia, PA: Quirk Books.

Venator-Santiago, C.R. (2006) 'Agamben's State of Exception and US Territorial Law and Policy', *Studies in Law, Politics, and Society* (39): 15–56.

Venator-Santiago, C.R. (2012) 'Marriage and the Denaturalization of Puerto Rican Women: Extending the Doctrine of Coverture to Puerto Rico, 1898–1940', *Latino(a) Research Review* 8 (1–2): 231–246.

Weston, R.F. (1972) *Racism in U.S. Imperialism: The Influence of Racial Assumptions on American Foreign Policy, 1893–1946*, Columbia, SC: University of South Carolina Press.

Wilkins, D.E. (1997) *American Indian Sovereignty and the U.S. Supreme Court: The Masking of Justice*, Austin, TX: University of Texas Press.

Willoughby, W.F. (1905) *Territories and Dependencies of the United States, Their Government and Administration*, New York: The Century Co.

Willoughby, W.W. (2nd edn 1929) *The Constitutional Law of the United States*, New York: Baer, Voorhis and Company.

Wolin, S.S. (1996) 'The Liberal/Democratic Divide, On Rawls' Political Liberalism', *Political Theory* 27 (1): 97-119.

Wolin, S.S. (2008) *Democracy Incorporated: Managed Democracy and the Specter of Inverted Totalitarianism*, Princeton, NJ: Princeton University Press.

Woodward, C.V. (3rd edn 1974) *The Strange Career of Jim Crow*, New York: Oxford

University Press.
Wooster, R. (1993) *Nelson A. Miles and the Twilight of the Frontier Army*, Lincoln, NE: University of Nebraska Press.
Yoo, J. (2006) *War by Other Means: An Insider's Account of the War on Terror*, New York: Atlantic Monthly Press.
Zizek, A. (2004) *Iraq: The Borrowed Kettle*, New York: Verso.

Index

Printed in Dunstable, United Kingdom

f8a86f9c-b811-4fe6-9d73-e9a242ed5abcR01